Contents

PART I
Early Berkley

PART II
Berkley Welcomes Traders and Travelers

PART III
Berkley Enters Its Heyday

PART IV
The Open Road Beckons

PART V
Coming of Age

Preface and Acknowledgments

*"The simplest things, don't you know, are
worthy to preserve just to show what things
were at a given time, what purpose they served."*
—John Clark
Interview, April 2000

This book is not "THE" history of Berkley, nor is it "A" history of Berkley, Maryland. It is a small journey through the history, lives, and events that deemed the Berkley Crossroads worthy of preservation.

On October 21, 1998, with support from the Dublin/Darlington Community Council, the residents of Berkley came together at the Hosanna School Museum in Berkley to discuss the possibility of preserving this historic crossroads. After two meetings, the community had decided what it wanted to do, how it should begin, and what the results should be. The residents wanted current and former older residents interviewed. They wanted to know more about the history of Berkley, particularly everyday life over the past two centuries, and they wanted the Berkley Crossroads nominated to the National Register of Historic Places. The community recommended people to be interviewed, developed a list of questions to be asked, and a list of the areas they wanted explored. A small, loosely structured committee was formed to coordinate and pursue the community's goals. The original committee members were Gwyneth Howard, Frances Huesman, and Connie Beims of Berkley, and Christine Tolbert, Executive Director of Hosanna School. Christopher Weeks, Harford County's Historic Preservation Officer, and John Clark, resident of Berkley, served as advisors to the project.

Word began to travel as the committee heard from former residents locally and as far away as Virginia, New Mexico, Illinois, and Arizona. Photographs, memorabilia, maps and other ephemera arrived in the mail, at our doorsteps, by telephone and e-mail. Each piece of new information provided more interesting stories and historical information. By 2002, the Berkley Crossroads Preservation Project, with a grant from the Maryland Historical Trust, had interviewed 23 current and former residents of Berkley ranging in ages from 65–96 including two former teachers at Hosanna School and two seventh-generation residents of Berkley. On November 11, 2000, the community reconvened at Hosanna to honor these individuals and celebrate their lives and stories. You, too, will meet them throughout the book.

The nomination of the Berkley Crossroads as a Historic District to the National Register of Historic Places was completed in 2000, supported by Harford County government and approved unanimously by the Governor's Commission on Nominations to the National Register in October 2001. Berkley was listed on the National Register as a Historic District in 2003.

And, finally, after a second grant from the Maryland Historical Trust, the story of the Berkley crossroads is ready to rest on the shelves for the next generation to explore more of this rich history.

Over the years Harford County has had serious and dedicated historians who, with great pride, persistence, and precision have captured the history of our county. We have turned to these researchers and writers to glean the events and significant facts and dates as they relate to the small hamlet of Berkley. In many cases, we have been able to enrich the history with excerpts from our interviews. Many stories and events were particular to Berkley and not previously published. For these, we have tried to rely on more than one source. In some cases, without corroboration, the stories were just too good not to be shared!

While this book may have broader appeal, it was written for the people of Berkley. Throughout the text, therefore, a special font has been used so the words and stories of the people interviewed may be readily identified. You will also find photographs and brief biographies of these individuals the first time their words appear in the text. For those interested in reading complete transcripts or listening to the audiotapes, they are available at the Maryland Historical Trust Library, The Historical Society of Harford County, Inc., and the Harford County Library in Bel Air, Maryland.

With a history covering over 250 years, one can expect changes in the language, descriptors, and spelling. For example, in the interviews, residents of color have referred to themselves as Negro, colored, black, or African-American. For consistency in most of the text, black will be used unless the context dictates otherwise. Spelling or grammar has not been changed in any quotes from old texts, letters or diaries or in the transcripts of the individuals interviewed except for clarification. Genealogical research and land searches are worthy subjects, ones that could have easily enticed us away from the journey. Therefore, genealogy has been undertaken only to ascertain the sequence of generations in telling a story; land and title searches were done only to determine the sites of various structures and ownership so we could, with some certainty, speak to the landscape and configuration of Berkley at any given time. We leave the exploration of these two engrossing subjects to others.

All illustrations, except those acknowledged with gratitude, belong to the Berkley Crossroads Preservation Project.

There are many people and institutions to thank. We acknowledge first the current and former residents of Berkley who had the confidence to pursue these goals and to cast their lot with the committee to make it happen. The individuals interviewed deserve a special "thank you" for their willingness to tell their stories—some funny, some poignant—and all rich with their remembrances of the crossroads. The list continues—the Maryland Historical Trust for its guidance and support, financial and otherwise, in particular, Elaine Eff, and Peter Kurtz; the Maryland State Archives and The Historical Society of Harford County, Inc. for their treasure troves of articles, photographs, and primary sources, and the helpful and knowledgeable staffs; and Christopher Weeks, historic preservationist extraordinaire, who was with us from the beginning and was instrumental in advancing the nomination to the National Register of Historic Places.

Lower Susquehanna Heritage Greenway, Inc. was the holder and administrator of the grants, and we specifically thank Judith Leonard, Donald Brand, Nancy Clark and Berkley resident and former LSHG Executive Director Bob Chance. The elected officials of Harford County provided real as well as moral support for the effort including: County Executive James Harkins and members of the Harford County Council for supporting every phase of this project including the allocation of matching funds for the final phase to restore the Hosanna School Museum; Harford County Department of Community Services Director Mary Chance, for her idea and support for the underwriting of the video, *Walking Around Berkley;* the Harford County General Assembly members, Senators Robert Hooper and Nancy Jacobs, Delegates Charles Boutin, Mary-Dulany James, Barry Glassman, Joanne Parrott and Daniel Riley who also supported the entire project and, in particular, for their leadership in acquiring the last phase of State funding for the restoration of Hosanna School. The work of our oral historians, Marya McQuirter and Carole Kolker; our transcriber, Susan Lanman; our photographer, Scott Perryman and the pro bono reproduction of the audiotapes by the library staff at Harford Community College made it possible for us to complete our first grant on time and within budget. We also appreciate the kindness of the Exelon Corporation in providing archival documents on the Conowingo Dam.

Many, many individuals provided photographs, articles, maps, documents and volunteer hours: Lillian Alston, Warren and Barbara Baity, William Beims, Charles and Verneal Cooley, Duane Cox, Charles Day, Megan Evans, Jean Ewing, Evangeline Ford, Jim and Fran Huesman, Ralph Gallion, Stephen Howard, Genevieve Jones, Edwin and Emalyn Kirkwood, Darlington Post Master Kenneth Moretz, Doris Toliver Presberry, Bob and Millie Riley, Stephen Sauers, Pastor Gary Sieglein, Deacon Sarah Standiford, Jeanne Thomas ... We know you are out there, so if we have forgotten your name, please forgive.

For a major part of its history, Berkley was one of many small settlements—Darlington, Castleton, Upper Castleton, Dublin—each with its own post office, stores, Justice of the Peace, and farms. Even then, Darlington and Berkley were linked intrinsically by family, business, faith, and friendship. Over the years, the transportation corridors changed, post offices closed, and the hamlet of Berkley is now identified as part of Darlington. This is true not only geographically but also in the friendships and neighborliness that flows from the Berkley Crossroads to the village of Darlington and back. So we thank our Darlington friends and neighbors who were so forthcoming with pictures, memories, and stories to aid in our quest for the past.

Special recognition is given to the following major contributors to this book: First to Berkley resident Gwyneth Howard, a founding member of the Berkley Committee, for her work on the first phase of the project and her research on the Conowingo Dam that resulted in a fine story on the construction of the dam. Resounding kudos also to: John Lamb, who, for over eight months, researched land records, books, articles, and historical documents that added significantly to the accuracy of the text and took us on many hikes up Peddler's Run, through cemeteries, to Bruninger's Tannery, and in search of the Woodpecker School; John Sauers, for the very special sketches that grace this book and for his wonderful bootleg story; Nancy Hume for her crisp critiques and review of the book-in-progress; Ann Gregory, for her research, photographs, and writing about the Towpath Tea House; Sharon Clark, Bob Chance, Art Johnson, Byron Young, June Bonham, Charles Day and Tanya Presberry for their writings on Berkley today; Yesmeen Healy-Day for her efforts in unraveling the art of indexing; Kari Beims for her rendering of the Berkley map, and former Berkley resident Roland Weldon Dorsey who volunteered his photographic talent to resurrect almost unusable photographs and prepare them for printing. And to our families who have had to live with the writing and rewriting of the book for almost two years, we thank you for your patience and encouragement.

A special bow is given to our editor, Louise White, whose style and wisdom sharpened and enriched these pages and, who, in editing the text, discovered that her great-grandfather of Baltimore fought in the same Civil War battle with a Berkley soldier, Phillip Webster.

We are particularly indebted to Ann Hege Hughes, President of Gateway Press, and Steven Meyer, Proprietor of The LetterEdge, for making the publishing journey an enjoyable one for us. Their professional advice, guidance, and talent have produced a handsome and readable book.

The stories and history belong to the people of Berkley. The errors are ours.

Constance Beims
Christine Tolbert

Introduction

The Berkley Crossroads

Berkley is one of the few remaining rural crossroads in Harford County, Maryland. Today, this unassuming, rural community, with its old structures and vista, can only evoke a glimmer of its past participation in the economic, political, and social growth of the region. Berkley was the site of a pivotal event in America's Revolutionary War, home to an uninterrupted history of free blacks in America, a station on the underground railroad, the location of Harford County's first public school for black students, and, until the 1920s, a thriving crossroads that served the travelers and commerce between Florida and Maine for almost 150 years. Berkley was an important part of Harford County's history, and, like many small villages and towns throughout America, was a contributor to the birth and growth of the nation.

Located on a gently contoured ridge of the Piedmont Plateau overlooking the Susquehanna River in northeastern Harford County, Berkley rests between the watershed of Hopkins Creek to the south and Peddler's Run to the north. The crossroads is one mile from present day U.S. Route 1 and one mile from the historic village of Darlington. With farmland, ponds, tree lines, and fencerows of wood and stone, the vista still has the ambience of an earlier time.

This journey is a story of blacks and whites living side by side for over two hundred years. It is a story of mutual respect and neighborliness that transcended the laws and mores of the time. It is also a story of economic interdependence and social separation. The names on the mailboxes today carry many of the family names that were here over a century ago—Presberry, Webster, Cooley, Sauers, Cain.

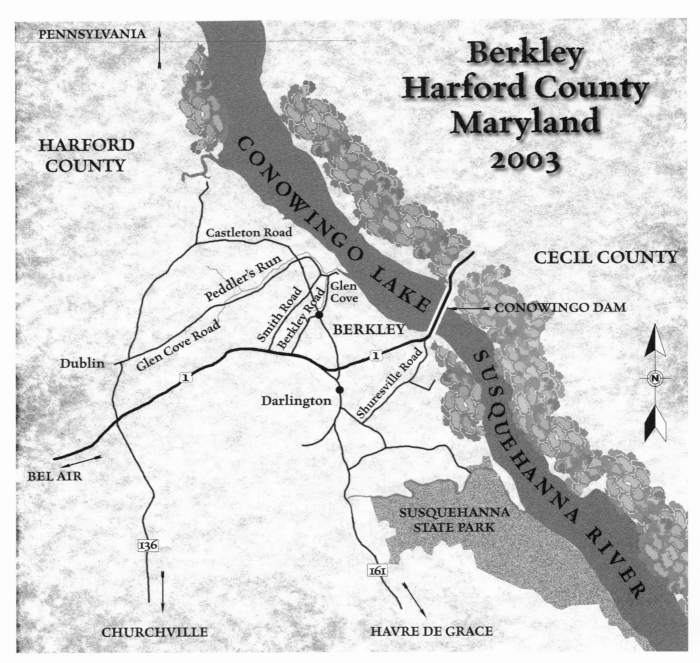

Rendered and donated by Kari Beims

The journey starts with the Susquehannock Indians and the beginnings of European settlement in the northern reaches of Harford County. The past is viewed through the writings of historians, land records, census records, diaries, newspapers, and ancestral stories from the early 1600s to the early 1800s when the Industrial Revolution changed production, transportation, and the way of life at the crossroads. The journey continues, recalling the impact of the Industrial Revolution on Berkley. No longer was the Susquehanna River forded at Bald Friar and no longer was the ferry necessary. The Conowingo Bridge was built across the Susquehanna River and Berkley opened for business. The book explores the effect of these changes on the daily lives of Berkley's residents in the 19th century, the area's participation in the Underground Railroad, the building of temples of faith, the community's experiences during the Civil War and the arrival of new entrepreneurs. This period also focuses on the passionate desire for education for all of the residents in the area, with an emphasis on the history of Berkley's Hosanna School, the first public school for blacks in Harford County.

The next segment of the journey looks at Berkley as its heyday was coming to a close and is devoted to the voices of Berkley. The Conowingo Dam was built and the Conowingo Lake formed. U.S. Route 1 was being re-routed to bypass Berkley and the industries and supporting commercial establishments began to close. Those interviewed for the book reminisce about life in Berkley in the early and mid-20th century—their childhood, daily life in Berkley, earning a living, the faith and education of the residents, World War II, and segregation. This journey ends in 2003 with Berkley part of the Lower Susquehanna Heritage Greenway and designated as a Historic District on the National Register of Historic Places, ensuring the preservation of the vista, the historic structures and sites, and the crossroads.

PART I

Early Berkley

"A commodious and delightful habitation"

Susquehanna River Vista by Walter Edge 1911
Private collection of Jean Sharpless Ewing

"Waking next day with an aking head
And thirst that made me leave my bed;
I rigg'ed myself and soon got up
To cool my liver with a cup
Of Succahanna, fresh and clear."

—Ebenezer Cook
The Sot-weed Factor

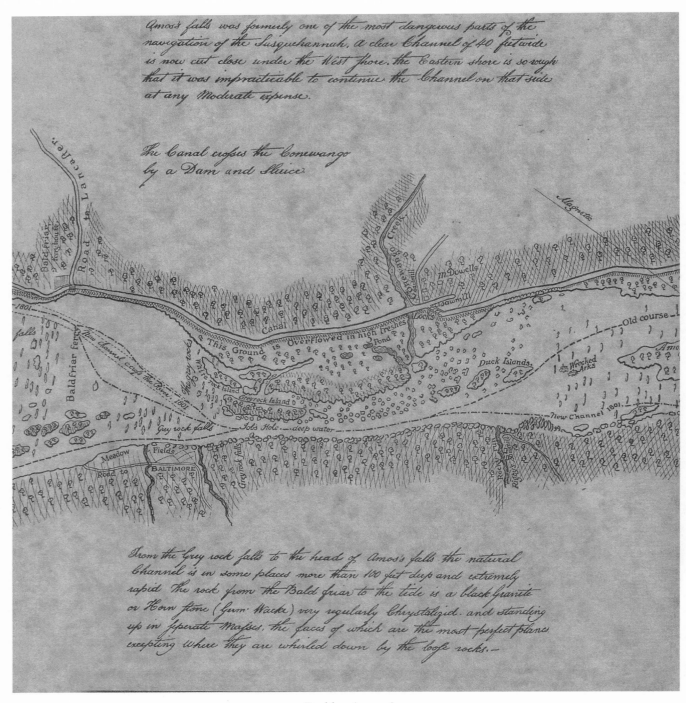

Berkley Area of
Benjamin Henry Latrobe MAP of 1810
Historical Society of Harford County

A Noble and Heroick Nation

Evidence and traces of Native American life in the lower Susquehanna basin, while sketchy and sparse, are cherished, and small hints of that past continue to be unearthed by today's inhabitants. There are, fortunately, the writings of the early European explorers who provide some understanding of the Native American existence along the Susquehanna River in Maryland.

The most noted European record of Native American inhabitants was that of Captain John Smith who encountered the Susquehannock Indians on his journey up the Susquehanna River in 1608. He wrote in his journal that they lived in "pallisaded townes and ... brested about very formally."[1] George Alsop, who conversed with the Susquehannocks, noted they stood "for the most part, seven feet" and "their 'gate' was straight, stately and majestic." He further observed that "Christian inhabitants and the rest of the Indians viewed the Susquehannocks as the most Noble and Heroick Nation of Indians that dwelt upon the confines of America."[2]

The Susquehannocks knew already what John Smith immortalized as he navigated the rock shoals and viewed the Susquehanna River and valley in May 1608 and recorded in his diaries, "Heaven and earth seemed never to have agreed better to frame a place for man's habitation ... Here are mountains, hills, plains, valleyes, rivers, and brookes, all running most pleasantly into a faire Bay."[3]

Before arriving on the Susquehanna shores, the ancestors of the Susquehannocks lived in the Upper Susquehanna Valley where early maize cultivation has been dated to the twelfth century. During the period 1400–1525, the Upper Valley was inhabited by the Iroquois. By the sixteenth century there was a split within the tribe and that splinter group became the Susquehannocks. They formed their own community and became the conduit for the trade of seashells in the sixteenth century and later brass from Europe to New England tribes.[4]

The Susquehannocks were close relatives of the Iroquois. However, when five tribes joined to form the Five Nations of Iroquois, the Susquehannocks went their own way and never became part of the Five Nations coalition. This decision eventually contributed to their demise. By the early 1600s the Susquehannocks were expelled from their original homeland and villages in lower New York State by the Iroquois. Wending their way south, they soon found settlement possible near the lower reaches of the river around Lancaster County, Pennsylvania.

The Susquehannocks were hunters. They lived near streams of fresh water in pallisaded enclosures and in the spring migrated to the salt waters at the head of the Chesapeake Bay for oysters and fish. By 1676 the Susquehannocks were widely dispersed from Pennsylvania to the Potomac River in Southern Maryland. A recorded map in Livingston's *Indian Records, 1666–1723*, gives the travel distance from the various "castles" of the Five Nations to the "Susquehanna Castle" on the Susquehanna River. There has been speculation that one of the "castles" was located at Bald Hill, north of Berkley. This information does raise the question of the origin of the name of

Castleton, located one mile from Berkley on what is now Castleton Road. This speculation about the castles of the Susquehannocks and subsequent forts established by settlers is reinforced in Samuel Mason's writing as he describes the Delaware and other Indians fording the Susquehanna at the Bald Friar Ford:

> The site of this fort is behind the first bald spot on Bald Hill, enclosing a spring, which has now almost dried up. From this eminence a clear view could be had of the entire breadth of the river and if a long line of Indians was seen, winding steadily across toward the Harford Shore, an alarm was sent out by "Heralds," summoning the inhabitants to the fort. It was known locally as the "Old Indian Fort."[5]

The permanent settlement of the Susquehannocks in Harford County is uncertain; however, a treaty with the Susquehannocks in 1666 suggests there was some permanent settlement in the area and cleared forestlands were used for the growing of corn and other crops "in a systematic way."[6] The treaty required the Susquehannocks to fence in their cornfields from the hogs and cattle of the English and, according to the treaty, "if any Englishman willfully throw (sic) down any of their fences they shall make the Indians full satisfaction for their damage."[7] During the mid-1600s the members of the Five Nations were at war with one another. In 1661, the Susquehannocks fought the Cayugas and Senecas, both part of the once united Five Nations of Iroquois. The conflict went on for over ten years, with the Susquehannocks almost victorious when, in 1671, another scourge—small pox—decimated them. In 1674 they were defeated by the Senecas and driven from their land. Their struggle for existence continued until a few survivors of the tribe "took refuge in Lancaster jail where they were cruelly put to death by a mob, thus ending a brave and high spirited people."[8]

Massacre of the Susquehannock Indians in 1763 by the Paxton Boys in Lancaster, Pennsylvania

Sinclair Lithograph, Gale Encyclopedia of Native American Tribes

As European settlement began to creep to the northern reaches of Maryland, Native Americans continued to be in the area, determined to defend their lands. To protect the expanding European settlements in these northern reaches of Maryland, Maryland Governor Copley, in 1692, ordered the establishment of rangers to patrol the "wilderness against roving bands of Indians."[9] The "Ranger's Road" extended from the main fort at Garrison Forest in Baltimore County to the Susquehanna River, thus the name most connected with these men—Garrison's Rangers. In 1692, the newly established government rangers recorded finding several Indian cabins in the wooded areas along the Susquehanna River but they probably were "the scattered dwellings of hunters and not permanent settlements."[10]

There are two documents that suggest there was a garrison post on what was later to become the Rigbie Farm. Jean Ewing recalled what she had been told by her parents and grandparents as a girl, *"Now the earliest accounts that I know of included a garrison set up on Rigbie's land … The Garrison was one of a string of forts built to keep the Indians from coming down along the river from Pennsylvania."*[11] Local historian Mary Bristow reinforces this account in her monograph on historic Rigbie House when she states, "Indians and settlers at battle. Red and White men had been at each other for years. And it **might** be true that the older part of the house stands on the very spot of an early ranger cabin."[12]

By the end of the seventeenth century signs of Native American habitation were beginning to disappear. Today, many of their important remnants are submerged under the Conowingo Lake. Before the waters of the Susquehanna River rose to form the lake behind the newly built Conowingo Dam in 1928, Indian petroglyphs were found in the caves along the Susquehanna River including the Berkley area. Many of these petroglyphs were photographed in 1916 by Martin G. Kurtz of Jarrettsville and William B. Marye of the Maryland Historical Society. Several petroglyphs were retrieved from the islands of the Susquehanna in the 1920s prior to the rising waters in the Susquehanna. Collected by the Maryland Academy of Sciences, they were reassembled for preservation at that institution.[13] Today, the Historical Society of Harford County is the repository of some of these petroglyphs and periodically places them on display.

JEAN SHARPLESS EWING's ancestors arrived in Berkley in the early 1800s. Ms. Ewing attended Germantown Friends School, the Wharton College, and the University of Pennsylvania. She taught school in Darlington and Bel Air and during World War II was a Technical Illustrator for the Martin Company and Bendix Corporation. A Quaker activist throughout her life, Ms. Ewing had been involved in most of the social issues of her time. In 1972, she surveyed Berkley's historic sites for the Maryland Historical Trust's survey forms for the National Register of Historic Places. She resided at a Quaker retirement home in New Jersey until her death on February 23, 2003 at the age of 89.

Interviewed 9 February 2000

Many of today's Berkley residents have their small collections of Indian arrowheads, soapstone mixing bowls, granite for flint, fire starters, etc., but the visual remains of this "most noble and heroick nation" are fleeting at best. What remains is the splendor of the river's shoreline, cliffs, outcroppings and forestland that still evoke a presence of the past as witnessed by Captain John Smith and the Native American tribes that roamed, hunted, and fished in this river valley.

Indian Petroglyphs located on rocks near Bald Friar in situ prior to the formation of the Conowingo Lake.

A Pretty Fair Prospect for a Pioneer

Historically, many villages, towns, and cities have risen at water's edge. This certainly was the experience for settlement and growth in Harford County. Old Baltimore on the banks of the Bush River was established in 1661. Governing bodies were established and the first Port of Baltimore had great sailing ships arriving and leaving the port to import and export goods and raw materials. While the lower reaches of what was then part of Baltimore County grew and flourished, the upper Piedmont lands of the county continued to have only small pockets of populations—mostly cabins for fur trappers, hunters, and scattered garrisons and forts to protect the citizenry from the Native Americans who roamed and hunted in the region.

Once the towns and cities bordering the ocean and bays became inhabited, the early pioneers began to move inland hoping to obtain land through homesteading or low cost. Many settlers, from New York to Virginia, discovered the richness of the Susquehanna River valley— "... A valley whose natural resources would provide the newcomers with vast quantities of timber; fertile soil for cropping; workable amounts of iron and copper ores and plenty of potential water power from the many fast flowing streams in the area. A pretty fair prospect for a pioneer."[14]

Indeed, a pretty fair prospect, but not necessarily peaceful. In addition to various Indian raids, a battle raged for many years between Pennsylvania and Maryland, known to many as an "acrimonious Border Dispute."[15] As a result of errors made by King Charles II of England, the boundaries of Maryland and Pennsylvania overlapped. And, as one historian noted, "No self respecting Pennsylvanian would lower himself to trade with the detested neighbor to the south."[16] Other Pennsylvanians, however, realized that their main markets lay to the south and navigation on the river was shorter and safer than overland transport. In fact, some settlements along the Lower Susquehanna were prospering, so it is easy to understand why William Penn began to make advances on the border. This dispute resulted in skirmishes and a shifting border.

King Charles II intervened finally and ordered a cessation of all land grants until the matter could be resolved. A settlement was reached in May of 1738. Charles Mason and Jeremiah Dixon were hired to identify and survey the border, marking the official beginning of the Mason-Dixon Line. This settlement benefited both Pennsylvania and Maryland—timber and ore moved south to the mills along the river and further down the Chesapeake Bay to Joppa and beyond to modern day Baltimore where mills and industry were flourishing. The return trip brought finished goods, foodstuffs, and other imports to the towns developing along the Susquehanna River in Pennsylvania. A new arrival to the area participated in the deliberations and settlement of the border dispute. His name was Nathaniel Rigbie.

Nathaniel Rigbie Comes North

The habitation and landscape around Berkley began to change in the early part of the 1700s when Nathaniel Rigbie, orphaned as a child and ward of Thomas Tench, inherited a 2000-acre tract designated as "Phillip's Purchase." The Tench will of 1708 stated: "to Nathaniel Rigbie, a grandson of my first wife, all of my lands within the Province,"[17] which in addition to the 2000-acre tract, consigned caretakers for him until his majority. Tench's first wife was a Rigbie. Her family had arrived in colonial America in about 1650. The family lived in Virginia and then moved to what is now Anne Arundel County, Maryland. James Rigbie, the first Rigbie in the colonies, had come from England as an Indian Agent and ran a store. He patented many land tracts, including lands along the Susquehanna River, and was a prominent Quaker in the middle colonies.

The original tract of land had spilled along the banks of the Susquehanna River from Worthington's Landing, later called Shure's Landing, to Glen Cove. Its western boundary passed through Darlington. Having come of age, Nathaniel Rigbie married Cassandra Coale and moved to "Phillips Purchase" in 1730. Prior to the move, Rigbie had sold several holdings, probably because of financial necessity. In 1725, John Hawkins purchased one hundred acres from Rigbie. Three years later, Rigbie sold one hundred acres to Thomas Jones and five hundred acres to Gerrard Hopkins. In 1731 Henry Coale purchased two hundred acres. This left twelve hundred acres in the Rigbie family. In 1732, "Rigbie House," which still stands today, was built.

After three generations of Rigbies, the house was owned by the Fletcher Jones family from the early 1820s until it was sold to John Clark in 1960. Rigbie House is on the National Register of Historic Places.

Photograph by Scott Prettyman

With his twenty slaves residing on his properties near Lapidum, Rigbie produced tobacco that was shipped to London from this landing in his own ships. In addition to his tobacco crop, Rigbie owned a sawmill located on the banks of the river, a trading post, and a store that serviced the small community growing up around him. Because his store was on the "Upper Route," coming from Joppa to the river ford at Bald Hill, it can be assumed that, as the only provision stop in the area, it flourished by providing needed supplies and foodstuffs for the travelers, including Native Americans still in the area. There is conjecture that, "this store was evidently at his dwelling and was patronized quite freely by friendly Indians, who came to barter for powder, shot and kettles."[18]

Over his lifetime Nathaniel Rigbie became a prominent citizen of the area and one of the two richest men in the county. Lord Baltimore appointed him Justice of the Peace, an important position in the county. Justices were not only responsible for maintaining the peace but also levied taxes. In 1735, he was appointed Lieutenant Colonel of the cavalry of Baltimore County, which, at that time, included Harford County. Rigbie was now a soldier as well, quelling flurries of uprisings between the settlers and Indians and skirmishes with Pennsylvanians over the Maryland-Pennsylvania boundary. At his house "were stored arms and supplies used in these forays and on the property not far behind the house, was a building of logs used as a prison for the captives ..."[19] In 1738, Rigbie was appointed High Sheriff, the most important civic position in the county and the high point of his career in public service.

Rigbie's wife, Cassandra, and their children joined the Deer Creek Presbyterian Church but Rigbie continued to belong to the Church of England, and served as a vestryman in St. George's Parish at Spesutia, located in southern Harford County.

Yet, probably because of his Quaker heritage, in 1737 Rigbie conveyed three and one half acres of his land to the Quakers who lived in the Darlington area. There they built the first Society of Friends Meeting House in the northern reaches of the county.

Rigbie was one of the wealthiest men of his time. His personal property was valued at about seven thousand dollars. He was a man who "dressed with care, wearing broadcloth and silk stockings, with silver shoe and knee buckles and gold cuff buttons. His dwelling was beautifully furnished with the usual silverware, books and paintings."[20] Nathaniel Rigbie died in 1752 at age fifty-seven and was buried in the Friends Meeting House cemetery.

John Clark of Rigbie House shared his knowledge of how Nathaniel Rigbie came to settle in this area, *"Well, in the early days ... this grant of land was given to the Calverts, and now here you are in England and this is just forest and rugged country, except where some people from Virginia had already come up and kind of staked out, you might say, a holding or what not, of the fur business and things along the river. And now you have to populate the place. So what they did was to grant patents to people. Many times, they were for services rendered for something, and sometimes they were sold, and a little bit of money*

JOHN EVAN CLARK,
born in 1910, had an illustrious life in law and public service. With ancestors in the Darlington area for generations, Mr. Clark moved back to the area in 1960 when he purchased the Rigbie Farm. A law graduate of the University of Maryland, he maintained a private law practice while serving as a magistrate, county solicitor and an elected Delegate to the Maryland General Assembly. He was a founding member of the Maryland Environmental Trust, The Maryland Historical Trust, and the Maryland Agricultural Preservation Program and served on the Berkley Cemetery Board of Trustees. He and his wife, Sharon, have continued to preserve and maintain the historic Rigbie house and farm. John Clark died January 3, 2003.

Interviewed 16 June 2000

put in the treasury, and a very large tract of land would go with it. This was a patent that was granted of two thousand acres. It was granted to a man by the name of Rigbie. He supervised or had gotten by some process, the land deforested, and the condition where he could rent it, or have tenants, or maybe get some tobacco for the rent. Eventually, when it started to get more populated, he'd sell it off. It was all the way down to a hundred and seventeen acres when I bought it."[21]

Seekers of Land and Freedom

That there are no known eighteenth century structures extant in the area, except for Rigbie House, does not prevent speculation that there was a Berkley already settled before 1800. The Rigbie House may have been the grand manor of Berkley but it can be assumed that, in addition to his twenty slaves, there were also many laborers and craftsmen with various skills who lived in the vicinity. These workers manned the Rigbie sawmill, labored in his forge, worked his extensive farmland, managed his stores, mined his quarry, and performed tasks for the upkeep of his home and surrounding structures. And some testimony suggests that the settlers expected growth in the area. A petition recorded in the Baltimore County Court Proceedings of 1751 requests the commissioners to "lay out a road from Colonel Rigbie, late deceased, to the Susquehanna ford at Bald Friar."[22]

The new settlers arriving along the banks and on the hills of the Susquehanna struggled to make their new land successful. Their greatest resource was the river, providing sustenance and opportunity for trade. Most of the land was forested and needed clearing before shelter could be built and planting begun. Having cleared the land, crops were planted, harvested, and preserved to carry the family and livestock through the winter.

The daily lives of these settlers required stamina and faith. They had to have an average of 50 acres, with about 35 acres in tillage, in order to survive. Tilled by oxen and by hand, this land produced corn, wheat, spelt, rye, barley, oats, and flax. These crops were supplemented by a vegetable garden that yielded potatoes, yams, sweet corn, melons, peas, beans, squash, pumpkins, cabbages, and turnips, and, "then, as now, gardening was a constant battle with bugs, the weeds, and other predators. By present standards the yields were small."[23]

Apple, peach and pear seeds also traveled north with the settler but "he didn't bring them to eat the fruits, he brought them because apples make cider, pears make sherry, and peaches made [sic] brandy."[24] Once the orchards were established, they produced peaches, plums, apples, and pears; harvesting the woods provided black walnuts, persimmons, pawpaws, and mulberries. In season, "blackberries, raspberries, gooseberries and huckleberries grew wild along the quiet paths and lanes only awaiting their harvest."[25] Most of the homesteads had domesticated fowl and hunting gave them a wide variety of meats for smoking and preserving—rabbit, deer, and bear were plentiful. Fur trading provided some revenue for other essentials.

*ELVA PRESBERRY CAIN
was born in Berkley in 1915 into
a family that included influential and prominent educators in
the black community. Her father,
Kenton Presberry, was the principal at Hosanna School during
the early part of the 20ᵗʰ century.
The family lived adjacent to the
Hosanna School in the dwelling
built by Cupid Paca in the early
1800s. She attended Hosanna
School and, after attending college,
eventually taught at the Hosanna
School in the early 40s. Until recently, she and her husband resided
on Smith Road in a house believed
to have been a Quaker school.*

Interviewed 15 January 2000

The settlers brought tobacco seed for their cash crop
—an easy crop to ship from this area. Unlike most of the
county, hogsheads of tobacco did not have to be rolled
to Joppa. They were taken to Lapidum Landing, south of
Berkley along the Susquehanna River, where the tobacco,
"usually a variety called Orinoco,"[26] was loaded on ships
for transport to England and other destinations.

Colonists fished the Susquehanna River primarily from
the shore and batteries, for their own sustenance and for
profit. Herring and shad were abundant, and fishing the
river was profitable, even from the shore. This abundance
was enriched by Asahel Bailey of Havre de Grace, who in-
vented the "float" around 1830 and "revolutionized the
whole business."[27] This invention permitted larger seines
to be used and more men hired for the fishing enterprises
along the river. As Alpert Silver recalled in 1888, "In former times, the water seemed animate with the finney tribe.
It was a frequent occurrence that the seine gathered more
than it could land."[28] Catches were as high as 600 barrels
a day.

Berkley's first dwellings were constructed of logs. For
the new arrivals' shelter, "it was probably done rather
quickly and crudely, and not too well done, because man
didn't have much time to get that house built to provide
shelter for that first winter."[29]

Log structures still exist in Berkley. The tenant house
on Ribgie farm at Castleton Road was built and owned
originally by Cupid Paca, one of the first black landowners in Berkley. It later became the home of Kenton Presberry, the principal at Hosanna School. Its interior was
built of logs and today, *"the log construction is concealed
indoors and out in this small and probably very old house."*[30] Elva Cain, who grew up in
the house, remembered, *"Where I grew up, was the house right next to the school house
[Hosanna]. All I had to do was scoot over the fence. Go around the bend, it still stands
there … It was once a log cabin, but my father had weather board put over it … while we
lived there he added on two rooms—a bedroom and a living room. And the roof raised.
That's what repairs he made and had shingles put on."*[31] This structure still remains
next to the Hosanna School. Another log structure located on the northeast corner
of Berkley Road is intact and restored. A black family named James owned the house
for over one hundred years. They lost it in the early 1900s when a loan could not be
repaid. White families have owned the house since then. The current owners, Stephen
and Gwyneth Howard, have continued to preserve the historical integrity of this log
cabin with the original fireplace and hand-hewn logs gracing the room. Other log
structures have vanished, including Shirley Thompson's childhood home on Castleton Road. *"It was part log. I can remember going into the basement. It was unusual to*

have part of the basement concrete and the other part dirt. 'Cause where the log part is, it was still dirt … and the dining area it had the log beams from the log part and an old fireplace in it."[32] A fire destroyed this structure in the 1980s.

Nearly all clothing was made using products from the farm. Flax and wool were "grown, spun, woven and tailored"[33] for the family's needs. Men's work clothes were "osnabrig (rough linen) shirts, leather britches or britches of stout wool … Women usually wore dresses of osnabrig or wool … For Sunday church—good muslin, gingham or silk … made proper clothing … So highly did Mother regard her Sunday clothes, they were bequeathed to her daughters in her will. Fortunate was the Mother who had a wardrobe sufficient to leave one silk dress to each of her daughters."[34]

Travel during this time was difficult at best. In addition to horseback, an oxcart or horse-drawn two-wheeled wagon sufficed for moving goods, produce and people. Only the very rich could afford a carriage and they were few. In fact, prior to 1776, in Philadelphia, a city of 50,000 residents, there were only 84 coaches in the entire city,[35] so one can imagine the scarcity of carriage or coach travel in Berkley during this pre-revolutionary period. The Conestoga wagon was the conveyor of heavy equipment and raw materials. With rear wheels up to 6 feet in diameter, 6-inch wide iron "tires," and pulled by four to six horses, these wagons could haul 6 tons over the roadways. Mail stages also carried passengers. "They were unsprung, swayed violently over the rough roads and were generally uncomfortable,"[36] making for quite a miserable ride.

SHIRLEY PEAK THOMPSON grew up in one of the older houses in Berkley. Born in Aberdeen, Maryland, in 1936, she arrived in Berkley at an early age and attended Darlington Elementary School and Dublin High School. Employed at Aberdeen Proving Ground for 18 years as an Education Technician, today she is a leading member of and unfaltering worker for the Darlington Volunteer Fire Company along with her husband, Alan. So respected by the community, they were awarded the Darlington "Apple of Our Eye" award in 2000. Residing in Dublin, she remembers Berkley as a "mixed" community, with blacks and whites living next door to one another.

Interviewed 9 February 2000

Much of the wares and commodities necessary for daily life came by packhorses. One rider could handle twenty packhorses and could carry 5,000 pounds of corn or wheat quickly and more cheaply than by cart. Packhorses also brought tinware, cloth, thread, needles and other small items essential for daily life. These peddlers traveled throughout the colonies and, if they were literate, they carried pencil and paper to write letters for the settlers to be sent to relatives in England or throughout the colonies. The shoemaker arrived with his leather and tools and stayed with the family until all the shoes were made. He was also welcome because he brought "neighborhood news."[37] The news of the world and the colonies came from the Baltimore and Philadelphia newspapers that, surprisingly, "were promptly delivered to the inns and taverns along the Post Road."[38] The newspapers were then carried by horseback to the taverns in the upper reaches of Harford County and to a few individuals who then shared the news with the populace.

Lafayette at Rigbie House

Nathaniel and Cassandra Rigbie, the first Rigbies of colonial Berkley, had ten children. Their son, James, inherited Rigbie House and through him Berkley's history became important.

James Rigbie became a distinguished citizen. He served as a captain of the militia and, like his father before him, was appointed High Sheriff of Baltimore County. He joined the Friends and was a prominent minister of the society.[39] He also had ten children.

In April 1781, his house was the site of one of Harford County's most momentous events. The revolution of the colonials against English rule emboldened a young Frenchman, the Marquis de Lafayette, to join the colonial quest for independence. More inspired to fight the British than to fight for the independence of the colonies, the 20-year-old Marquis sailed to America on his own ship. He arrived in 1777, along with other adventurous French soldiers. He so impressed the Continental Congress that he was designated a major-general of the Continental Army without pay and he became part of General George Washington's staff. He was wounded at the battle of Brandywine and was at Valley Forge with Washington during the disastrous winter of 1777–78. Anticipating a war with England, he returned to France, and when that did not materialize, he returned to America to resume his rank and role in the Colonial Army, this time not as commander of French soldiers but as a leader of a small Colonial force.[40]

In early 1781, as the Revolutionary War was reaching a pivotal point, Washington ordered Lafayette to take a detachment of troops south to join General Nathaniel Green in Virginia in anticipation of the Battle of Yorktown. Lafayette began his march south with 1200 troops in two brigades and arrived at the east bank of the Susquehanna River in early April 1781. In his memoirs, Lafayette described how his men had to make a "diabolic crossing" across the rocky, bitter-cold Susquehanna River near Bald Friar.[41]

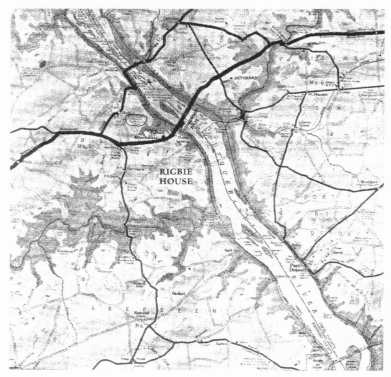

Lafayette's Route across the Susquehanna River to James Rigbie's Land.

Lafayette in Harford County. J. Alexis Shriver, 1931

Having reached the banks on the western shore, General Lafayette and his troops "followed the river from the fording place down to Glen Cove by way of Berkley to the Rigbie home."[42] Swarming over the hills and across fields they arrived at the estate and pitched their tents in the fields surrounding Rigbie's house. "Wet and exhausted, ill-clad, ill-fed, shoeless, and unpaid, many troops threatened to desert; others threatened outright mutiny."[43] Lafayette and his officers held a council of war in Rigbie's house on the night of April 13, 1781, and drafted a proclamation to inspire the troops. According to some accounts, the resulting proclamation read before the troops quelled the incipient uprising. Writing to Washington, Lafayette recounted his efforts to inspire the troops:

> *April 18, 1781*
>
> *My Dear General,*
> *Every one of my letters were written in so lamentable a tone, that I am happy to give you a pleasanter prospect.*

CHARLES MARVIN COOLEY,
a descendant of the Jones family who owned Rigbie farm for over 100 years was born in 1924. As a youth he attended Bel Air High School and the Darlington Academy where his great-grandfather had taught. A World War II veteran serving from 1943–46, Mr. Cooley said he was never leaving Berkley again and he has not. He resides with his wife, Verneal, in his grandmother's house that was designed by Philadelphia architect, Walter Cope. A career employee of the Chesapeake and Potomac Telephone Company, he is now retired enjoying his garden and family, particularly his grandchildren who also reside in Berkley. Charles Cooley's interview is rich in the physical details of the Berkley of his youth. He regales the listener with his stories of skunk hunting, mistletoe gathering, raising goats, and the life of a farm boy. Charles is holding a 1931 photograph of the Sesqui-Centennial celebration of Lafayette at Rigbe House.
Interviewed 21 February 2000

> *When I left Susquehanna Ferry, it was the general opinion that we would not have six hundred men by the time we should arrive at our destination.*
>
> *… On my arrival on this side of the Susquehanna, I had an order for the troops, wherein I endeavored to throw a kind of infamy upon desertion, and to improve every particular affection of theirs. Since then, desertion has been lessened. Two deserters have been taken up; one of whom has been hanged to-day … The word lessened does not convey a sufficient idea of what experience has proved to be true, to the honour of our excellent soldiers. It has been announced in general orders, that the detachment was intended to fight an enemy far superior in number, under difficulties of ever sort …*[44]

While Lafayette was drafting his proclamation, a local miller, Walter Piquot [also Pigot], having been accused of selling flour to the British, was hanged.[45] That hanging may have held some sway over the mood of the troops.

The event of Piquot's hanging, possibly referred to in Lafayette's letter to Washington, has evoked many stories among today's residents and historians. To some, the hanging tree is on the northeast corner of Berkley and Castleton Road. Charles Cooley,[46] whose family dates back to the 1820s in Berkley and owned Rigbie House, remembers that *"it was a walnut tree that had stood about 200 feet from the Rigbie House."* There is also debate on whether Piquot met his final hour at Rigbie's farm or elsewhere. In all accounts a Major McPherson was transporting Piquot to military authorities after his unsuccessful attempt to escape. In one scenario Piquot was taken from Joppa to Colonel Rigbie. Serving in his capacity as the High Sheriff, Rigbie imprisoned Piquot in the jail located on his estate and ordered his hanging at that site. In other accounts, Piquot was turned over to military authorities and hanged at Susquehanna Ferry. According to Mary Bristow, a Harford County historian, who conjectured whether Piquot's ghost haunted Rigbie House, the hanging occurred elsewhere:

> The first alleged spectre is that of a hanged man: a spy or traitor or deserter or a wayward miller. Digging into published *Archives of Maryland,* Vol. XLV and into local texts, I found that indeed one Walter or Heathcote Pickett or Pigot was hanged by order of Lafayette sometime between Friday 13 and Friday 20 April 1781. Most likely in the small hours of Saturday the 14th, since the general needed a deterrent to restless, bone-tired troops threatening rebellion. Pigot came to his untimely end at Susquehanna Ferry after imprisonment at Joppa and an aborted escape. Susquehanna Ferry is the old name of Lapidum on Herring Run between Rock Run and Havre de Grace. Now a footnote to history—a "little" guy—killed on a charge of treason may be forgiven if his spirit does not rest easily in the hereafter. But why haunt Rigbie House?

Historic marker commemorating General Lafayette and his troops at Rigbie House in 1781.

> A better haunting place would be the hanging place or the Joppa "gaol." James Rigbie had nothing to do with the arrest and imprisonment or with the execution. Neither had the deed been on Rigbie's plantation. Besides, James Rigbie, a gentle, soul-searching person, had long ago foresworn anything to do with killing.[47]

Christopher Weeks noted, "It would be futile to try to determine whether actions or words—the hanging or the speech—spoke more loudly that April morning."[48] But Lafayette and his troops did continue to Yorktown, routed the British General Charles Cornwallis, and the genesis of a nation was assured.

Later that same year Comte de Rochambeau made two trips south through Harford County in preparation for the battle at Yorktown. On his second movement south, on September 10, 1781, Rochambeau traveled the same route as Lafayette, bringing troops and supplies down from the North and fording the Susquehanna River at Bald Friar. But it is Lafayette's successful efforts to quell the rebellion of his troops that are commemorated on the historical marker in Berkley.

Early Laws Governing Berkley

The settlers' everyday life can give some insight into the daily struggle to survive and, with good fortune, thrive. It is equally important to understand the legal restraints and privileges that controlled their environment, particularly the kinds of laws that the High Sheriffs and other officials had to enforce. While the State of Maryland enacted hundreds of laws by the late 1700s, it is interesting to explore a few that were important at that time but less so today.

Several forms of currency were used in colonial times and the first United States currency was not produced until 1793. One of the common currencies must have been tobacco judging from the penalties for breaking some of the following laws. The 1799 digest of the Laws of Maryland included:

DRUNKEN INDIANS—Act of 1715—Persons carrying liquor to any Indian town or within three miles thereof and selling to the Indians, shall forfeit five hundred pounds of tobacco, one-half to support the government and the other half to the informer. To prevent disorders by drunken Indians, no person shall sell to any Indian, above one gallon of rum, wine, brandy, or spirits, or above five gallons of cider, berry quince drink, or strong beer, in the space of one day on penalty of three thousand pounds of tobacco.

HOG STEALING—Act of 1715—Persons killing any unmarked swine about three months old (not being upon their own land or in company with their own flock) shall be judged hog stealers and suffer such corporal pains as in the act of thieving and stealing.

BOUNDARIES OF LAND—Act of 1722—No person shall on any pretense whatsoever cut down or destroy any boundary tree, either on his own or any other persons land, even though such boundary tree should stand within his own land, on penalty of five thousands pound of tobacco for every offence, one-half to the informer and the other half to the free school of the county.

SABBATH BREAKING—Act of 1723—Persons working on Sundays or suffering their children or slaves to work or profane the Lord's day by gaming, fowling, hunting or other unlawful pastimes, shall on conviction before a single magistrate forfeit two hundred pounds of tobacco for the use of the county, and any housekeepers selling strong liquor on Sunday (except in cases of absolute necessity) shall forfeit two thousand pounds of tobacco; one half to the use of county and the other to the informer.

CURSING, SWEARING, DRUNKENESS—Act of 1723—Every person profanely cursing or swearing in presence or hearing of any magistrate, minister, secretary, sheriff, coroner, vestryman, church warden or magistrate shall be fined for the first curse or oath, two shillings, current money; and for every other or curse after the first, five shillings, to the use of the county. Persons drunk in presence of any of persons aforesaid shall be fined five shillings for every offence.

BOATS—Act of 1737—Persons convicted of willfully burning any ship or any other vessel, sloop or boat of seventeen feet keel or upwards, and their aiders and abettors, shall suffer death without aid of clergy.

HORSE STEALING—Act of 1744—Every person who shall feloniously take or steal any horse, mare, gelding, or colt within this province and all their aiders and abettors and accessories before or after the act, shall on conviction, outlawry, or refusing to answer directly, or standing mute upon arraignment, suffer death without benefit of clergy.

FORGING OR COUNTERFEITING COINS—Act of 1767—Persons forging or counterfeiting foreign gold or silver coins (commonly current in the Province) for the first offence shall be whipped, pilloried and cropped; and for the second offence, be branded in the cheek and banished.

WOLVES—Act of 1788—When any credible free person shall bring before any Justice of the Peace the head of any wolf actually caught and killed within the limits of that county, the Justice shall judge the age of such wolf and if he believe it to exceed six months, shall, after causing the ears to be cut off and tongue taken out, issue a certificate, and persons producing such certificate, shall for every old wolf's head be allowed five pounds, and for every young wolf's head, twenty shillings in current money.

DELEGATE'S SALARIES—Act of 1796—Four dollars and fifty cents shall be allowed the Speaker of House of Delegates and three dollars and fifty cents to each member of the General Assembly for every days attendance as such, besides the itinerant charges and ferriages.

CROWS—Act of 1796—If any person shall bring to any Justice of the Peace of the county in which such person resides, the head of any crow or crows, such person shall for every such head be allowed in the county levy six cents, and the Justice shall cause the head or heads be burnt or destroyed.[49]

Through Maryland's colonial period, Harford County was part of Baltimore County. In 1774, Harford County was established as a separate county with its own governance, giving the county some autonomy in its public decisions. The Governor of Maryland and the State Legislature, however, continued to be the fount of all major laws governing the citizenry of the state—particularly in providing funding for road, bridge, and waterway construction.

Getting from Here to There

As the century advanced and population expanded inland, dirt roads, most of which were privately owned, began to join homes and farms. In 1782, when the town of Bell Aire (today's Bel Air) was first laid out, there were five roads converging in the town, including one leading to Conowingo connecting by way of the Bald Friar Ford. This route to the ford would open commerce to Lancaster and Philadelphia. In an Act of the 1795 Maryland Legislature "every farmer or landowner must have a right to a road to his dwelling or farm and the county surveyor was directed to lay out such road on application."[50] The specifications in the law required a width of 16 feet including ditches and the upkeep and maintenance were to be paid by the property owner. In 1791, the Maryland General Assembly required that roads be straightened including "one other road leading from the Bald Friar Ferry, on said river to Belle Air and from thence in as straight a direction as the situation of the ground will permit toward Baltimore Town as far as the Baltimore County line."[51]

At the end of the 1700s travel became better along the river. No longer was it necessary to ford the river by foot or scow or attempt to raft across. In 1791, the Bald Friar Ferry became the transport of choice to cross the Susquehanna for points north and east. For over 25 years, goods, produce, and passengers traveled through Berkley to board the Bald Friar Ferry on their way to Philadelphia, New York, and many villages and towns in between. The name Bald Friar has been traced to the individual who operated the scow across the ford and then the ferry. "A bald headed man, named Fry, gave the area a slightly abridged edition of his name."[52] Over the years, Bald Fry's Ferry was transformed into Bald Fryar's Ferry and finally into Bald Friar's Ferry.

While early settlers were trying to navigate the river, rafts, boats, or arks were not regular sights on the river until after 1800. In 1796, a Pennsylvania German by the name of Breider owned a flour-mill and is said to have built an ark, loaded it with flour and ran it down the Susquehanna, and thence to Baltimore. This is believed to have been the first venture of its kind and Breider, having demonstrated the practicality of navigating the perilous river as well as the profitableness of the Baltimore market, was followed the next year by several others. In 1797, the bed of the Susquehanna River was declared to be "a public highway, free for any person or persons whatever to work thereon in clearing the obstructions to its navigations."[53]

Early ark on the Susquehanna River
Historical Society of Harford County (The James T. Wollon Collection)

These arks were 75 to 100 feet long and 15 to 20 feet wide with a very shallow draft of only 3 to 5 feet. The early goods rafted down the river were wheat and corn. The corn was concentrated into corn whiskey and the wheat into flour; they were then placed in barrels before rafting the river, making the products more portable.[54] In fact, rafting goods and raw materials down the Susquehanna was dependably successful only in the spring when the river was running high from the spring melt and rain upriver. This successful means of navigation, however, began an era of commerce on the Susquehanna River that used every means available—rafts, arks, bridges, ferries and canals—to transport raw and finished goods to the many markets opening up beyond the river's mouth.

Another Century Approaches

By the latter part of the eighteenth century, industries had begun along the Susquehanna River. The "Cumberland Forge," built by Nathaniel Rigbie in 1749, was producing iron and metal works for farming and industry. His quarry was producing stone for building and roads, flint for tools, and his sawmill provided finished lumber for construction and woodworking.

The Susquehanna was bountiful with fish and, at the head of the Chesapeake Bay, oysters were plentiful, providing a market opportunity for the settlers. It was a fine transportation corridor—logs were rafted down the river for construction in more populated areas and travel on the river was adequate—provided that one was going downstream.

While industrial and transportation ventures were erupting along the river's edge, the Haudecoeur's Map of 1799 shows Rigbie, Worthington, Stump, Coale, Hawkins, and Hopkins as the only major landholders.[55] These early settlers, with their supporting labor forces, would soon witness and be part of the changes in their landscape. Darlington would become a thriving village and the hamlet of Berkley would be an important stop for those crossing the Susquehanna. The number of mills and other business enterprises would increase and prosper, as both communities would become home for many entrepreneurs and farmers of the nineteenth century.

The importance of spiritual nourishment was already beginning to blossom. The Deer Creek Friends Meeting House had been an important center of fellowship and worship for the citizens of Darlington and Berkley since the early part of the eighteenth century. During this time the Quakers undertook the spiritual care of the free blacks in the area. "The [Friends'] Meeting … conducted many meetings for worship for Negroes, which were well attended. In 1779, the Meeting formed a committee for the oversight of manumitted slaves, to protect freed blacks from being kidnapped and resold into slavery; in this instance, freed men and women were legally placed under the care of the Meeting."[56] The Deer Creek Harmony Presbyterian Church was serving its communicants in a wooden two-story structure before the close of the 1700s and, by 1837 the congregation had erected a new structure.

At the latter part of the eighteenth century, James Rigbie continued to subdivide the remaining 1200 acres and since he had no sons, inheritance rights were shared with his sons-in-law. For Berkley's history, the life and decisions of son-in-law John Corse and his wife, Cassandra, are significant. This was the couple who, in 1822, sold land to Cupid Paca.

PART II

Berkley Welcomes Traders And Travelers

"Use Conowingo Crossing"

The Conowingo Bridge and Toll House

Berkley Welcomes the Farmer, the Entrepreneur, and the Craftsman

By 1810, land records started to show more land purchases for settlement in the area. Over the next 40 years Berkley began to emerge as a residential as well as commercial community along the upper reaches of Maryland's portion of the Susquehanna River. And the settlers began to arrive: English, Welsh, Scots, German, Irish, African, and re-settlers from Virginia, North Carolina and southern Maryland—free, indentured or in slavery, bringing with them their faith, values, skills, and fortitude from the Old World and carrying the dreams and promises of the new one. As these settlers arrived, the woods were cleared, acreage tilled, and farming began in earnest —for sustenance and for market. As industry along the river increased, the craftsmen came—quarriers, millwrights, wheelwrights, carpenters, coopers, sawyers, blacksmiths, stonemasons, brickmakers, bricklayers, joiners, and millers.

Through all this it was still the river that attracted the new population—for its water to drive machinery, for its food, for its pleasure, and for its vistas that nourished the soul.

Freedom and Emancipation Come Early to Berkley

Slavery in Maryland, particularly in the Berkley/Darlington area, was being rejected long before the 1863 Emancipation Proclamation. Many slaves were released upon reaching a certain date or age, and existing court records show that the blacks in the community had some standing in the courts—appearing because of offenses or as witnesses. In one such case in 1835, Margaret Stump v. Negro Stephen, the court recorded that "said Negro Stephen was a slave for a term of years and entitled to his freedom on the first day of July Eighteen Hundred Thirty-Five. ..."[57] This short phrase provides significant information. The absence of a second name for Stephen was a practice common during the time and a practice carried well into the twentieth century. Also, most of the blacks in the area were indentured, working for a family rather than a farm manager, which, while bleak, at least provided some the hope for freedom. Fortunately, the hope of freedom became a reality for most blacks in Berkley and Darlington long before the Civil War.

The historical census data show the growth of free blacks in Harford County.[58]

Date	Free Blacks	Slaves
1790	755	3,417
1830	2,058	2,947
1850	3,644	1,800
1870	4,855	0

Free Negro Passes.
After the Fugitive Slave Act of 1793, free blacks were required to carry passes on their person at all times to avoid being captured as fugitive slaves. The top pass was issued to John Presbury who was born free and the lower to Charles H. Hooper who was manumitted.

Donated to Christine Tolbert by Mary Bristow

Few of the slaves listed in the 1790 census resided in Berkley or Darlington. There are, however, a few traces of slave ownership. R. I. Jackson, a successful businessman in the area, owned slaves before the Civil War. During renovations long after Jackson's death, Alfred Edge, a carpenter and builder in the area, repaired the rear part of the second floor, where, as author Samuel Mason recorded:

> On hammering here a hollow reverberation was heard and on removing the plaster, a door was disclosed barred with iron, closing the entrance to the room behind it. Here they kept some of the slaves. On Investigation, I [Samuel Mason] discovered an old colored woman, whose sister, now dead, with some others, was regularly locked up in this room by Mrs. Jackson each night. She said her sister was born a slave here and one day she did something which displeased Mrs. Jackson, who picked up a butcher knife and slashed her across the back of the hand, these scars remained with her till her dying day. I have been told this tale from both sides and there can be little doubt of its truth.[59]

The statistics do show some families in this area held slaves in the early 1800s but "around Darlington most slaves were freed by the Quakers before 1805."[60]

21

CHRISTINE PRESBERRY TOLBERT,
born in 1935, can trace her African-American ancestry in Berkley to the late 1700s. Attending Hosanna School and receiving degrees from Bowie State College and Loyola College and completing a certificate for administration and supervision at the Johns Hopkins University, she served as a teacher, counselor, and Supervisor of Elementary and Secondary Education in Harford County. Christine has served her community as a member of the Harford County Human Relations Commission, the county Historic Preservation Commission and, most importantly, has served as the volunteer Executive Director of the Hosanna Community House for over 20 years, preserving the Hosanna School as a museum for future generations. In 2001 she was inducted into the Harford County Educators Hall of Fame.

Interviewed 21 February 2000

By the mid to late 1700s, blacks had arrived in Berkley and records show landholding by free blacks as early as 1812. On June 10, 1812, Joseph Worthington, white landowner, sold a piece of land to Moses Harrison (or Harris), a freeman of color, for 20 pounds.[61] This piece of land was located on the north side of Deer Creek on part of a tract of land called Phillips Purchase. Later, on November 9, 1816, Moses Harrison sold a parcel of his land in the vicinity of Darlington, known as Arabia Petrea, for 50 pounds to Cupid Paca.[62] James James, the great-great grandfather of Christine Tolbert, was born in Berkley in 1782 and built a house for his family in 1836 on property that he owned. With extensive genealogical research on her family, Christine found some answers illusive, *"I have no evidence that my great-great grandfather was a slave. But I also don't have any evidence that he wasn't. This area here had a great Quaker presence and it also had a great presence of free blacks. And so I don't know how far back it would have been, but I do know that he wasn't a slave prior to the Emancipation Proclamation because he was a property owner."*[63]

Cupid Paca's Influence Begins

In 1822, Cupid Paca,[64] freeman of color, became a major black landowner in Berkley. He purchased, in cash, fifty acres of land "on the main road leading from Bald Friar Ferry to the (Darlington) Friends Meeting House."[65] The land was purchased from James Rigbie's daughter, Cassandra, and her husband, John Corse, for the sum of seven hundred dollars. Paca has been described as "one of the most interesting mid-nineteenth century countians of any color."[66]

Local residents have pointed out that Paca showed good sense in his choice of residence, for others in the county were not as welcoming to the blacks, free or otherwise, as the many Quaker residents in the area, particularly in the village of Darlington and the hamlet of Berkley.

Paca built his first home along Castleton Road (then called the Berkley Road). His house still exists today and sits next to the Hosanna School Museum. Paca purchased the freedom of his wife and infant daughter "and spent the rest of his prosperous life investing in real estate, farming, practicing cobbling and masonry and taking steps to ensure the material comfort for the next generation."[67] Cupid Paca and Moses Harris were considered "the principal builders

PACA HOUSE
Free black and landhold-ing Cupid Paca built this house for his family in the early 1800s. The house was owned later by Kenton Presberry, a principal and teacher at Hosanna School in the first part of the 20th century. The house sits adjacent to Hosanna School and his spring was the source of water for the school children.

Photograph by Scott Prettyman

of stone fences"[68] in Darlington and Berkley. Many of those stone fences stand today.

In 1831, Paca obviously had a setback. He borrowed money from William Worthing-ton on the condition that "the said Cupid Paca's daughter Charlotte should depart the State of Maryland immediately, never to return …"[69] He put his total parcel of fifty acres up as security and, obviously, fulfilled his financial obligations since the property remained in his and his children's hands. As for Charlotte, while one is curious, the end of her story is hidden in the shadowy past.

While Paca was a landholder and a contributor to the community, the laws at that time did not ensure or protect his freedom of movement or commerce. In 1807, the Maryland Legislature passed a law stating that "no free black coming into Maryland could stay more than two weeks."[70] Conversely, if black residents spent more than two weeks out of Maryland they legally returned to slave status. And in order to sell the corn and wheat grown on his land, Paca, by law, had to sign a written statement attesting that he did not steal the crops.

In his will, Paca subdivided some of his holdings to ensure a mortgage-free op-portunity for each of his children. His son, Robert, donated land for the first house of worship for African-Americans in the Berkley and Darlington communities. Located in Berkley, the church sat on the knoll behind today's Hosanna School Museum.

The first Hosanna Church, a log structure, opened around 1835 and may have been established under the aegis of the Deer Creek Friends Meeting. The quiet Quaker influence could be felt in this early church for the services were very sub-dued and the preaching was absent the fervor that may be found in today's services. People worshipped quietly in their pews with perhaps an occasional amen. The more robust shouting, hand clapping and foot stomping was viewed as a practice for other denominations. But while the original Hosanna service may have been modeled after the Friends Meeting, changes were occurring in Philadelphia that would affect the Hosanna Church.

Free blacks in Philadelphia were seeking their own religious foundations and began this search under the leadership of Richard Allen. He attended St. George's Methodist Church where blacks were, at first, welcomed into the congregation. After years of worship at St. George's, it was becoming clear that the parishioners were growing increasingly uncomfortable with its burgeoning black population so they relegated these black parishioners to the balcony. On April 12, 1787, along with Absalom Jones, Allen formed the Free African Society (FAS), organized to extend aid to widowed, sick, and jobless blacks. It regulated marriages, taught thrift, censured drunkenness, condemned adultery, and attempted to improve morals. Even though this was not a religious movement, admiration for the Quaker philosophy and its views on moral rectitude persuaded the FAS to emulate the Quaker culture. Allen then began preaching in Delaware, Pennsylvania and Maryland to encourage blacks to join together to unite under one religious body. John Wesley, founder of Methodism, aroused Allen's interest in the new denomination. Allen said, "The Methodist is so successful in the awakening and conversion of colored people [because of its] plain doctrine and having a good discipline."[71] He felt that "to a mostly unlettered flock an easy to understand doctrine would help to stimulate spontaneous worship and permit extemporaneous sermonizing."[72] On April 9, 1816, a convention was held in Philadelphia and resolved "that the people of Philadelphia and Baltimore and other places who may unite with them shall become one body under the name and style of the African Methodist Church of the United States of America and that the book of Discipline of the Methodist Episcopal Church be adopted as our discipline ..."[73] This church then became known as the African Methodist Episcopal Church (A.M.E.).

When the Hosanna Church officially joined the African Methodist Episcopal Church the congregation resisted the more exuberant method of worship. The new order of service followed the plan of the Methodist Episcopal Church, not the more reserved format of the Quakers. While the congregants enjoyed singing hymns there were few hymnals and, in a congregation that was not well read, the practice of "lining" was prevalent. The preacher would read or say a line or lines of the hymn just before it was to be sung.

It is also likely that the catechism and church doctrine were taught in a similar way; the preacher would read and the people would repeat. Slaves in the south were taught in this manner when they were being converted to Christianity. Some older residents report experiences in their families of relatives who could not read anything except the Bible. Roland Dorsey recalled his uncle this way, *"Uncle Will didn't have no education, never went to school, but do you know what he used to do? He would take the family Bible that thick (gesturing with his fingers about four inches) ... on Sunday mornings if you went there, he'd make you sit down, he'd pray with you, read four or five verses out of the Bible ... He couldn't read no paper, but he could read the Bible."*[74]

In 1850, the church that now bears the name St. James A.M.E. Church in Havre de Grace petitioned the A.M.E. Conference to provide a pastor to give spiritual guidance to the newly formed congregation. The conference sent the Reverend W. M. Waters and "People came in horse and buggy, buckboard and on foot from as far away as Darlington."[75] As a consequence the black residents of Berkley chose to affiliate with the A.M.E. Church and sometime after 1850 Hosanna Church assumed the name of Hosanna A.M.E. Church.

Harry Webb Farrrington had fond memories of the music that emanated from the Hosanna Church and the camp meetings. In his biography he harkened back to "hearing black men singing from the store porches with the 'jew's'[76] harp, stamped their feet or rattled the bones." But even better to Farrington were the camp meetings. "When they had their camp meetings near Newlin Smith's farm on the way to Berkeley (*sic*), as I lay in my bed, although it was far, far across the fields, and in a wood, their songs would drift into my window."[77] When Farrington was older he went to the camp meetings and remembered:

> Old Alec Berry was their most respected preacher, esteemed alike by the white people. They said he could use words as long as any white preacher! ... And Joe Butler, driver of the mail stage to Havre de Grace ... preached so learned, that the colored people could not understand him ... I never forgot the old hymns I heard from the colored folks' Saturday night; and I can still hear them singing, going down the road before midnight, when the stores closed ... We had a choir in our church, but they could not sing like the colored folk.[78]

This log church served the community until the Hosanna School was built in 1867. The school then began to be used as the site for religious services until the current Hosanna A.M.E. Church was built on land donated by the Paca heirs in 1880.

ROLAND EDWARD DORSEY, affectionately known as "Bus," *was born in 1924. He remembers walking almost five miles to and from Hosanna School every day, including many cold winters of snow. He did farm work as a boy and, at the age of 12, began to work for Jourdan's tomato cannery in Darlington. He worked for the Pennsylvania Railroad running the spike master and other equipment put before him. Retired from his railroad work, farming and gardening are still his passions as he plows, mows, plants and nurtures his land. Roland Dorsey has attended Berkley's Hosanna A.M.E. church since he was a young boy following in the footsteps of his ancestors.*

Interviewed 28 March 2000

In addition to the Paca family providing the land for the first Hosanna Church, Cupid Paca's son, Joseph, and his siblings continued their father's struggle for equality, viewing education as the key to full citizenship and playing a significant role later in the century in the establishment of the Hosanna School.

While the lives of Paca and his descendants can be documented by land and court records, the recollections about some other free blacks in Berkley and Darlington are more informal. George Hensel, whose great-grandmother was a Rigbie, could recall events dating back to 1828. Of "Notable Colored Men" he wrote:

> The old colored people too! Notably among them were Abram Wilmer, Jimmy James, Cumberland Cain, Cupid Peaker, Robert Peaker, Nero Johnson, Tom Nosey, Bob Giles, Bill Kenley, Zeke Wilmer and the two Moses Harris, one of them known as "Mason Mose," and the other "Blacksmith Mose" ... There were not many slaves in that neighborhood at that time. Ephriam Hopkins had a slave woman "Fanny" the wife of Tom Nosey; her children Charley, Jim and John, were slaves but obtained their freedom at a given age, I think 28 years ... The country abounding with stones ... They were utilized for fencing—Cupid Peaker, Cumberland Cain and Moses Harris (Mason) were the principal builders of stone fences.[79]

And of his friend, Moses Harris (the blacksmith), Hensel wrote:

> ... My old friend Mose Harris, who was a neighbor of ours during my boyhood. He was a blacksmith by trade, having at one time worked in Darlington. He removed to a small property between Darlington and Dublin [Berkley] where he continued to work his trade until he became so afflected (*sic*) with rheumatism he could no longer work—being compelled to walk with two canes ... He managed to cultivate his little patches and dry his peaches ... We boys called frequently to see the old man and his old wife, Jenny, and sample their peaches ... My acquaintance with Mose and others of his color and time gave me a high appreciation. ...[80]

The Harris family members will appear again in these stories as they became important participants in the Underground Railroad in Berkley and Darlington, rowing fugitive slaves north to freedom in Pennsylvania and beyond.

William James, who resided in Berkley with his wife, India Anna, prepares food for preserving for the winter meals. c. 1910.
Private collection of Evangeline James Ford

Mose Harris has lived on in the memories of many current residents of the area. John Lamb remembered that his mother would call his father "Old Man Mose" when he walked painfully or stiffly. According to Lamb this was a local phrase she used that, after a century, harkened back to Blacksmith Mose Harris who suffered mightily from rheumatism in his elder years.[81]

In describing this period, Christopher Weeks stated, "This is also the era that the county's black citizens, too, came into their own, when real, documented faces—such as that of entrepreneur Cupid Peaker—began to emerge from the county's sizable and heretofore dimly defined African American population."[82] Or as Samuel Mason wrote about the black residents, they "made Harford County what it is. They were the wheels that made our clock tick."[83]

Building Bridges and Roads

While the Susquehanna River could be crossed by ferry and ford, it continued to challenge the residents, travelers, and entrepreneurs to find dependable and relatively safe ways to move people, goods and produce across its rocky and, sometimes, treacherous waters. An act of the Maryland Legislature in 1815 spoke to the State interest in creating good transportation corridors when it authorized the County Commissioners to "lay out a road from Belle Air to the place contemplated to build a bridge at Rough Island or Conowingo across the Susquehanna River and said roads shall be laid out not exceeding 60 feet wide, of which 20′ shall be artificial road composed of stone, gravel or other material."[84]

There was stiff competition on both sides of the river to build a bridge. The competition was so fierce that in 1818 two new bridges spanned the Susquehanna River, one at Rock Run, south of Berkley, and the other, the Conowingo Bridge at Berkley. Fortunately, one of the most famous bridge architects of the day, Lewis Wernwag, had settled down in the town of Conowingo in Cecil County to run a sawmill. So the competition was on. Wernwag was enticed from his sawmill duties and became the architect of one of the finest bridges built in Maryland at that time—the Conowingo Bridge. This covered toll bridge had ten sections totaling 1,744 feet spanning the river.

After construction, the competition continued and, according to news coverage "sparked one of Maryland's first outdoor advertising campaigns. Posters up and down the turnpike between Baltimore and Philadelphia urged travelers to 'Cross Susquehanna by Rock Run Bridge' or 'Use Conowingo Crossing.'"[85] The Conowingo Bridge later became known as the Upper Crossing.

A letter to the *Baltimore American* from John W. McGrain gave a fine, firsthand description of the architect and his bridge:

Gentlemen, I have now the pleasure of announcing to you, and through your useful paper to the citizens of Maryland in general, the successful issue in raising the last Arch of the Conowingo Bridge, over the Susquehanna, which was completed on the 12th instant, contrary to the expectation of many, who know the great risque and almost insurmountable difficulties that Lewis Wernwag, the contractor, had to content [sic.] with—there being a depth of upwards of 30 feet of water, passing a current covered with whirl pools, that presents difficulties almost insurmountable, perhaps altogether so for the genius of any other architect than Mr. Wernwag; who has deservedly established himself as the greatest Bridge builder in America, perhaps in the world ... Three pier abutments have an elegant appearance, as well as that of great strength, forming almost solid columns of hewn stone, all being clamped and bolted together at the upper end-which is perhaps as well calculated to resist the immense force of ice and water that descends this proud stream at different periods, taking along almost everything that comes in contact with it.

The final completion of this magnificent bridge, that perhaps is not equaled in America, will afford resources of great wealth to your city, and no doubt will be a means of your market being supplied with butter, pork, beef, &c. at an average of 15 per cent less, the year round, than it is now, of more than sufficient to build such a bridge annually—the cost of which when finally completed, will not exceed $82,000 ... [86]

This first "Upper Crossing" bridge continued as a major corridor for goods and travel until it succumbed to the dramatic whims of the winter ice and spring freshets that buffeted the structure. In 1846, a severe winter of thick ice on the river resulted in fatal damage to the bridge and a new crossing would not open for thirteen years.

By 1835, newcomers to the area, in addition to farming, embraced the entrepreneurial spirit that was sparking the nation. Manufacturing, mining, and new modes of transportation began to be viable and profitable along the Susquehanna from Shure's (formerly Worthington's) Landing to Bald Friar.

The roads leading to and from Berkley began to take the configurations that a twentieth century resident would recognize. The early road leading through Berkley

The Conowingo Covered Bridge viewed from the banks of the Susquehanna River
Historical Society of Harford County (The Elizabeth Ewing Collection) ref. 1657

stretched from Darlington through the Rigbie estate and down to the river. Although the hamlet of Berkley existed, the crossroads had not yet been established.

Soon, horse and hunting paths and farm roads developed into throughways. This major corridor of travel stretched from Old Joppa Road in the southwestern part of Harford County, crossed Deer Creek on what is known now as Sandy Hook Road, leading into Scarboro (Union Crossroads) to Dublin then to Bald Friar. According to John Lamb,[87] a respected local historian, there are traces of an old road into the Berkley area coming from the Sandy Hook Road, through the Trappe Church area to his property located southwest of Berkley and connecting with Smith Road leading into the Berkley community. The dry-stacked stone fences that banked most of the roads in the early nineteenth century still sporadically identify this route.[88] Remnants of these stone sidings traverse his property and align directly with the present day Smith Road. Similar stone walls can still be seen along Castleton Road in Berkley.

Education in Early Berkley

According to Andrew Guilford, author of *America's Country Schools*, "The country school [has] always been important in rural areas of this nation, as a symbol both of cultural continuity and of opportunities to be gained from education."[89] The early schools that served the children of Berkley, like other country schools, served to reinforce the important beliefs and values of the community. In the past, the early Berkley residents came together in homes and churches to hold meetings, to raise funds for community purposes, to celebrate their heritage, and to educate their children.

Before there were public schools in Harford County, the clergy, black and white, and private citizens educated the children of the area in their churches and homes. Schooling in the home began shortly after the arrival of the Quakers in the Darlington and Berkley area. By 1796, in addition to educating their own children, the Society of Friends was providing classes for black children. A report to the Meeting that year by Silas Warner was "on behalf of the black school children."[90]

In 1723 the Maryland General Assembly provided that one school be opened in each county of the state. From 1724 until 1784 a fledgling school operated near Old Philadelphia Road close to Joppa. Between 1784 and 1825 there was very little activity toward providing public education in Harford County.

Public education for whites in Maryland was slow to emerge and schools for blacks materialized at an even slower pace. As Maryland began to build public schools, there was a disparity between rural and urban schools as well as between black and white schools. Educational facilities for whites in rural areas were among the last to be provided and were not as well equipped as those in urban areas. As meager as rural school facilities were, favorable conditions for black children were non-existent.

A Maryland law in 1825 provided for primary schools in all communities. Harford County was one of thirteen counties out of twenty-four to take advantage of this new law. In fact, almost all communities in Harford County had a school building by the time of the Civil War.

In addition to the Quaker "homeschooling," the first known provider of education in the Darlington and Berkley area was an Englishman, William Watson, who started a private school, presumably in his home. George Hensel remembered him as "A man of considerable learning, and wrote a beautiful round hand. Although he used the rod and the ferrule, he was a mild and pleasant gentleman, and was looked upon with awe by us small boys, with whom the wonder grew that one small head should carry all that he knew."[91] This school was located at the corner of Shuresville and Quaker Roads.

The first "schoolhouse" school was in existence in the early nineteenth century; the date of its origin is uncertain. W. Stump Forwood provides a description of this early school:

> Previous to the year 1841, school facilities in the vicinity of Darlington were chiefly limited to the small log schoolhouse at the foot of Bosen's Hill, called the Deer Creek School … It stood upon the edge of the "woods"; several large forest trees—and especially a very large chestnut tree stood quite near; and in the summer they afforded fruit for the pupils, as well as umbrageous shade for protection from the noon-day sun. At the foot of the hill were springs of drinking water. And what to our young minds was a beautiful flowing stream, winding around the base of the hill, under the spreading limbs of the grand old tree; in which stream we "waded," and made "dams," which afforded us excellent bathing, and as much pleasure, doubtless as adults of the present day derive from their bathing at the seashore.[92]

This early school was located near the present corner of Stafford and Price Road. Dr. Forwood also wrote about one of the teachers at the Deer Creek School, William Purvell.[93] "At this school, from William Purvell, we received our early lessons in school studies; after a preliminary ABC course with good Mrs. Daggs, the mother of Mrs. Henry W. Hopkins."[94] William Purvell is believed to be the last instructor at the Deer Creek School. In its later years, according to John Lamb, the school was called the Woodpecker School, possibly because the insects in the old logs provided a tasty lunch for the birds! A set of stone steps along Stafford Road provides the only remaining evidence of the school today.

In 1832, William Waring, an Orthodox Quaker from Cecil County established a school in the Orthodox meeting-house. He was credited with introducing new branches of study and new methods of teaching. He later moved his school to the old Deer Creek schoolhouse at the foot of Bosen Hill on Stafford Road and changed the name to Lawn Villa Seminary. George Hensel described his childhood memories:

> How vividly I recall to mind this old schoolhouse! An old rough log, chunked and daubed inside and out, with long seats and desks ranged around the sides.

Occupied by the larger boys and girls, who sat on low rough benches without backs. The teacher occupied a small raised platform at the rear of the room. But it was a good school. Mr. Waring was a painstaking and conscientious man, having the happy faculty of infusing into the minds of his pupils his own enthusiasm for learning, which brought forth fruit, awakening an interest in the cause of education which had never been felt before, and out of which grew the Darlington Academy.[95]

When William Waring married, he moved his residence to the Ephraim Hopkins house located on the road to Berkley a short distance from the Quaker Meeting House. There he continued his school until he moved back to Cecil County. But this is not the last time the Waring name will appear in Berkley's story. Waring descendants returned to Berkley in the early twentieth century to again influence the lives of many of the residents.

Early in the nineteenth century the state of Maryland encouraged the movement to establish academies to "prepare students for entrance into institutions of higher learning and for public life." A Board of Trustees was to control the academies and was given the authority "to acquire property, appoint teachers, and adopt regulations for the conduct of the school."[96] Thus began the hundred-year history of the Darlington Academy.

The record book of the Darlington Academy shows that the Maryland General Assembly approved the trustees for the academy on March 30, 1836. These first trustees were John Quarles, William Wilson, Henry C. Stump, William Worthington, Samuel Worthington, Christopher Wilson, John Sappington, and Richard Jackson. With this approval, the trustees elected John Quarles as president and Richard Jackson as secretary and began to secure a site for the Academy.

At a meeting on October 20, 1836, three sites were considered: the site of the Deer Creek School at the foot of Bosen's Hill, a half acre lot offered by John Quarles in front of Wilmer's house (a house then occupied by a well-known black woman of that day named Polly Wilmer), and a quarter acre lot in front of the Methodist Church offered by Aquilla Massey. After long deliberation the Trustees decided on the Massey offer and purchased the site for a sum of forty dollars. Work began on the 22-foot by 27-foot two-story structure on June 15, 1841, and the first floor was open for school on December 13, 1841. Preston D. Park Taylor was the first teacher.[97] John M. Cooley, the great-grandfather of current Berkley resident Charles Cooley, was the headmaster at the Darlington Academy.[98]

The original state donation to the Academy was $150 annually and while it was a "public" school, it was not free. Tuition was required for attendance. As a "consideration" the Trustees obligated themselves to have two or three deserving pupils whose parents did not have the means to pay for their education. In its operation, the academy was clearly a community school particularly when one reviews the list of local contributors to its construction, its upkeep, and its fiscal viability. Fortunately, the patrons and pupils of the Darlington Academy were indebted to Benjamin Silver, Jr. for much more substantial aid. While a member of the State Legislature in 1868, he exerted influence and by his own efforts succeeded in having the amount of the state donation increased from $150 per year to $400—thus saving the academy from certain demise. The donations from the community exceeded the contributions of the state, and financial assistance from the county was not received until 1877.[99]

DARLINGTON ACADEMY—1840

Historical Society of Harford County

There is very little evidence to determine if blacks and whites attended the Academy together; however, a copy of an interesting picture found at the Historical Society of Harford County suggests that it might have been so. In the picture are equally well-dressed whites and blacks standing for a portrait at the stone front of the Darlington Academy. The manner of dress seems to imply the blacks were probably not slaves or servants. The early education of blacks by Quakers and the picture at the Darlington Academy, clearly including blacks, raised several questions about the early education of black Berkley children. Are the black people in the picture students? If they are students, were they from the families educated earlier at the Quaker school? And, further, if there were black children educated at the Darlington Academy at some point, what caused the halt to that practice necessitating the construction of a public school for black students in Berkley in 1867? Since blacks in Berkley and Darlington were taught to read and write in the eighteenth century why were they still signing their legal documents with an X in the nineteenth and early twentieth centuries? Since Maryland did not have laws which prohibited teaching blacks to read and write as did some Southern states, could the signing of documents with an X have been a deliberate concealment of this ability to read and write? The answers to these questions have not been discovered.

Grist for the Mills

By the early 1800s the population of Berkley was increasing. These Berkley farmers and entrepreneurs were making use of the water resources around them and were encouraged further when there was talk of a canal being constructed along the banks of the Susquehanna River. They now would have the possibility of a dependable way to move goods and raw materials up and down the Susquehanna as well as across the river. John Fletcher Jones was one of these new arrivals. In the mid-1820s, he became the proprietor of Rigbie's land. During the nineteenth century he and his descendants farmed this rich soil raising grains and corn that were ground at the local mills and shipped to cities and towns in the new nation. The Jones family would retain ownership of this land until 1960 when John Clark purchased the land.

Bruninger's Tannery

The steep gradients of the streams descending into the Susquehanna River provided ample waterpower for the many enterprises established along their banks. Hugh Jones, one of the early settlers in the Castleton area, arrived about 1835. He built a sawmill along Peddler's Run, a stream falling from above his property, along the lower reaches of Berkley to the river. Jones was "a millwright, having built many of the old grist mills in Baltimore and Harford Counties, as well as on the eastern shore of Maryland. He was a man of affairs, for his time, and in addition to his trade was a large land owner, and also possessed some $20,000 invested in stocks in the best banks in Baltimore."[100] Hugh Jones' property was part of "Brother's Discovery" and reached as far as Glen Cove. As the population increased, so did the use of Peddler's Run as the power source to run the various mills and industry along the stream, including Smith's Tanbark Mill, a flint mill, and the San Domingo Flour Mill. In hiking Peddler's Run today one may find remains of millponds, millraces, diverter dams, and the stone foundation of the flourmill. Bruninger's Tannery stills stands nearby, located on an unnamed tributary of Peddler's Run.

Richard I. Jackson was another major businessman and civic leader during this era. Jackson was a founding member of the first Darlington Academy. W. Stump Forwood eulogized him in his historical address at the 1890 cornerstone ceremony for the new academy:

> Mr. Jackson was perhaps better, and more widely known throughout the county than either of his fellow-incorporators. Nearly all of his life he was more or less engaged in the iron business; first as a clerk at Harford Furnace, and afterwards as the active partner of the firm of Stump & Jackson in establishing the "Deer Creek Iron Works." Subsequently he kept iron for sale to the blacksmiths throughout the county; it being a business of which he had a thorough knowledge, and for which he had a great fondness.

In his latter years, as the most of you know, he opened up the rock-bound region along the river, hitherto inaccessible, except to the foot-steps of the fisherman, and hunter—opened broad avenues to travel, and established a flourishing business in lumber, coal, iron, lime, and various other products of industry needed by the people of our county. He named this place of business, opened in this wild region, *Glen Cove*; and had he been permitted a few more years of life, and of health and strength, he would have reaped golden returns for his wonderful business provision ... But that was not to be; death terminated his labors in 1871, in the 63 year of his age ... He was noted for his judgment in the laying out of new public roads, and for the improvement of the old ones.[101]

Ephraim Hopkins' homestead bordered the Rigbie land on the road to Darlington. George Hensel recalled the Hopkins family of 1828:

One of the families best known to me was that of Ephraim Hopkins—"Uncle Ephraim" we always called him. Father did a great deal of work for him ... The old house with a green lawn in front of it; ... choice of fruit, especially the red-cheeked "ashmore" apples, I well remember.—Near Uncle Ephraim's gate lived Olivia, known as "Livy" McNutt, who kept a cake and beer shop ... It was generally understood that she sold something stronger than beer. Her house was the resort of many "characters" well known at the time, among them George Harris and John Ford ... George Harris was the local oak shingle maker and John Ford was a simple-hearted fellow, whose funny sayings and songs were very attractive to the small boy at the time. He was one of the most expert watermen on the river, the roughest of water had no terror for him in the lightest of boats.[102]

The black landowning population in Berkley was already well established by the mid-1800s. The descendants of James James, Cupid Paca, and others had married, had children, and surnames such as Presberry, Webster, Cain, Harris, and Jones became familiar in the community. The James family had several landholdings including the ancestral home of Christine Tolbert, *The property of the house that my mother lives in has been in the family since 1836. My grandmother was born in the house where my mother now lives, and she was born in 1888 and the house next door was built in 1924 by my grandmother and grandfather. But the property originally belonged to James James, my grandmother's great-grandfather, and he had sons and he divided the land among his sons, and so that was part of that division where my mother lives now.*[103]

Many of these black residents earned their livelihood by farming, both for family sustenance and for market. Others were stonemasons and were considered masters in their day, as they built many of the stone fences in the area, foundations for ice-houses, cisterns and houses, and, in many cases, the construction of some of the stone houses in Darlington. They were workers at the flint and limestone quarries, the mills, and other industries along the river. According to Tolbert, *"Most people were either farmers or stonemasons in the area. Women were domestic workers, laundresses, or sold eggs, butter and produce from their farms."*[104]

Building a Canal

Looking north along the Tidewater Canal and Towpath.
Private Collection of Megan Evans

The building of canals began to take precedence over all other water-related transportation modes in the early 1800s. Canal fever struck both sides of the Susquehanna and competition, just like the bridge building earlier, was fierce. On the western bank of the river, the Susquehanna and Tidewater Canal opened for business as a transportation corridor in 1839. Running from Havre de Grace, Maryland, to Wrightsville, Pennsylvania, the canal had twenty-nine locks, and a fall of about a thousand feet. Each lock was 170 feet long and 16-½ feet wide. There were ten locks in Maryland, one of which was located at Berkley, down by the river at Glen Cove. From scows to passenger boats as long as sixty-five feet, passengers and goods were towed by mules pulling the boats at about three miles an hour. The boat tolls for use of the canal ranged from $.60 to $1.90 depending on the distance traveled. The type of cargo determined the cost per ton. For example, pine carried from Havre de Grace to the paper mill near Berkley was $.14 per ton and poplar from York Furnace to the paper mill was $.20.[105] The *Baltimore American* (May 16, 1840) noted that a "new era for Baltimore trade opened with the arrival of four canal boats from Havre de Grace." Baltimore began to get shipments from Pennsylvania and could send return cargos such as groceries, sugar, coffee, salt, fish, dry goods, and plaster.[106]

According to Samuel Mason, "the lock keepers lived in white washed houses near the locks"[107] and in his book he lists the lock keepers, including one Theodore Richie at Glen Cove. With the approach of a canal boat, the captain would blow a conch shell, the lock keeper would close the gates "crossing the lock with a plank pivoted near one end and weighted with stones so as to swing across easily."[108]

After the boat was in the lock, the gates were swung shut, and the lower ports opened and water admitted or let out depending on whether the boat was going up-river or downriver. Mason's reminiscence of the canal cannot be improved upon:

> The Canal Boat Hands and the Lock Keepers of the Susquehanna and Tidewater Canal dwelt in a world apart, the fishermen and the river "rats" being their satellites. Life here was happy and thoroughly satisfactory. Barges passed and repassed going up and down, now in the shadow of the overhanging trees and next in the glare of the hot sun and always the company of the grand old river with its countless rapids and sunny islands.[109]

Not all of the travel on the Tidewater Canal was business. Dressed for an outing, the Joshua Smith family enjoys a day on the canal.

Private collection of Ann Hopkins Gregory

The canal became the major impetus for industrial, commercial and residential growth in Berkley for the next sixty years.

But it was not all peace and prosperity in the valley, for the bridges crossing the Susquehanna were being buffeted every year by ice floes, floods and fires—finally taking a toll on both bridges. A portion of the Rock Run or Lower Crossing Bridge was damaged by fire in 1823 when the runner of an iron shod sleigh scraped a nail head on the dry wood floor igniting some bits of straw.[110] The Lower Crossing was closed for five years for repairs.

A View of the Susquehanna Canal and Warehouses at the Conowingo Bridge c. 1900.

Maryland State Archives Special Collections (Robert G. Merrick Historical Photographs Collection) MSA SC 1477-1-6145

The Conowingo bridge was to be even more severely damaged in 1846 when a spring flood destroyed all ten sections of the spans. Privately owned and operated as a toll bridge, this disaster bankrupted the owners. The need for the bridge to support the growing economy was obvious. Even though it took thirteen years to garner the funding for the bridge, it was rebuilt and opened for transit in 1859 and continued in operation until the completion of the Conowingo Dam in 1928.

The Rock Run Bridge met its final demise in 1854 when a herd of cattle panicked when crossing the bridge. As the newspaper reported, "The vibrations of the stumbling animals toppled two spans into the river sending beef on the hoof to delighted scavengers downstream."[111] The bridge was not repaired from these harmonic vibrations and three years later an ice floe completed the demolition of the bridge; it was not to be rebuilt. The competition between the two bridges was over—the Conowingo Bridge survived.

The Canal Encourages More Industry

R. I. Jackson, an early resident of Darlington, established several mercantile businesses in the 1840s. In addition to these businesses in Darlington, he built four limekilns at Glen Cove to burn lime for marketing to local farmers in the region. Jackson also constructed warehouses and a store along the banks of the canal near Peddler's Run. This stretch of industry in the river valley was like "entering a kind of canyon white with lime dust and redolent of bone meal."[112] Mr. Jackson was married, had no children, and has been described as wearing "a long white beard up to his eyes … giving the impression of a man at least one hundred and fifty years old, but he died in 1872 at the puerile age of sixty-two."[113]

By 1853 John Sharpless and his partner, Gideon Smith, had purchased some of John H. Worthington's holdings which included parts of the original patents of Arabia Petrea, Paradise, and Brother's Discovery. While a homestead existed on the property prior to 1800, it was the Sharpless and Smith families who began to farm in earnest and become entrepreneurial leaders in the area. Their new homestead was named Swallowfield.

Prior to moving to Berkley, Gideon Smith had a producing tanbark mill along the river's edge south of Berkley. The large black oak groves in the area were the sources of the tannin necessary for tanning leather. The trees were harvested in the late spring when the bark would peel easily. The wood from the tree became firewood and the bark was hauled to the mill, broken into small pieces, and ground into a fine powder, "filling the cart underneath and the air above with a quantity of choking dust which settled in your hair, eyes and ears."[114] He later moved his enterprise to Berkley, located near today's Smith Road, labeled in early records as Gideon Gilpin Smith's Lane.[115] Smith's property on which he built his tanbark mill was located on the banks of Peddler's Run, a good running stream that produced energy for many of the power-driven activities in the area.

Daily Life in Berkley

Beginning with the Swallowfield purchase in 1853, the Quaker family of Sharpless-Smith-Cope-Ewing-Waring would live at Swallowfield until 1960. Swallowfield was a productive farm in the nineteenth century and a summer home for the Philadelphia members of the family in the twentieth century. When purchased from John H. Worthington, the property had a small two-story house with a barn and springhouse. Elizabeth Ewing wrote about a special event that occurred on the property when John Worthington owned it:

> In 1829 or 1832 while stumping for his election for President of the United States, Andrew Jackson happened to come to Berkley and was entertained here by the farmers in the Oak Grove just above the stream, by an ox roast. There were two oxen barbecued and the fire pits fifteen feet apart are visible today (April 1936) as two shallow depressions above Rebecca Gould's spring house. These pits are just outside of the overhang of a large White Oak now standing. This was told to me by Gilpin Smith and the pits pointed out by him in 1921.[116]

During the nineteenth century, in addition to the grains and corn that provided grist for the mills at the river, Swallowfield thrived for many years as a dairy farm. The dairy products were transported to Philadelphia and to hospitals in New Jersey. The house and barn expanded with the prosperity of the residents. The final additions to these structures were completed in 1880. Jean Ewing interviewed her mother, Elizabeth Sharpless Ewing, in 1970. From their conversation, Jean Ewing drew a picture of daily life and farm production at Swallowfield as it would have been during her grandfather's time.

While the upper part of the bank barn was used mainly for hay and equipment storage, "the lower level of the barn had stalls for about 10 horses and mules, 12 cows, calf pens on the upper level and in the barnyard was the pigsty and bullpen."[117] Near the house, was "a string of multipurpose areas under one roof, forming with the ice-house and the house itself, a courtyard centralizing farm and household work. The covered area included the woodshed, the chicken house, tool shed and smokehouse."[118] In addition to the storage and work areas, there was a root cellar. This important asset provided cool, dark storage for root crops such as carrots, potatoes, turnips, and onions, and for apples, pears and other hardy fruit.

Swallowfield, a Quaker Homestead since the early 1800s, was a stop on the Underground Railroad and home to many of the late 19ᵗʰ century entrepreneurs of Berkley.

Photograph by Scott Prettyman

The icehouse was "one of several buildings supplying work space and storage for goods thru several seasons, part of the domestic activity of a large family trying to be self-sufficient. The room above was for storing chicken feathers for pillows, weaving, painting chinaware, mending harnesses and anything any member of the house did not want to mess up the house with."[119] Icehouses served as today's refrigerators. These above ground structures had stone pits beneath them averaging 12 feet in depth where ice and straw were layered for storage of perishables, particularly fish from the river. In his family's history, Benjamin Stump Silver noted that the ice was harvested from ice ponds or the river and maintained cool temperatures well into the summer. "The preservation of food in large quantities during the summer months was a particularly difficult problem. The solution was the construction of icehouses. Filling them each winter with enough ice to last through the hot summers was a major task."[120] Giles Benjamin Silver, an ancestor who lived in northern Harford County, observed that on September 5, 1860, "ice put in the icehouse lasted until today, Monday."[121] Icehouses were particularly useful in the storing of fish caught in the Susquehanna. Bernard Waring, a former owner of Swallowfield, reminisced in his 1954 interview about fishing the river, "... *go down in the spring to watch the trees, and when you could tell a poplar tree a half a mile away, it was time to go down to the river to get your herring, because they would be running. We used a conestoga wagon creaking up our hill to go down to the river and got a load of fish, chiefly herring but I'd catch some bigger shad in there, take them up to York County and there they would prepare them, salt them down or dry them. We put ours up in a log cabin where we'd keep it cold. It was very, very good.*"[122] The log cabin Waring used is gone but the icehouse at Swallowfield still stands and has penciled notations of the storage of food, particularly shad.

BERNARD GILPIN WARING was the head of the last Quaker family to own Swallowfield and resided there in the summers from 1929 to 1960. His voice may be heard in a 1954 audiotape interview conducted by his son. Memories of his family's stories about Swallowfield, the people who lived there and their role in the Underground Railroad are captured in this interview as well as information about his business and life in Philadelphia. The language of the Quakers is reflected on the tapes with "thee," "Thy," and "thou" gracing the interview.

Photograph from private collection of Genevieve Webster Presberry Jones

These outside structures were the heart of production and upkeep and certainly found their place at every homestead in some fashion. Though they surely existed, few remain and those few may be found at some of the properties in Berkley, including the Rigbie Farm, Swallowfield, and the Chance residence on Berkley Road.

The water supply for these farms and dwellings came from hand-dug wells lined with rock and equipped with hand pumps to bring the water to the surface. There were wells, too, where one dropped a bucket tied to a rope and pulled the water out. In some cases, hydraulic rams moved the water from the springhouse into the dwelling. The hydraulic ram was an engineering marvel for those whose water source was a spring. These rams, consisting of pipes, valves, and tubes, lifted the water by using the energy of falling water. Water flowing through a pipe from the springhouse closed a valve, setting up backpressure forcing the water into a pipe leading upward. This upward pipe had an air chamber at the top. When the water pressed against the air, another valve opened to move the water higher. Only part of the water moving in this direction actually was lifted so an overflow pit collected and discharged the uncaptured water. This ingenuous mechanism lifted water from the springhouse at Swallowfield to provide water for the residence and neighboring Red Gate farm. Huge water barrels were placed in attics of the houses and, by gravity feed, furnished indoor water to these houses. Parts of the ram structure, including the overflow pit, still remain. Megan Evans and Dorothy Strang, on visiting their ancestral home at Swallowfield, remembered the water barrel. *"It had clamps around holding together, but it did echo. Mossy feel on the inside and we would dare each other to put our hands in."*[123]

DOROTHY SHARPLESS STRANG and MEGAN EVANS
were interviewed in January 2002. Megan, a retired federal employee, is a granddaughter of Bernard Waring, the last member of the Quaker family who owned Swallowfield. Megan continues to foster the Quaker tradition of viewing the world as one family of people regardless of race, color, or creed. As an eight-year-old visiting her grandfather in the summer she met and built a life-long friendship with her new black friend, Christine Tolbert. Dorothy, a teacher and poet, and also a Waring granddaughter and cousin to Megan, resides in Chicago and has devoted years providing enriching experiences for children who have limited opportunities. This interview was a closing chapter in a long history of the Smith/Waring family influence on the lives of the residents of Berkley in the early 1900s.

Interviewed 30 January 2002

The springhouse provided water, and also was an important storage place for perishables such as milk, cream, and butter for the family. Equally as important, it kept the perishables cold until the wagons arrived to take the dairy products to institutions and markets.

Such was the daily life of the Smith family whose entrepreneurial spirit contributed to the economic vitality of Berkley. However, it is this Quaker family's extraordinary courage in freeing the human spirit that marks their place in Berkley's history.

Secret Passages to Freedom

Underground Railrooad Routes through Northeast Harford County.
Wilmer H. Seibert, *The Underground Railroad: From Slavery to Freedom* Meridian Press

One only needs to understand the structure of the Underground Railroad (UGRR) system to know why little documentation of many lesser-known stations is available. Oral histories are invaluable tools for filling in the gaps.

Nearly everyone has heard of the amazing efforts of Harriet Tubman as she assisted runaway slaves from Maryland to the free states and on to Canada. And Thomas Garrett of Delaware is well known for the courageous, committed and unselfish activities he conducted on behalf of freedom. Few, however, have heard of the many lesser-known acts of bravery performed by black and white people in little known locales all **41** along the route of the UGRR. This network of people, safe houses, river pilots and secret passages was found in numerous places. Berkley was one of those places.

Henrietta Buckmaster in her book, *Let My People Go,* first published in 1941, described how this network came to be known as "the Underground Railroad."

> The system of help, the illegal activities, the journeys in the dead of the night had no name at this time [1831]. They were merely the passing on of fugitives, the outstretched hands. But when the naming finally came, the news spread gleefully on that invisible telegraph which spoke an intelligible language only to the men who knew the code. The hand, the system, the journeys had a name, and a slaveholder had given it—the Underground Railroad.

> According to those who were best informed, around 1831, a fugitive named Tice Davids crossed the river at Ripley under the expert guidance of those river operators who worked within sight of slavery. He was escaping from his Kentucky master, who followed so closely on his heels that Tice Davids had no alternative when he reached the river but to swim. His master spent a little time searching for a skiff, but he never lost sight of his slave bobbing about in the water. He kept him in sight all across the river and soon his skiff was closing the distance between them. He saw Tice Davids wade into shore, and then he never saw him again. He searched everywhere, he asked everyone, he combed the slavery-hating town of Ripley where John Rankin kept so formidable a watch. Baffled and frustrated he returned to Kentucky, and with wide eyes and shakings of the head he gave the only explanation possible for a sane man, "He must have gone on an underground railroad." The phrase spread like a wind, and the friends of the fugitives completed the name in honor of the steam trains that were nine-day marvels in the country. Underground Railroad! How could such things be? Was there really a long tunnel dug miraculously, into which runaway slaves were poured? The mystification was enhanced logically by the good humor of the operators who forthwith called themselves "conductors," "stationmasters," "brakemen," and "firemen," called their houses "depots" and "stations," talked of "catching the next train," and began sedulously to cultivate a wonder and a marveling in the minds of the uninitiated.[124]

Clearly, for this UGRR system to be effective certain conditions must be present: "stationmasters" who were willing to risk life and limb to escort the fugitives to freedom; "safe houses" where the fugitives would be sheltered, hidden and fed; "depots" a place to meet and get safe passage; wooded areas or swamps where the fugitives could move clandestinely to the depot; and a means of transportation to travel north.

Gideon Smith of Swallowfield operated one of those stations, strategically located near a heavily wooded area, about a mile from the Susquehanna River and ten miles from the Mason-Dixon Line. This location and the abolitionist temperament of the owners of Swallowfield were a natural fit for providing a safe haven on the Underground Railroad network. According to Elizabeth Sharpless Ewing, Gideon Smith's granddaughter, the phrase "There are people in the corn" was the signal to prepare for the fugitives. Jean Ewing recalled her mother's story, *"Isaac had been a retainer on the place [Swallowfield]. He was one of several wonderful black people that lived in the neighborhood and had a permanent job here at Swallowfield. But, Isaac was descended from some of the people who came through with the Underground Railroad, and didn't get any farther than Berkley. The Smith family and the Worthington family, the Worthingtons were in Darlington—but they set up a station in the Underground Railroad and people were coming through—what we were told about them was, someone came to the door and said, 'There's people in the corn.' That was the language to say that the people had come through the Underground Railroad and were hiding outside someplace. And they stayed in the barn or in the icehouse right outside the main house at Swallowfield. And they were carried across from Worthington's landing, which later became Shure's landing. Up the river in the north and ended in Chester County. ... Mother was very proud of them. We were very proud of being part of the Underground Railroad. I don't know whether they were ever threatened by local people, but certainly a lot of the local people didn't approve at all of getting the Negroes through."*[125]

Isaac and Frances Washington at their home in Berkley (1890)

Maryland State Archives (Machean Collection of Harford County Photographs) MSA SC 1751-13-05-B

Writing about the Underground Railroad in Harford County, Christopher Weeks stated:

> Documenting such stations now is extremely difficult because secrecy was so important then; if discovered, the slaves would be returned to bondage and certain punishment and those who aided them would be fined and/or imprisoned.

The Swallowfield Ice House

The Darlington area, settled by Quakers, became a center of abolitionist activity but only two sites—this property [Swallowfield] and the ruins of the William Worthington house nearer Conowingo—can be documented as such with any certainty ... the most poignant of these must be the icehouse, "a kind of eerie place" recalled Tolbert. "I could not imagine people would go down there, let alone huddle and hide—it's just a dark, damp pit."[126]

Worthington's Landing, located along the banks of the Susquehanna River on the Harford County side, was one of the routes up the Susquehanna River north to Pennsylvania. The Conowingo Power Plant now occupies this land. Samuel Mason gave this account of "Uncle Billy" [William Worthington]:

> … In the evening one of his men would come to him and whisper, "Uncle Billy, there's people on the hill"; thereupon Uncle Billy would order a sheep killed and cooked for the escaping slaves then hiding in the cornfields, and after dark a boat would be available at the landing to take them across the river.[127]

Bernard Waring's testimony was similar to Samuel Mason's account of efforts undertaken to provide safe passage, *"When they got across the river, the Cecil County side, then they would stride north and follow the North Star. They got across the Mason-Dixon line when they'd be free, theoretically. And sometime, the old colored man down at Worthington's place would say to his boss, Billy Worthington, 'Mr. Billy, there's people on the hill.' That meant that there were some slaves, escaping slaves, were down over the hill waiting. And Mr. Billy would say—he knew there was a very heavy fine, you know, for helping these people, so he'd say, 'kill a sheep, kill a sheep. Don't tell me.' He didn't want to have anything to do with it, but they wouldn't mind if they killed a sheep to feed these people."*[128]

The Richard "Had" Harris House was the "jumping off place" for fugitive slaves to be rowed across the Susquehanna River to head north to freedom. The house, located along the Susquehanna River not far from Hopkins Creek, was buried under the waters of the Conowingo Lake in 1928. Photograph taken in 1890.

Private collection of Jean Sharpless Ewing

Worthington (Shure's) Landing was the "jumping off place" for many a traveler on this railroad. As the fugitives made their way north a black man named Richard "Had" Harris, who lived at Worthington's Landing would row them up the Susquehanna River into Pennsylvania or across the Susquehanna where they would be met by other "conductors" who led them to other "stations." The passengers coming north from the southern states were joined by some fugitive slaves residing in Maryland—all of them moving from station to station making their way to points north, and in some cases, as far as Canada.

As a young girl, Christine Tolbert recalled working with her mother, Genevieve Webster Jones, at Swallowfield. Her mother served as a domestic for the Waring family for twenty-six years beginning in 1944. She helped her mother with cleaning; she also served the meals, and worked in the garden. Bernard Waring, the owner of Swallowfield at that time frequently took her for walks around the property. She poignantly remembered those occasions and the importance he placed upon some of the stories he told her as they walked, *"Mr. Waring, who was here, used to take me by the hand when I was a little kid—take me to the icehouse and say, 'Christine, this is where we used to hide the slaves when they were*

44

on their way north.' He wanted to make sure I knew that. And he did it. I used to get so tired of hearing it over and over again. He didn't want me to forget it. And I didn't. I've forgotten a lot of things, but I did not forget that. Jean Ewing found this picture for me. Jean Ewing was a part of this family too ... and she couldn't remember what book she got it out of, but she gave me a copy of it—of a little house that sat down on the Susquehanna River. And in the article the little caption under it said that this was the house of Richard Harris, better known as Had Harris, and when the slaves would come, he would row them up the Susquehanna River into Pennsylvania to their freedom. Well, if you just went out here [out the door from Swallowfield] and walked down through what used to be over there, you would walk right down to the river."[119]

There was a strong and abiding connection throughout this clandestine and secret undertaking between Berkley and Pennsylvania. Aiding and abetting these seekers of freedom often brought harm to those who dared to help. An abolitionist named Jacob Lindley from Chester County, Pennsylvania, was especially active in assisting the fugitives who were passing through Harford County. Some Harford Countians viewed him as a real threat. A man named James Lindley was mistaken to be Jacob Lindley as he walked the streets of Havre de Grace. Thinking he was Jacob Lindley, "A large piece of iron was thrown at him. He was then beaten until three of his ribs were broken, a number of teeth knocked out, and he, unconscious, left on the street for dead."[130]

Slaves were sent to such places as Harrisburg, York, and Columbia, Pennsylvania, to be given refuge then aided in their passage under the cover of darkness. According to Samuel Mason, "So great was the exodus at Columbia that slave owners posted men along the route and paid teamsters to give information, but to no avail."[131]

Philadelphia was one of the primary stops and sometimes the final destination for the fugitive slaves. There they were received by a group of Philadelphia abolitionists who formed a General Vigilance Committee as a part of the Anti-Slavery Society. Dr. Benjamin Quarles noted in the foreword of William Still's book, *The Underground Railroad*, "Of the blacks who worked in the Underground Railroad all names pale before that of Harriet Tubman, whose base of operations included the slave states themselves. But second only to Mrs. Tubman was William Still of Philadelphia."[132]

It was Still, a former slave, who as secretary and executive director of the General Vigilance Committee, received the railroad passengers and kept records. This was not a common practice but Still felt a need to keep accounts of the slave stories, hoping someday they might help reunite former slaves with their relatives. A strong veil of secrecy protected the slaves and the abolitionists. Still kept the records hidden until 1872, and then, long after the Civil War was over, he published an 800-page book, replete with anecdotes, personal letters, legal papers, and pen and ink drawings.

Were it not for the effort and works like Still's, no one would know of the passengers arriving in Philadelphia from Arlington, (Darlington), Maryland, in 1857. Still wrote about John Alexander Butler and his party from [Darlington]. "This party made, at first sight, a favorable impression; they represented the bone and sinew of the slave class of [Darlington], and upon investigation the Committee felt assured that they would carry with them to Canada industry and determination such as would tell well for the race."[133] It was comforting to know that even the fugitive slaves of the Berkley/Darlington community made a favorable impression on others they encountered.

Nonetheless, Butler and his three travel mates, William Henry Hipkins, John Henry Moore, and George Hill, hated to be the property of another human being and as such, the suppliers of free labor. Butler said his master was a man named William Ford who belonged to the Methodist Church at [Darlington]. Ford, he charged, "defrauded him of his rights ... compelled him to work on his farm for nothing; also had deprived him of an education, and had kept him in poverty and ignorance all his life." He said Ford "was a hard man and his wife and children were of the same evil spirit. He spoke fondly of his own wife and children whom he had to leave at Cross-Roads."[134] Although this was 1857, ten years before a public school for blacks was established, Butler's statement about being deprived of an education is significant. He seemed to imply that, had his master not thwarted him, he would have had the opportunity to get the schooling that was available to blacks in the Darlington and Berkley area.

The second in the party, William Henry Hipkins, escaped from Ephraim Swart whom he described as "a gambler and spree'r."[135] He said Swart treated his wife badly as well. His wife would sometimes stand up for the servants and when she did he would knock her down. The third member of the fugitive group, John Henry Moore, escaped from David Mitchell of Havre de Grace. He claimed that Mitchell and his wife treated their slaves cruelly. Moore was one of the most willing in the [Darlington] party to continue on the Underground Railroad.

George Hill, the fourth slave in the party, reported that Dr. Savington [Sappington] of Harford County "owed him for years of hard and unrequited toil, and at the same time was his so-called owner." He declared that he had never received enough to eat the whole time he was with him, and continued, "The clothes I have on I got by overwork of nights. When I started I hadn't a shoe on my foot, these were given to me. He was an old man, but a very wicked man and drank very hard. I left because I had got along with him as well as I could. Last Saturday a week he was in a great rage and drunk. He shot at me."[136]

Seven years after the Civil War, William Still published his recollections of the period. He eloquently and pointedly characterized the structure of the Underground Railroad:

> The slave and his particular friends could only meet in private to transact the business of the Underground Railroad. All others were outsiders. The right hand was not to know what the left hand was doing.
>
> Stockholders did not expect any dividends, nor did they require special reports to be published. Indeed prudence often dictated that even the recipients of our favor should not know the names of their helpers, and vice versa they should not desire to know theirs.

> The risk of aiding fugitives was never lost sight of, and the safety of all concerned called for still tongues. Hence sad and thrilling stories were listened to, made deep impressions; but as a universal rule, friend and fugitive parted with only very vivid recollection of the secret interview and with mutual sympathy; for a length of time no narratives were written.[137]

Still had written these stories to help others and at great personal risk to himself. He acknowledged that his writings of escapees' experiences documented only a few of the brave men and women who were involved in the Underground Railroad. He anguished that more were not told. "Good men labored and suffered, who deserve to be held in the highest admiration by the friends of Freedom, whose names may be looked for in vain in these pages."[138]

The brave whites and blacks in Berkley who participated would fall into this category. The sealed lips and the absence of documentation were taken very seriously in Berkley, particularly when history shows the Quakers to be excellent and prolific diarists. The Berkley oral histories, especially those of the black citizens, displayed residual evidence of this past practice of sealed lips. The older the interviewees the more this adherence to silence seemed to be true, perhaps suggesting the closer the interviewees were to the time when silence was absolutely essential, the less forthcoming they were.

Berkley's Role in the Civil War

Compared to much of the nation, Berkley, like most of Harford County, was spared from the serious and deadly conflagrations and strife during the Civil War. In Berkley, there are no battles to document and no monuments to photograph. Berkley's main contribution was the secret, silent, and dangerous commitment to advancing freedom for fugitive slaves.

Strong loyalties and allegiances, did arise, however—for the North and for the South. As a border state, Maryland had many strong Southern sympathizers who pushed the state to the brink of secession. The Berkley and Darlington area reflected those opposing loyalties.

The county population numbered about 21,000 people in 1861, and of them, 1,087 men had volunteered for the Union—including some black citizens. Because sentiment was split in Harford County, one can assume there were significant numbers of Confederate supporters also. As has been written in many texts and recalled by oral histories, neighbors and families were pitted against each other, many times brother against brother and father against son. The Silvers, of northern Harford County, illustrate how many families, even those holding to the pacifist tenets of their Quaker faith, coped with the split:

> It is a credit to the Silver Family, all of whom had strong minds, bodies and wills that during the Civil War no major family disputes concerning that war occurred.

When the Civil War erupted, the family members entered into an agreement that the war would never be mentioned within the family circle. This agreement was kept to the credit and benefit of the family. Several family members had diverse views ... some, for instance Benjamin, were red-hot Southerners who would go out on a hilltop with their families and sing the "Long Meter Doxology" in thanksgiving for Confederate victories ... Others for example John A. and Jeremiah, favored the North.[139]

As the war advanced, one in five men in Harford County had taken up arms. By then the Federal Government had invoked the draft in an effort to swell the ranks of the Northern army. A draftee could escape service if he could find a substitute or, if he were wealthy, could purchase his release for the sum of seven hundred dollars.

Black residents of Harford County also joined in battle. Philip Webster, for example, had been born and raised in Berkley. He was the son of Moses and Diane Webster and an ancestor of current resident, Genevieve Jones. President Lincoln had issued an executive order giving the Bureau of Colored Troops the authority to raise an all black regiment in Maryland. According to Agnes Kane Callum's research:

This maneuver opened the way for the government to enlist the aid of Negro men as volunteers in the different branches of the Armed Services. It was at this time, July 15, 1863, that Philip Webster made his way from Harford County to Baltimore to volunteer in the 4th Regiment United States Colored Troops and was assigned to Company C of that unit. Thusly, Philip Webster had the honor to join the 4th Regiment on the day of its origin. He was mustered in July 24, 1863, at Baltimore. He acclimated to the regimentation of army life and went on to earn the rank of corporal.[140]

His regiment was part of the Negro Troops of the Army of the James where he participated in the "Dutch Gap Canal" engagement by digging the canal "almost under siege."[141] At Deep Bottom, the "4th Regiment's gallant action was bold, daring and executed efficiently. Their effectiveness earned them a commendation from the General-in-Chief of the United States."[142] Discharged on May 8, 1866, Philip Webster returned to Berkley to resume his trade as a stonemason and raise his family. He died in 1915, and was buried in the Hosanna Cemetery behind the Hosanna A.M.E. Church. Webster's descendants still reside in Berkley.

During war, bridges become indispensable for moving troops, ammunition, and supplies and so it was in the Civil War. Both sides recognized the importance of controlling and protecting access to significant bridges or, if more beneficial, destroying them. Sympathizers from both sides understood this and both attempted to control the Conowingo Bridge. At the beginning of the war in 1861, Southern sympathizer and supporter, Captain Stephen S. Johns of Berkley, took possession of the Berkley side of the bridge to stop the passage of Federal troops. That year, Harford County secessionist, Herman Stump, Jr., did attempt to burn the bridge but failed. When Johns could no longer continue to hold claim to the West bank on behalf of the Confederacy, Squire James Cummings, a Union loyalist, came to the rescue. He protected the entire bridge by "taking a keg of powder located on the span, near the middle and connected it with the shore by means of a train of coal oil, and held himself ready at a moment's notice"[143] to send the Confederate soldiers to their watery graves, or as Mason stated, "into the seething waters of the well-known maelstrom."[144] This maelstrom was known as "Job's Hole," a violent rotating swirl in the river that had frightened residents since early settlement along the banks of the river.

Later in the war, the 18th Regiment of Connecticut was stationed in the Berkley area to protect the bridge and carried out the responsibility of capturing deserters and transporting them to a war prison in Baltimore. As the war was drawing to a close, 3000 Federal troops were dispatched to Berkley and Conowingo areas to protect both sides of the Conowingo Bridge. Harry Gilmore and his Confederate troops had burned the railroad bridge crossing the Gunpowder River in south Harford County. The fear of another "Gilmore's Raid," destroying transportation corridors elsewhere in the county, precipitated this buildup of troops at the bridge. The Union troops prevented the

A close look at the strong foundation and structure of the covered Conowingo Bridge.
Maryland State Archives Special Collections (MSA SC 1477-6145)

raiders from crossing the bridge by cutting through the lateral bracings across that section that traversed "Job's Hole." The bridge did survive the Civil War, was repaired, and served as a rejuvenator for commerce, trade, and travel for the recovering nation.

The Smith family records harken back to Joshua Smith's remembrances of a surprise visit of Federal troops to Swallowfield:

> Joshua C. Smith, who lived north of Darlington and on the hills above remembered that, as a small boy, there were Union Soldiers stationed at the old covered bridge, to prevent it from being burned or captured. To make it easier to guard, the flooring was taken up on one side of the bridge, which had a partition in the middle. These soldiers were friendly to our peaceable-non-fighting family, and also came often, and ordered meals.
>
> One day 20 of them came, ordered dinner and marched on. Later Joshua came to sit on the porch steps, looking at the stacked guns of the soldiers who were eating in the house. He looked up and was terrified to see a row of soldiers with their guns trained on the house. He fled inside, and when the commanding officer came out, all was well, for the later arrivals were the first comers who had ordered the dinner, the fast feasting ones, a second detachment who had happened along. But it was not funny for our family, who had to feed them all, all Union men of course.
>
> He was a boy of six during the Battle of Gettysburg 50 or 60 miles away, and never forgot having heard the guns booming, booming all the daylong.[145]

Another member of this family, Bernard Waring, spoke of his family's memories of that day and of the difference between Philadelphia and Berkley during the war, *"We were in a foreign country to our own people, so to speak. A certain number of Philadelphia people came over the river and established their homes in Harford County. But we were a relatively small number of people and most of the people there were southern in their sympathy ... It was quite an event in our isolated country there, for these people to have a squad of nice soldiers come up, nice young men. Now there were many odd numbers of our aunts around the place who were then young girls, and this was quite a notable event ... They [Union soldiers] scoured the country to get equipment for the Federal Army, and they went out to the barn and were going to take our horses, what we used for farming and hauling flint later, across the river to the flint mill ... When mother found that they were really serious about taking our horses, she went down and told them that we were, we are northern people and these horses are the only thing we have to get a living from and I want you to leave them here. And they did."*[146]

Hannah Watson Harper, wife of Samuel Harper, the Darlington blacksmith, wrote to her son-in-law, Frank Hopkins, on August 4, 1864. She described the presence of Federal troops at the bridge and how the Harford residents had protected their livestock during Gilmore's presence in the County.

> You wished to hear some of the particulars of the raid into Maryland, there was quite an excitement for a few days on Sunday night we heard such traveling all night. We could not imagine what it could mean but the next day we found that it was the people from the lower county taking their stock across the river and brought the news that the rebels were in this state—they all appeared to be very excited.[147]

She continued to lament the conditions of the country. "When will this country have peace again everything is so high shougar [sugar] is from 30 to 35 cents per pound flower [flour] 14$ per barrel hams are selling in Baltimore for 45 cts per lb and every thing in proportion."[148]

Throughout the Civil War period and afterwards, the Conowingo Bridge continued to be a blessing and a bane to the economy of Berkley. Just as the war was over, on March 18, 1865, a flood carried away a span on the Cecil County side of the river, halting the transport of dairy products, cattle, grains, and quarried materials. Writing in his diary, Silas B. Silver recorded trauma up and down the river, "18 March great freshet in the Susquehanna River! Tremendous rise! Bridges—canal banks are carried away. 20 March—the bridges far up the river are all swept away. One span of the Conowingo Bridge was carried away. It is said the river has not been as high since 1832."[149] And so the bridge was repaired again, as it would be many times before the end of its productive life.

Unlike many parts of the country where the strife and loyalties of the Civil War years strained relations permanently, where shunning and expulsion occurred, and where businesses and friendships were ruined, the Berkley area began a growth period that would exist until the construction and opening of the Conowingo Dam in 1928. The animosities and hard feelings were laid to rest and the families and the community embraced the industrial age and the progressive era that would provide employment for the residents in an environment where people wanted to live, raise and educate their children.

Education Takes a Different Path

Black and white education was definitely separate at the close of the Civil War. It was at this time that the first public schools for blacks in Harford County were built. Following the Civil War, the Federal Bureau of Refugees, Freedmen and Abandoned Lands, usually referred to as the Freedmen's Bureau, was established. As part of the reconstruction of the country, one of the Bureau's missions was to create schools for the newly freed slaves. Quaker families were still living in the Berkley area, and by the outbreak of the Civil War, slavery was all but extinct. Perhaps these were the reasons that the Bureau, looking for success, chose Berkley as the site on which to build Hosanna School, the first public school for blacks in Harford County.

The Bureau needed to be able to demonstrate some success for the program because U.S. President Andrew Johnson was not one of its supporters and did not approve of assisting blacks. In 1866, the U.S. Congress passed a bill that extended the Bureau's powers to assist destitute free blacks in addition to the newly manumitted slaves. It was passed over President Johnson's veto.

Hosanna School was built the following year on land donated by Cupid Paca's son, Robert. Even though the one-room school was the norm in Harford County, as it was in most rural communities in the United States, Harford's first public school for blacks was a two-story clapboard structure. The Freedmen's Bureau provided financial assistance for building materials and teachers' salaries. The men in the community provided labor and used recycled lumber to erect the building. Like most schools for black citizens at that time, the Hosanna School was inextricably linked to the church. At nearly every site of a school for blacks, one would find a church adjacent to it or very close by. Hosanna School was no exception. When it was built, blacks abandoned the adjacent old log church where they had worshipped and used the new building not only for school but for church services and lodge meetings as well.

Hosanna School
1867–1954

51

The students most likely used the roughly chiseled benches without backs and wrote on slates held on their laps. "Early in the nineteenth century the three R's, readin', ritin' and 'rithmetic were the only subjects taught … School furniture was very crude homemade wooden benches of oak and chestnut, with a master's desk of the same rough material. Slates were used in Harford County until 1916."[150] Each of the two floors had its own wood/coal burning pot-bellied stove. The earlier furniture was probably much like the original furniture in the Darlington Academy.

In his writings, Booker T. Washington vividly portrays what the black citizens of Berkley must have been feeling when they saw their dream of securing an education was being realized:

> Few people who were not right in the midst of the scenes can form an exact idea of
> the intense desire which the people of my race showed for an education. As I state,
> it was a whole race trying to go to school. Few were too young and none too old,
> to make an attempt to learn.[151]

It did not matter if Hosanna's students were adults or children, finely dressed or in rag-tags, homeowners or renters, if they had some skills or none at all. It did not even matter if they had to walk for miles through rain, wind, or snow. They enthusiastically embraced this opportunity. Nothing in the school—including the building materials—was new. Nonetheless, their spirited enthusiasm was not the least bit diminished.

Initially, some early documents record the school as the Berkley School named for the community in which it was built. Later, with a sense of pride and ownership, the Hosanna trustees named it the Hosanna School. The Harford County School Commissioners took over operation of the Hosanna School in 1879. The earliest records found at the Board of Education listing the names of students attending the Hosanna School date back to 1909 and continue until its closing in 1946.

PART III

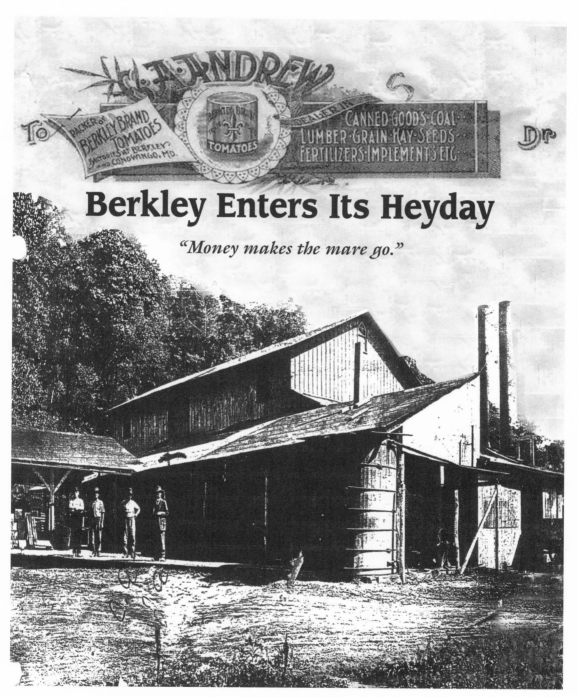

Berkley Enters Its Heyday

"Money makes the mare go."

The Berkley Tomato Cannery
Historical Society of Harford County (Reeves Family Collection)

Berkley Area of
Martenet Map of Harford County—1878

Special Collections (Maryland State Archives Map Collection)(MSA sc 1427-224.B5-1-1)

Berkley Enters Its Heyday

By the 1870s Gideon Smith had established his Swallowfield homestead, had added a wing to the house and barn and was planning a second wing to both. The tanbark mill was still operating as was the farm, and his children were coming of age.

Two of the children, Joshua Cowgill Smith and Bernard Gilpin Smith became business partners in the Berkley area and carried on their father's entrepreneurial spirit. When Joshua married Edith Mason in 1881, Gideon Smith had a house built for them. This majestic stone house, Roscrea, named for Gideon Gilpin Smith's ancestral home west of Dublin, Ireland, still stands on the outskirts of Berkley on U.S. Route 1. It has been exquisitely preserved and maintained by the Clifford Brown family.

For his son Bernard, Smith engaged a renowned Philadelphia architect and relative of the family, Walter Cope,[152] to design a house to be built next to Swallowfield. Known as Red Gate, the house still stands today. This cruciform-shaped house is one of the first examples of modern suburban housing. It "sports prominent gables with ridgelines that meet at a central chimney; … and is a reminder of Cope's (and Smith's) awareness of modern technology; Red Gate was among the first houses in the county equipped with central heating, and the large chimney was centrally placed so it could efficiently serve a huge coal furnace."[153]

Redgate, one of two Berkley houses designed by Philadelphia architect, Walter Cope, was built for Bernard Smith, a co-owner of the Susqehanna Pulp and Power Company. It was one of the first "modern" houses designed with a central chimney to provide central heating. The house was later owned by the Gregory family who ran a flourishing turkey farm on the property, in addition to owning the Towpath Tea House.

Photograph by Scott Prettyman

In their first enterprise the brothers purchased the Stafford Mill farther down the river. The mill had been built by Thomas Symington to manufacture soapstone. The Smith brothers used it for grinding flint. The flint arrived on canal boats from a quarry near Bald Hill. The brothers operated the Stafford Mill for several years. They sold it and opened the Conowingo Flint Mill on the Cecil County side of the river opposite Glen Cove. The flint was "quarried by the Presberry boys (colored) and hauled by mule team across the old Conowingo Bridge to the flint mill."[154] The flint, in some cases, was burned and ground for local use. This fine white powder was shipped to factories producing porcelain or pottery. It was also crushed and shipped to the Grasseli Chemical Company in Cleveland, Ohio, where it was used to filter liquid gas.[155] The 1880 census observed that the Smith's:

kaolin and ground earth [flint] works was worth $12,000 and that their fifteen employees produced $8,400 worth of goods. Flint, a hard white rock, was commonly quarried throughout northern Harford; transported to mills by mule cart or barge, it was broken up, then tossed into stacks … where it was heated and then ground to a fine powder invaluable to the production of china. This stack [at Stafford], roughly 30 feet tall, had a square, rubble stone base, a cylindrical shaft, and a brick cap; solitary and sentinel-like, it is all that remains of the Stafford industrial complex.[156]

By 1881 the two brothers had lost interest in the flint industry and had turned to paper manufacturing. The Susquehanna Power and Paper Company had its birth "in the fertile minds of Joshua C. and B. Gilpin Smith."[157] Their brother, N. Newlin Smith, joined them later. The brothers were enthusiastic about this new enterprise but knew nothing about paper manufacturing, so they lured Harry Carter of Cecil County who was knowledgeable in the field to manage the mill and teach them the trade. Before building the mill, they pursued possible stockholders, and together with their investors, envisioned a dam spanning the width of the river. To advance this prospect, they appealed to the Maryland General Assembly in 1884. The company was granted a charter that gave it the authority to "acquire, with rights of condemnation, any property needed for the development and extension of a dam to be used for water power. This authority extended to cover acquisition of any property liable to be overflowed or injured by backwater from the dam."[158] With this authorization, the construction of the mill began and used both waterpower and coal as the energy sources. "A wing dam was built out into the river"[159] which carried the water to the headgate. The grindstone run by the turbines was imported from Nova Scotia—especially made to withstand the intense grinding necessary to prepare the wood for papermaking. Over the years of operation the mill produced "brown wrapping paper, wallpaper, and 'chevroettes,' a paper product used extensively in women's skirts as bustles."[160] While the company built the wing dam complete with an intake channel, headgates, and waterwheels to accommodate the power needs of the paper mill, it did not build a dam that spanned the river. It did, however, take advantage of the authority in the charter to purchase significant amounts of land along the riverbank.

This enterprise became the major user of the canal that "ran past the mill with convenient docks for unloading supplies."[161] The company owned at least one scow, The John H. Hughes, usually captained by Charles White who lived at Castleton.[162] According to Reverend Scriven's treatise:

> The paper mill of the Susquehanna Water and Power Company accounted for much of the canal traffic during this period (1892) with about 300 tons of pulp wood and some tamarack coming from Pennsylvania … Spruce pine from the mouth of the Susquehanna—5112 tons of it … many canal boat loads of coal, 120 tons at a time came up the canal for the paper mill, and probably sulfur.[163]

The Susquehanna Power and Paper Company was a "$3,000,000 investment and was one of the important centers of trade on the canal. The mill worked continuously three shifts a day for seven days a week and employed as many as three hundred people."[164] Fred C. Jones, a farmer and mill-owner along Peddler's Run gave a vivid picture of the location and workings of the mill in his 1940 recollections:

The paper-mill was located directly on the west shore of the river and the Susquehanna and Tidewater canal passed along the western shore of the river between the paper mill and the mainland. In order to reach the paper mill from the mainland, it was necessary to cross a short bridge across the canal and this bridge was raised to permit the free use of the canal and then lowered to permit the traffic from the mainland to the towpath and the paper mill. There was a small body of water in the front of the mill and it was called "forebay." There were some iron racks where the water from the forebay passed on the wheels to make the power. The racks located at the lower end of the forebay were usually kept clean of driftwood by an old man named Bill Webster ... so that the full power of the water could be utilized ...

The paper was made from rags and pulp of soft wood. The ingredients were mixed together and were ground by large wooden wheels called "beaters" and then ground mixed pulp was passed on to a wire and felt cloth so that the water would pass through, while the solid part of the pulp went on to the driers. The driers were heated to absorb the moisture and from them the pulp passed on to the machines. Unless the pulp was handled very carefully, the paper would break and the broken paper was deposited in a large container and taken back to the beater room, and so it was a waste and made a lot more work for the machine tenders. From the machines the paper went to the calendars, which were a series of steel rolls placed one on the other, the paper passed between them. They were very heavy and the feeder frequently got his fingers mashed in them when the paper was fed into them on its way to the finishing room where it was wrapped into bundles and prepared for market ...

When the paper mill was first built the only contact it had with the railroad was by means of a team of mules that hauled the paper to the railroad from the mill. The mules were usually gray in color and they had some bells attached to the harness so the paper mill team could be heard long before it could be seen crossing the covered bridge over the Susquehanna River ... There was no light in the bridge and the night users frequently carried a lantern. The mules were kept in a stable at the old paper mill ... The team was later abandoned and an endless chain was erected to run from the mill across the river to the railroad siding on the east side of the river. The ferry was called "twickinham" and there was a high tower built on the paper mill island over which the endless chain passed ...

The paper mill provided work for many people at Darlington as well as at Conowingo and other places and the pay was looked forward to each two weeks for it was never known to fail to pay on time and of course was depended on, and was highly regarded by the community to which it meant so much.[165]

Harry Webb Farrington worked at the paper mill when he was about 15 years old. His narrative captures his memories as a young worker at the mill:

One day Amos Ely stopped at Gorrells' and asked me to go down and work a night for him on the "chipper." "Go down" meant the slab mill of the Susquehanna Pulp and Power Company, the greatest industry in the county, three miles away on the river … The whole plant … was a sort of gateway to fairyland to such boys as, tired of the hardships of the farm, wished to try something else, or are fascinated by the lure of the world of machinery.

From five that evening to seven the next morning I simply handed these three-foot slabs to the man who shoved them into the chipper. So well did I take to this new work that I was given a job of five dollars a week.[166]

Because of the complexities in operating a paper mill, there were many stoppages—jams, breaks, and, at times, a less than dependable water source, enough so that Farrington noted the demeanor of the machine men in stating "Next to sailors, paper makers are said to be the most profane of men."[167]

Samuel Mason's childhood memories evoke a sense of how the children in Berkley viewed the mill works. "Below the mill a quarter of a mile, was the settling pond from which clean water was secured for washing the pulp when the river was muddy, and we boys used to haunt its shores in attempting to shoot the huge 'snappers' that lived there … There was always a strong sulphurous smell at the mill and in front, were often large piles of yellow sulphur and barrels of rosin, the latter for sizing the paper."[168]

As for its owners, Fred Jones recalled Joshua Smith in particular. He was a "very close attendant at the paper mill and seemed to be very efficient in his work there. The paper mill was very active especially in its earlier days, and so was very popular for it made a very important contribution to the community; and so, its passing was very much regretted by those who knew it best. Smith brothers stood very high in the estimation of the community and the old paper mill employed a great number of people during the many years that it operated."[169]

As industry and commerce were growing and prospering so was the agricultural community. During the late 1800s, Fletcher Jones, a descendent of the Jones family at Rigbie House, continued the family tradition of productive and profitable farming. A letter to the editor of the *Aegis Intelligencer* in 1878 boasted of the fertile and productive farmland in the area, particularly the Fletcher Jones farm. The letter writer highlighted the importance of rail service to the farmers in the area, and then continued his text to give his own, somewhat acerbic, view of the world around him.

Letter From Darlington.

Darlington is located about 2½ miles from the West bank of the Susquehanna river. Six miles northwest of Lapidum and 4 miles southwest of Conowingo. It is situated about 400 feet above tidewater. Our soil is red and sand loam, very fertile, producing this year from 30 to 40 bushels of wheat to the acre. Mrs. John M. Cooley had by measurement on three acres nearly 99 bushels of wheat, or by weight 104½ bushels.

We have some model farmers, too. Mr. Fletcher Jones's farm will compare favorably with any farm in the State. He raises full crops always, and as to weeds—they seem to be afraid to grow, either in a field or alongside a fence.

The largest farm near us is owned by William and Albert Holloway. They have about six hundred acres, and feed about sixty head of cattle yearly.

The dairy business is pursued by three of our farmers: Isaac H. Thompson, who has about forty cows; and B. Gilpin Smith and his brother N. Newlin Smith, who have about one hundred cows. You see, Mr. Editor, the advantages that a railroad affords. If these dairymen did not have a railroad near them, they could not follow this most lucrative business.

We have the advantage of four churches, Methodist Episcopal, Protestant Episcopal and Orthodox and Hicksite Society of Friends. I cannot say that our morals are correspondingly good.

The health of this vicinity is generally good, but at the present time the three resident physicians seem to be quite busy. They certainly have patients, or they would not be riding; they have practiced too long to ride for fun.

Now, one would think with all these blessings with which we are surrounded that we lived in the midst of brotherly love; but we do not.—Society is so divided, that it is brought down to the old adage—"Money makes the mare go."
                                                                MAX.

The Cooley House was the second Berkley house designed by Walter Cope with the same "modern" features as Red Gate. Built for Helen Esther Jones and her new husband, Marvin Lord Cooley, by her father, Fletcher Jones of Rigbie farm, it is now owned by her grandson, Charles Cooley.

Photograph by Scott Prettyman

When Fletcher Jones' daughter, Helen Esther Jones, married Marvin Lord Cooley, her father gave her five acres and had a house built for her. This house, the second in Berkley to be designed by Philadelphia architect Walter Cope, was built by John T. Lamb,[170] a well-respected local carpenter and great-grand-father of John Lamb who currently lives near Berkley. The house is located on the private road to Rigbie House. Helen Cooley gave the house to her grandson, Charles Marvin Cooley, and his wife, Verneal, and they live in this ancestral house today. Charles Cooley recalled that, *"my grandmother got this house and five acres from the farm up here as a wedding present when she got married … he built this house for her and give it to her as a wedding present plus some furniture from the house up there to take care of her mother if any thing happened to him … and I still have his will which deeded her this house and property, a horse, a cow, and chickens, and feed and a certain amount of stock."*[171]

Other business moguls found their way to Berkley, including Charles A. Andrew. Born in Darlington and the third generation Andrew to live in Harford County, he completed his "literary studies at the Darlington Academy"[172] and came to Berkley in 1887. Andrew purchased significant pieces of property, and built his three story Victorian house, Oak Winds, at the corner of Berkley and Castleton Roads. He was described as possessing "untiring energy, is quick of perception, forms his plans readily and is determined in their execution; and his close application to business and his excellent management have brought to him the high degree of prosperity which to to-day is his."[173] He has also been described as "very fat, and always rode around behind fast horses."[174]

Charles Andrew, businessman and politician of late 1800s and early 1900s Berkley.

Harford County Historical Society

The year he arrived he opened a cannery in Berkley and engaged in general farming. On the corner of his property, he opened a general store and sold food, yard goods, kerosene, and other commodities to the community and to the increasing numbers of travelers passing through on their way to the Conowingo Bridge. He had numerous and varied enterprises. He owned a coal

Oak Winds, home of Charles Andrew

Photograph by Scott Prettyman

The limestone kilns produced lime for farm-land and industrial use until just after the end of the 19th century. The offices above were the headquarters for the various enterprises of Charles Andrew. The kilns were torn down when the Berkley Road was widened to accommodate the increase in "horseless" traffic across the Conowingo Bridge.

Private Collection of Edwin and Emalyn Kirkwood

company and a lumber company; he owned warehouses at Glen Cove. He was president of the Berkley Savings and Loan, and he built the Berkley Raceway, a sulky track located near the crossroads that was the source of fascination and enjoyment for many. Andrew owned a mercantile business in Glen Cove and sold supplies for many years. His office was located there, too, in a whitewashed building that "stood on the top of one of the abandoned lime kilns and was known locally as the 'Castle.'"[175]

Andrew's tomato cannery was located on the Berkley Road towards the river. It was a local market for the farmers in the area and provided employment for many of the residents of Berkley and the surrounding communities. Lois Steele Jones was one of many residents who remembered the cannery, *"I think the canning house was operating during the time we were there. It was whitewashed on the outside; the boards were painted that way. I remember being down there while they were canning."*[176]

And Jean Ewing remembered it as a place of employment, *"… the road that runs east from Berkley had a canning house that Mr. Charles Andrew ran and that employed a lot of people. And that may have been when he wanted to build up Berkley as an employment center. That may have been when the houses were built up in, right near the middle of town, near the blacksmith shop."*[177]

Berkley Raceway attracted horsemen and horse lovers from around the area. It provided employment for many, the thrill of the race for a crowd—and one of Charles Cooley's fondest memories, *"I can remember the harness track where they drove harness horses, and trained them. Charles Andrew had a lot of horses and he trained them. Colored guy by the name of Winnie James worked for him. And Winnie knew horses."*[178]

Harry Webb Farrington was fond of Nancy, an old racehorse, and he took her to the Berkley racetrack for her to experience the track one more time:

At the village of Berkeley (*sic*) was the nearest race track to our stock farm at Darlington. Here was where we exercised our young trotters. On that particular day Nancy did not know where she was going. She certainly had not seen a race-

LOIS STEELE JONES and PHYLLIS STEELE PRICE
*are sisters who grew up in Berkley between the late 1930s and early 1950s.
Their family lived in one of the four structures at the Berkley crossroads. Both
sisters attended Darlington Elementary School and Dublin High School with
Lois attending the Darlington Academy before it closed. Phyllis attended
Goldey Beacon College to be become a secretary while Phyllis, upon graduating
from Church Home Hospital Nursing Program worked as a registered nurse
for 38 years. Their interview evokes a past in Berkley that provided a pleasant and warm childhood with remembrances of ice-skating on the Berkley
ponds, going to Glen Cove to swim, eating fresh-baked bread at the McNutt
house baked by Flo Cain, and trips to the Berkley store. As they recall, "It was
a great place to grow up."*
29 February 2000

track for years. As she jogged along, everything seemed as usual until we came to
the race track and Dr. Windolph tried to drive her across the track and hitch her
behind the now empty stand where, on racing days, the judges stood to start, time,
and watch the race.

Scarcely had her front feet touched the hard yet soft loam of the track, scarcely had
her eyes caught the contour of the judges' stand, than her ears stood erect, her tail
was raised, and a little snort flew from her nostrils. It was no longer dear little old
Nancy, but Nancy 2.23 ½ … even before the Doctor could gather up the reins that
Nancy had wheeled to the right, made a dash up, and obliquely across the track
to get to the inside rail … She had not gone ten yards before her rapidly moving
body flattened out so low that her chest seemed to touch the ground. Berkeley
had become Boston; the old buckboard a high-wheeled sulky … and with a rein
that had not time to guide or restrain her, with the full speed of her inspired spirit
and body, she tore down the track as in the days of old … The time of the heat is
chalked up on the judge's stand … Nancy 2.03 ½.[179]

It is unknown whether Nancy ever had such a thrilling run again but to the pleasure and enjoyment of many Marylanders, near and far, the sulky races continued for
many years thereafter.

Andrew was instrumental in establishing the Berkley Permanent Building and Loan Association. It was founded in 1894, according to Harford County land records, and continued to operate until 1906.[180] Andrew served as President of the Association for at least four years. The treasurer was W. F. McNutt, also a resident of Berkley. No documentation suggests that there was a separate building for this enterprise. Because there were limited state regulations at that time, the building and loan association was probably located within Andrew's offices with very few hours of operation. In fact, many of the savings and loans during this period were small offices where the officers met with individuals by appointment in the evenings to make decisions about loans and investments. And as historian C. Milton Wright noted, "Since 1865 Savings and Loan Associations have served a dual role in the promotion of our economic system. Small investors have had the opportunity to add to their savings and receive a fair rate of Interest," thus providing money "for the construction of thousands of homes with payments on the installment plan extending over a number of years."[181]

The Andrew family belonged to the Darlington Methodist Church but Andrew also built the Berkley chapel. This was a non-denominational chapel for family worship located on his property along Castleton Road between his home and Swallowfield. According to construction receipts, the chapel was built between February 1892 and June 1893[182] by Alfred P. Edge who worked under the supervision of John Lamb, a well-known local carpenter. The chapel cost $430. It was later used as a private residence and burned in the 1980s.

The Berkley Chapel was built by Charles Andrew on land next to his house as a private chapel for his family.

Private collection of Edwin and Emalyn Kirkwood

Andrew was his party's candidate for High Sheriff in 1891, and in 1897 his name was again placed on the ticket as the nominee for county clerk. But it was not until he ran for the Maryland State Senate in 1910 that he won an election. He served two terms in the Maryland General Assembly as Harford County's senator. Throughout the rest of his life and, even today he is referred to as Senator Andrew. His business acumen later led to his appointment as one of two citizen members of the Government Committee on Awards to reimburse Harford landowners for damages incurred for loss of their properties when Aberdeen Proving Ground was established in 1918. His responsibility as a committee member was to "fix the value of the land and settle all damages made by the War Department in establishing the proving ground."[183]

The widening of the road to the bridge in 1911 signaled the demise of the limestone kilns and the end of Andrew's office space. Andrew moved his offices to Conowingo on the other side of the river.

Transportation and Communication
At the End of the Nineteenth Century

Travel over the century changed dramatically—from oxcart, two-wheeled carts drawn by horses and mules, and riding horseback over rutted, privately owned roads —to the beginnings of integrated road systems operated and maintained by government.

In the mid-1800s, four-wheeled carts and buckboards were in daily use, taking products to markets. If one could afford it, one used a buggy to take the family to church on Sundays. Wagons drawn by mules carried mined ores such as flint and soapstone to the canal for passage up or down the river, across the Conowingo Bridge for points north and east, or to the boats at Lapidum to transport these raw materials to Baltimore and other ports.

And rail transport had arrived! By 1835, railroad service was available in Harford County. The first was the Baltimore and Port Deposit Railroad with a line from Baltimore to Havre de Grace. While building trestles and bridges across streams was daunting, crossing the Susquehanna River proved formidable; in fact, the rail cars were ferried across the river until 1866, when the first railroad bridge was constructed. The Baltimore and Port Deposit Railroad was eventually taken over by the Pennsylvania Railroad, and by 1880 the Baltimore and Ohio Railroad had also laid its rails and competed for customers between Baltimore and New York.

Berkley's farmers, entrepreneurs, and craftsmen benefited from this new mode of transportation. The canal goods could be transferred to and from the railways on the west side of the Susquehanna. Other commodities and produce were taken across the Conowingo Bridge to connect with the Columbia and Port Deposit Railroad that went north to York and Lancaster and south to join the major railroads traversing the southern part of Harford County.

Many grand and glorious rail plans were afoot that would have affected Berkley —but none came to pass. A third railroad company in the area, the Maryland Central Railroad, had such plans. Begun in 1884, its plan called for "a railroad from Baltimore to Philadelphia by way of Bel Air, crossing the Susquehanna at the Conowingo Bridge, as indicated in a charter by the State of Maryland to the Maryland Central Railroad Company."[184] However, the local influential investors in Harford County changed the route to go through the richer farms in the western part of the county, and the plan was abandoned.

Upon completion of the altered route, the investors sought a line connection with an anthracite coal railroad, "… the projected expansion to be built northward to reach the Reading." The Reading was an anthracite railroad, and the investors hoped to construct "a standard gauge line to the Susquehanna along Deer Creek." This was to be known as Deer Creek and Susquehanna Railroad. After reaching the mouth of Deer Creek, the Maryland Central plan envisioned "building from Stafford up the river four miles and there crossing to Conowingo, possibly on the existing vehicular bridge"[185]—the Conowingo Bridge—to connect to the Lehigh Valley Railroad in Bethlehem, Pennsylvania. Contracts were actually let to begin the grading along Deer Creek, but after five years, "the Maryland Central wasted enough money on the project to weaken itself financially."[186] The Maryland Central Railroad later became the Maryland and Pennsylvania Railroad, a narrow gauge railroad known affectionately by its passengers and in memory as the Ma and Pa.

Privately owned roads were the main corridors of transportation during the major portion of the 1800s. In many cases, payment for passage was required and as Mason noted:

> Harford County, 1895, had no pikes or hard roads. They were dirt; narrow and crooked, overhung with trees and grapevines, muddy in spring, dusty in summer and dark at night when spooks walked abroad … In front of our house there used to be one of these narrow dirt roads such as I have described. Cedar trees lined it; wild cherry, walnut and locust grew there, and over all a tangle of fox grape, which at night shut out most of the light from the moon and stars.[187]

By 1890, "private ownership had been abolished and responsibility for the building and maintenance of roads was vested with county governments."[188] The authorization for this building and construction rested with Maryland state government mainly because the funding for this construction came from state resources. Just after the turn of the century, in 1907, the state took over completely the major roads traversing Harford County, including the road through Berkley to the Conowingo Bridge. The turnpike was called the Monumental Trail,[189] and later the Baltimore Pike—the major north-south route on the Eastern Seaboard.

By the 1900s, services were booming at the crossroads—the carriage and wheel shop provided an exceptional product for those beginning to travel greater distances from home and offered "roadside services" for travelers. The blacksmith, Sam Sauers, known as one of the finest in the area, served both the local farming community and the many travelers seeking help for their horses. The roads leading to and from the bridge were bustling with carts and wagons hauling produce, canned tomatoes, dairy products, hay, and grain; the cattle rumbled down the road and, hopefully, broke stride before galloping across the bridge.

The other major transportation mode, the Tidewater Canal, required constant repair, vigilance, and labor. Because of the uncertainties, particularly the financial liabilities connected with the canal, the directors wanted to relinquish their responsibilities. They found an interested party in 1881 when the Reading Railroad agreed to assume all of the debts of the canal and be responsible for the regular repairs resulting from the unpredictability of the Susquehanna waters. But by 1887, Reading, with its deep pockets, was ready to "relinquish its lease of the Canal from the State of Maryland."[190]

Floodwaters continued to rupture the embankments of the canal requiring frequent rebuilding and this, coupled with the emergence of the railroads as the major transporter of goods and raw materials, signaled the demise of the canal in 1894. In May of that year:

> The river rose out of its banks inflicting a mortal wound on the canal. The Pennsylvania portion of the canal never reopened. The Tidewater section was returned to operation but only for local traffic. The flint mills, paper mill, and icehouses still had a means of transportation available to them. However, by 1900 even the Tidewater portion was closed, and the sounds of mules, the blare of the boatmen's trumpets, and the rush of water in the locks were gone.[191]

This final closure also wrote the last chapters of many of the enterprises along the river's banks including the flint mills, the tanbark mills, the tannery, the soapstone quarry, the paper mill, the lime kilns, and other related industries. The Tidewater Canal property was sold in 1902 to the Harlow and McCall Company—a company that would later play a pivotal part in the beginnings of the Conowingo Dam.[192]

Travel across the Conowingo Bridge continued at a brisk pace. Cattle drives were a regular occurrence to get to the markets, particularly in Lancaster. Raw materials like flint and soapstone crossed the bridge to mills along the east side of the river and to the train in Perryville headed for Wilmington, Philadelphia, and Camden, New Jersey. The dairies in the area depended on this quick system to get their fresh milk, butter, and cream to institutions and distribution facilities. And personal travel was flourishing as some residents chose to shop or go to the church in Cecil County. Samuel Mason returned to Berkley as a child and recalled the move from Philadelphia in his 1940 book. Those childhood memories of his family's return trip to take up residence again in the Darlington area were an "ordeal." Coming from Philadelphia, they arrived at the covered bridge in Conowingo Village on the east side of the river. He described in colorful language the last leg of the journey as they passed through the covered bridge and on to Berkley on the other side:

> We approached the end of the Conowingo bridge by a kind of causeway raised above the flood plain. On the left stood a toll gate, always occupied, but no toll was ever collected on this side in my time, and then came the first section of the bridge with its double barrelled construction. Overhead a large sign in black letters marked "Walk your horses." After passing through this covered space, we came to a second short causeway, protected by low stone walls on each side, and from here the main bridge continued across the river at an angle of ten or fifteen degrees toward the South. We entered the right-hand barrel and were enveloped in semi-gloom, the horses' hoofs reverberating in a muffled way on the dirt-covered floor boards. Overhead, the telegraph lines rattled and sang as they all crossed the river inside the bridge above the tie beams … The interior was scaly with old white wash and the beams covered here and there with stimulating advertisements such as, "H.H.H. Good for Man and Beast"; Lydia Pinkham's Pink Pills for Pale People; Castoria; Early Bird Chewing Tobacco; Sloan's Liniment, and many others. As we progressed, the great wooden arches rose regularly beneath the floor. Under them was a space through which we could see the water, perhaps thirty feet below, gliding swiftly along with a swirling motion, which when high, has been known to suck down saw logs, also canoes and people … We passed the

heavy wooden gates at the Harford end of the bridge, paid the toll keeper, and started on the River Road. This was a narrow dirt road overhung with large trees on either side. Frequently we would meet a wagon pulled by four or six head of mules hauling flint to the flint mill. At Glen Cove the road forked; one part continuing down river past the paper mill, while the other turning around the lime kilns. The horses now walking, now trotting, take us past the abandoned lime kilns, the haunt of the copperheads and Carolina wrens; across the wooden bridge over Peddlers Run, past the beds of smooth false foxgloves and finally bring us to Berkley with its blacksmith shop and general store.[193]

By 1911, almost all of the original wood structure of the Conowingo Bridge had been replaced with iron, providing a safer, but probably less romantic, crossing over the Susquehanna.

Private collection of John and Stephen Sauers

On June 6, 1907, a serious fire destroyed half of the Conowingo Bridge and "The missing spans were replaced, not by the old wooden covered bridge, but by modern metal spans."[194] The bridge had continued to operate as a private toll bridge throughout the 1800s and until 1911 when the State of Maryland purchased it and took over its maintenance and upkeep—of which there was a lot! "Subsequent fires leveled other wooden sections until, by 1927, when the bridge was blown up, only two of the ten wooden covered spans remained."[195] But between the 1890s and 1927, the bridge served as a major corridor for trade and commerce—adding to its travelers a new "buggy"—the automobile.

Until the middle 1800s, the only form of distant communication was through the written word. Early settlers depended on messages being carried by horseback, stagecoach, pony express for a very short time, and by ships. As recorded in the annals of U.S. Postal Service history:[196]

> ... mail delivery evolved from foot to horseback, stagecoach, steamboat, railroad, automobile, and airplane, with intermediate and overlapping use of balloons, helicopters, and pneumatic tubes ... By the turn of the nineteenth century, the Post Office Department had purchased a number of stagecoaches for operation on the nation's better post roads—a post road being any road on which the mail traveled ... In 1831, when steam-drive engines "traveling at the unconscionable speed of 15 miles an hour" were denounced as a "device of Satan to lead immortal souls to hell," railroads began to carry mail short distances ... and by 1836 the Postal Service had awarded its first mail contract to the railroads. As early as 1896, before many people in the United States were aware of a new mode of transportation that would eventually supplant the horse and buggy, the Post Office experimented with the "horseless wagon" in its search for faster and cheaper carriage of the mails.[197]

Postal Delivery along the Towpath.
Historical Society of Harford County (895-5)

By the late 1800s, Berkley, Castleton, Dublin and Darlington had their own post offices. The Berkley Post Office was established in 1892, located on the corner of Berkley and Castleton Roads in Andrew's store. This postal service continued to serve the Berkley community until 1928, except for a brief hiatus from 1919–21 when it was combined with the Darlington Post Office. The advent of Rural Free Delivery began to make many of the small hamlet postal stations unnecessary. Postal history points out another benefit of this new delivery system to the county:

A byproduct of rural free delivery was the stimulation it provided to the development of the great American system of roads and highways. A prerequisite for rural delivery was good roads. After hundreds of petitions for rural delivery were turned down by the Post Office because of unserviceable and inaccessible roads, responsible local governments began to extend and improve highways. Between 1897 and 1908 these local governments spent an estimated $72 million on bridges, culverts, and other improvements.[198]

This need for postal service explains some of the impetus in the Maryland General Assembly during this period to approve so many transportation funds for roads and bridges.

By the end of the nineteenth century, the telegraph had been in use in the United States for over 50 years. Congress had provided funds to build a line from Washington, D.C. to Baltimore, and Samuel Morse had used the line in 1843 to tap the famous message, "What hath God wrought!" By 1851, about 50 telegraph companies had been established in the United States. This was the first nationwide communication service and provided an access for trade and communication that had never before been possible. The telegraph system was available to Berkley and telegraph lines crossed the river through the inside of the covered bridge. Bernard Waring spoke about the great inventions of the time: *"The friction match, in the country was the most important thing, one of the great inventions. The other invention in the country was the telegraph and Grandfather Waring came back from Baltimore and told the family that he had paid twenty-five cents in Baltimore to have his name telegraphed over to Washington and back on the new electric telegraph. That was about 1840."*[199]

This extraordinary communications phenomenon was followed by two other technologies that were to change the shape and form of daily life in Berkley—the availability of electricity and the magic of the telephone. Telephone and electric poles began to spring up like daffodils along rural roads throughout the county—and Berkley was no exception. By 1910 about 15 Berkley residents were listed in the Chesapeake and Potomac Telephone Directory.

The Darlington Academy Rebuilds

While black students were attending the Hosanna School, white children in Berkley continued to attend the Darlington Academy, which occupied its same building until 1890. By then, the old stone Academy that had served the community for over 50 years had deteriorated beyond repair and was too small for the burgeoning white population. It was torn down and was replaced by a 34 by 42-foot frame building. The new, colonial-style Academy was properly ventilated and heated and had a large room in the basement for gymnastic exercises.[200] It was designed by George T. Pearson of Philadelphia and John T. Lamb was selected as the contractor.[201] James H. Whitaker built the foundation using stone from the old Academy. Harford County appropriated $1500 for its construction and private donors provided the remainder. The trustees of the new Darlington Academy were Dr. W. Stump Forwood, John H. Price, R. S. McNutt, Joshua S. Gorrell, R. J. Williams, F. J. Hopkins, Dr. John Sappington, A. S. Holloway, Isaac Wilson, D. F. Shure and D. E. Wilson—names that may still be recognized in the Darlington area. A. Finney Galbreath was principal and Mattie S. Richardson served as his assistant.

Darlington Academy

The Stephenson Masonic Lodge of Lapidum conducted the cornerstone laying ceremony for the new "public" school. A tin box was placed in a receptacle in the cornerstone. It contained lists of the trustees of the Academy and Public School, the names of the current teachers, and documents of various kinds, including copies of Baltimore, Philadelphia and New York newspapers, the county papers, a poem by Mr. Caleb Emien, records of the Shure Family, a statement of the population of Darlington, and two pieces of Continental money 150 years old, given by Dr. H. C. Whiteford.[202] The new Darlington Academy would serve the white children of Darlington, Berkley, and the surrounding countryside until 1938 when it was replaced by a new public school built in Darlington.

During this time in Berkley there was another school for the Quaker children in the community. As Bernard Waring remembered it, *"The school room was at Swallowfield. We didn't want to send our children to public schools—a lot of rough kind of people and just the same we wanted them to have a school which was a little bit better in quality so the third story, where Nannie sleeps now, they had to call it the schoolroom. Aunt Mary Smith, who was quite a person, she taught school there. She's my mother's sister. She was matron later at Haverford College."*[203]

68   Jean Ewing recalled that, *"Mother (Joshua Smith's daughter who was raised at*

Roscrea) and her two sisters, who lived over by Route 1, used to come over to Berkley to go to school up in the school room, over the dining room here at Swallowfield. And Aunt Becky [Rebecca Gould] *used to teach them too, and get them ready to go to Germantown Friends School."*[204]

Faith of Our Fathers and Mothers

Berkley and Darlington residents were diligent and faithful in the construction and use of their places of worship. By the end of the nineteenth century, all of the churches extant in the area today had been built. These churches were solidly constructed to welcome communicants for centuries to come. In the past, as in the present, blacks attended Sunday services at Hosanna Church in Berkley. Unless they could use the private Andrew chapel in Berkley, the white residents—Quakers, Presbyterians, Episcopalians or Methodists, attended church in nearby Darlington. Those of other faiths traveled some distance to worship and this continues to be true today.

The first Deer Creek Friends Meeting House was established in 1737 on land acquired from the Rigbie family. The Meeting subsequently moved across the road to its current location on the same property. The dates on its cemetery tombstones speak to the historic importance of this place of meeting.

In the late 1820s American Quakerism divided into two branches. The Hicksites, followers of Elias Hicks, had a more universal individualistic approach to the Deity. They stressed the doctrine of Inner Light, which was more apt to be followed by rural Quakers than urban ones. The others, the Orthodox Quakers, were more evangelical and stressed the authority of the elders. They were Christ centered and emphasized the Bible. After they split into two groups the Hicksites remained in the present Meeting House, while the Orthodox met in private homes.[205]

Jean Ewing's grandfather, Gideon Smith, was personally involved with the dispute. She said, *"Hicksite Friends were more liberal and didn't take the Bible quite so literally. And my grandfather thought the Hicksites were right, but he didn't want to join them because they were breaking up the Meeting. So, he stayed an Orthodox Quaker."*[206] Eventually, the two groups reunited. The Quaker presence is still strong in Darlington and, in 2000, an addition was added to the Meeting House to accommodate its members.

The Presbyterians began their congregation at about the same time as the Quakers built their first Meeting House. Deer Creek Harmony Church can trace its existence to 1734 and according to its records, "It can also be shown, beyond a reasonable doubt, that its first members were of those sturdy puritans from the Severn, who had pushed their adventurous way thus far into the Deer Creek forest."[207] Built of logs, it was called the Whitefield Meeting House, named for George Whitefield who preached there in 1739. Almost a century later, a meeting was held at the Prospect School House on January 18, 1837, to organize and build a church. The first resolution of the meeting stated: "That in the opinion of this meeting, it is necessary and expedient that a house should be erected for the purpose of public worship and to be occupied for a Sunday School." Furthermore, "that measures be immediately taken to collect funds for that purpose." The following individuals were to form a committee to "superintend the building: William Wilson, Benjamin Silver, John H. Price and Samuel Harper."[208]

Within a fortnight they met and agreed upon the plans, delineated the site and hired the builder:

> First that the church should be located at or near the junction of the roads lead-ing from William Wilson's mill, and Dr. Thomas Worthingtons; second, that the church should be built of stone, thirty by forty feet, sixteen and one-half feet high, with a gallery of twelve feet across one end and covered with slate; third, that if Zephaniah Bayless can get workmen to quarry the stone and put up the wall for one dollar per perch, he be authorized to employ them.[209]

The parishioners held their first service in the new church on Friday, October 13, 1837.

The Hosanna Church in Berkley was the third church in the area, tracing its ancestry to the log structure built around 1835 on land provided by Robert Paca. The Hosanna A.M.E. congregation moved its church ser-vices and activities from the old log struc-ture to the Hosanna School in 1867 and re-mained there until 1880 when a new church was built and used exclusively for religious services. The following excerpts from the deed detail the action taken to acquire the land to fulfill a long held dream:

The "new" Hosanna Church was built in 1881 and still has a flourishing congregation.
Photography by Scott Prettyman

> This deed made this Sixteenth day of March in the year Eighteen Hundred and eighty by Robert Peco and Rosa Peco his wife in the one part and William E. Bond, Joseph Peco, Hampton Washington, Jacob Lee and Sylvester Washington Trustees in trust to the said Robert Peco and Rosa his wife ... for in consideration of the sum of twenty-two dollars ... have granted to the said trustees and their successors ... all that piece or parcel of land called "Phillips Purchase" ... that they shall erect ... a house or place of worship for the use of the members of the African Methodist Episcopal Church in the United States of America according to the rule and discipline of said church.

Until recently a parsonage was always provided for the minister at Hosanna. Prior to 1903, the congregation rented homes in Berkley for the Hosanna pastor and his family. In that year, a house was purchased *"for a reasonable price"*[210] on Berkley Road and served as the parsonage until the church no longer had a full-time pastor. The church still owns the parsonage and has rented it for many years. An excerpt from the church's 100th Anniversary Journal captures the dedication of the many pastors and parishioners who worked to sustain the soul and maintain the church:

Much time was spent in worship in the early years, for services were held two or three times on Sundays and at least one night each week. During those years, also there were many faithful workers who gave much of their time and made outstanding financial contributions ... Many members spent much of their time visiting the sick and helping the needy ... During 1915, The Rev. F. S. Dennis, pastor, the church was painted on the inside ... During 1919 ... a long standing mortgage was paid off and concrete steps were built ... 1927, the chimneys were rebuilt and a new roof was put on the church ... During 1947 to 1949, the Reverend Melvin C. Swann, Sr. supervised the completion of the roofing, burned the mortgage, had shingles put on the church, redecorated the interior and refinished the church furniture. Eight memorial windows were installed and a few rooms of the parsonage redecorated. He liquidated outstanding obligations against the church and during his pastorate, the building which is now the kitchen was constructed, the labor being contributed by an organization known as the Berkley Brotherhood.[211]

The Episcopal Church, formerly the Church of England, has had a long and distinguished history in Harford County beginning with the establishment of the Spesutia Church in Perryman around 1672. It was the parish of Berkley's first resident, Colonel Nathaniel Rigbie. By 1750, St. James Chapel was the closest parish church for Darlington communicants. Known originally as Deer Creek Chapel and then Trap (Trappe) Church, it was located at Priests' Ford on Deer Creek about three-and-one-half miles from Darlington. According to James Wollon in his brief history of the Episcopal Church in Harford County, there were "difficult years following the Revolution and the disestablishment of the Church of England."[212] Sometime around 1842, the Episcopalians in the Berkley and Darlington area tried to form a congregation but it was not until 1861 that, "the Reverend Edward Colburn, the rector of Deer Creek Parish, gathered a congregation in Darlington and established services in the Darlington Academy."[213] The first Episcopal Church in Darlington was constructed in 1872. The board and batten structure stood on the site of the present day rectory. It was used for a very short period and, according to Wollon:

> in 1876, Mr. D. C. Wharton Smith of Philadelphia and Darlington offered to assist in the construction of a stone church in Darlington to be designed in the manner of a small English medieval church. The parish borrowed $2,000, and with five guarantors—Mr. Wharton Smith one of them—the present church was built. Upon its completion Mr. Smith offered to refund all of the money raised and to close the expense account so that the church might stand as a memorial by him to his father, Milton Smith. The offer was accepted and Grace Church thus became known as Grace Memorial Church. The cornerstone was laid on October 4, 1876; the first service was held in it on June 17, 1877, and it was consecrated October 5, 1882.[214]

Philadelphia architect, Theophilus Parsons Chandler, Jr. was the architect of the church and, according to Wollon, approached the design with great skill and attention to detail. He noted, "The care in design, and the attention to authentic medieval details which this structure shows is characteristic of examples of the Gothic-revival, the architects of which had the opportunity to visit England, personally studying, and sketching, medieval structures and details."[215] The new rectory was designed by

Walter Cope, the Philadelphia architect whose architectural accomplishments still grace the landscapes and vistas of Berkley and Darlington.

What happened to the original board and batten church? The frame building was moved to Scarboro, about five miles from Darlington, renamed the Church of the Ascension, and remains consecrated and in service today for the Episcopal communicants of the Dublin area.

Methodism was a popular and influential faith of the early settlers in Harford County, and there was an abundance of Methodists who lived in Berkley and Darlington. As early as the late eighteenth century, Methodists and Quakers alike struggled mightily over the concept of slavery and the ownership of another human being. Early on, Methodists in Havre de Grace and Philadelphia opened their doors to include people of color within their congregation. C. Milton Wright confirmed the strength of the Methodist Church in Harford County when he observed, "According to the *Scott Gazetteer*, Harford contained in 1798 two Episcopal churches and two chapels, two Presbyterian churches, one Catholic church, one Baptist church, six Methodist churches, and three Quaker meeting houses."[216] In the late eighteenth and early nineteenth centuries, before the establishment of nearby Rock Run Methodist Church, the Methodists in the Darlington area shared space in the Whitefield Meeting House with other denominations.[217] The records of the Methodist Historical Society at Lovely Lane Museum document the existence of a Methodist Class meeting in Darlington as early as 1807 and the journal of John Wesley Bond records that he preached at the Darlington Meeting House on April 29, 1817.

LAURA M. BRADFORD
is probably the most remembered individual in all of the interviews. Born in 1904, she came to Darlington at age six and lived on the Jourdan farm. She attended the Darlington Academy, Maryland State Normal School, Johns Hopkins University and UCLA. Her first teaching assignment was a one-room schoolhouse in Glenville, a small village south of Darlington. She then taught at the Darlington Academy and, in 1938, when the Darlington Elementary School was completed, she was the first grade teacher and continued teaching for 46 years. In her interview she reflected on some of her students and her memories of Berkley. Laura nurtured hundreds of former and current residents in the area, many of whom filled her beloved Darlington United Methodist Church to overflowing to honor her life when she died in 2002 at the age of 97.
Interviewed 13 June 2000

In 1832, a Board of Trustees was formed and land, where the church still stands, was purchased from Joseph Worthington. The first church was built of logs. According to Christopher Weeks' eloquent description, a simple and timeless structure replaced the early log church in 1852:

> That structure, of log construction, became too small for the popular sect and was replaced with the present handsome frame church. With its simple, classic lines, oak-shaded lot and attractive cast-iron fence, the Methodist church has long figured in village vignettes. Its very construction was a cooperative community effort; one person donated lumber, someone else woodworking skills; in all probability blacksmith Joshua Gorrell contributed the fence.[218]

*GENEVIEVE WEBSTER
PRESBERRY JONES,*
*a descendant of the James family, was
born in Berkley in 1917, lives in the
home in which her mother was born on
Castleton Road. Her family has owned
this property since the early 1800s.
This property is one of only two parcels
of land purchased by her ancestors in
the early 1800s that is still owned by
James family descendants. Like her
mother, she attended Hosanna School.
Genevieve worked for several Quaker
families in the Berkley area, including the Waring family at Swallowfield
for whom she worked for 25 years, both
in Berkley and Philadelphia. Having
only one child of her own, Christine
Presberry Tolbert, she became revered
as a mother figure to her nephews and
nieces as well as the children in the
Waring Family. Like many involved
in Hosanna School, she put education
first for her child to make certain her
daughter would receive a college education. In her interview, she recalled
her school days at Hosanna School and
her love of driving. Her warm spirit
continues to draw children like a
magnet, whether relatives or friends,
black or white.*

Interviewed 15 January 2000

A vestibule and a belfry with bells were added in 1892. Every day, even now, Darlington residents are calmed and soothed by the belfry bells and when it is quiet, those joyous sounds can be heard in Berkley, as well. In her history of the church, Elizabeth Gorrell in-cluded recollections by the old members. "They one and all recalled the pastorate of the Reverend L. M. Dutton from 1895 to 1897. It was then that the church had its greatest revival, lasting six weeks with 185 con-verts."[219] Berkley chronicler Harry Webb Farrington was converted at one of these meetings. On Christmas Eve, 2001, a fire erupted in the Educational Building, a wing that had been built in 1956. The fire was con-tained, the church and educational building were saved, and the community, representing many faiths and all walks of life, stepped forward to embrace and support the Methodist congregation and immediately provided space for services on Christmas day.

Churches were the places where people came togeth-er for fellowship and communion with their neighbors. Charles Cooley, a member of Grace Memorial Episco-pal Church said, "*You had to go to church on Sunday ... I served on the altar as an acolyte from the time I was nine 'til sixteen, seventeen. In the summertime, we had what you call camp meetings where they had pavilions. Every-body sang together.*"[220]

To Laura Bradford, a Methodist, the church was a uniting force, "*I think people were connected more through church activities. We would have groups from church that would meet at different places ... we would have picnics, take walks ... kids from the Methodist Youth Group would play.*"[221]

The Hosanna Church continues to raise money through its superb chicken dinners. In the early twen-tieth century, the church also staged another benefit, an annual Tom Thumb wedding, where people would pay to see children, dressed up as a wedding party, perform the wedding rituals. Genevieve Jones remembered it clearly because one year she was the reluctant bride, "*They had a Tom Thumb wedding and I had to be the bride. I don't know why they put me up to such a thing. I have always been awful shy, always ... and, oh, my goodness, the floor wouldn't open for me to fall through or nothing ... they just got two poor children and one of them made the bride—the bride and the groom and they had to go through the ceremonies like they was having a real wedding. I did not appreciate it,*" she laughed, "*Oh dear, I did not appreciate it.*"[222]

All of the churches that have served the current and former residents of Berkley are at least 150 years old; some of them are over 250 years old. And, equally as important, some of today's parishioners can trace their lineages back to those early beginnings.

Monuments to the Departed

There are several cemeteries in the area. The oldest markers may be found in the Quaker cemetery adjacent to the Meeting House, the Presbyterian Cemetery behind the Presbyterian Church, and the Berkley and Hosanna Cemeteries located on two sides of the Hosanna Church. In 1881, the Darlington Cemetery Company was formed. It purchased three acres, and "turned that site into a veritable picturesque park, complete with winding, oyster-shell paths, informally clumped trees and shrubs and …" with the leadership of D. C. W. Smith, "made certain that from the beginning the cemetery was open to all regardless of race, creed, or color."[223] The cemetery's focal point, its sanctuary, is visible across the hills and valleys of the surrounding community. Christopher Weeks described this white building with green trim as "octagonal in shape, crowned by a steep conical roof topped by a terracotta chimney pot."[224]

There are also private cemeteries and cemetery remnants extant in the communities. Each provides a wealth of information about the people who lived here over the past centuries.[225] There are two stories, however, that belong directly to Berkley— the evolution of today's Berkley Cemetery and the story of the watering trough.

The Berkley Cemetery

In the 1800s, blacks owned a significant amount of Berkley acreage. It is remarkable that these people who had little access to education, political power, legal expertise, or professional occupations were able to have the foresight to take steps to acquire land and hold on to it legally. Older black residents tell story after story of how acres of land belonged to their grandparents, great-grandparents, or great uncles. Often, when the relative died, however, the land slipped away from black ownership. The older relatives talked about "buying" land, but in many cases there was no written documentation available to establish claim to the property even though it had been in the family for many years and had been subdivided for the next generations. In other cases where there was documentation, the black landowner did not wish to be confrontational about property lines and would decide to just "leave well enough alone."

Genevieve Webster Presberry Jones' story is a case in point. Her mother, Annie Webster, was approached by Mervin Pomraning when he purchased the land next door to their property. Pomraning told Annie Webster that when he had his land surveyed he discovered that the Webster property line went right through his front door. He asked what she wanted to do about it. She told him she would do nothing about it, but she could not say what her children would do after she died. No action was ever taken, and could not be after a period of time because of the law of adverse possession. As a result, she and her family "lost" part of their property.

This tale has a bearing on the story of the Berkley Cemetery—involving over 175 years of history and land ownership. Berkley's first cemetery dates back to the Rigbie family. This cemetery was located next to the first black church in Berkley. It occupied the knoll behind what is now the Hosanna School Museum and is believed to have been a cemetery for both blacks and whites connected with the Rigbie family. Later, it was used exclusively for Berkley's black residents. That assumption is based upon the tombstones that have been moved from the site and placed against the foundation of the Hosanna School Museum. John Clark, the owner of Rigbie House, explained how this came about, *"And I remember one Sunday I was just driving out there in my car and they* [church members] *were standing right there looking out right over this old cemetery, all grown up, see. And the only evidence of any markers or anything were stones that looked like they'd been specially, you, know, placed. But anyway, I took each and every one of those stones that I found, and down there* [Hosanna School] *right now in a pile in back of the church, and, I cleared that all off. Matter of fact, I'm a little ahead of the story. These two or three members of the church* [Hosanna A.M.E. Church] *said to me, 'Mr. Clark, this old cemetery here, why don't you clean that up and use that for your farm?' They said, 'We can't use it anymore, it's just an eyesore.' And I said, 'Well, I'll tell you, you can't, but I can, I can clean that off, and I can hold title to it, or I can occupy it for twenty years, and then I'll have title, and I can convey to you, that's what I want to do.' And I'm having a bit of trouble getting it done right now, but I'm going to do it before I die, I hope. Just to give that, convey that either to the cemetery company, probably, to take care of, see? But, that's the first cemetery, right there."*[226]

Christine Tolbert, who traces her family back to 1793 in Berkley, said, *"Well, I remember that there was a cemetery, because we were always warned not to go in those woods and play because there were sunken graves, and I remember seeing them—that there were graves back there where John Clark's horses are now ... I have no evidence of any of my relatives being buried there ... there were a lot of stones there but most of them were not inscribed. And in the old days what they would say was, 'Aunt Sadie's over here by the such and such tree,' and 'there's a such and such bush here,' or 'It's five or six rocks from so and so.' And that's how they determined where people were buried."*[227] And David Gordon added, *"But the stones are laid up behind there somewhere in this pile. They never did remove bodies from under ground; they just removed their tombstones."*[228]

This old cemetery was probably used until shortly after the construction of the current Hosanna A.M.E. Church in 1880. Then, the congregation began to establish a new cemetery behind the new church. On July 16, 1887, William B. Wilson, James Tucker, Horace Prigg, and Hampton Washington formed the Hosanna Cemetery Company and incorporated it under the laws of the State of Maryland. Incorporation was meant to assure the perpetual maintenance of the cemetery, but "in perpetuity" was fleeting at best.

During that same year the Hosanna Cemetery Company prepared to purchase land adjacent to the church fronting on Castleton Road. The parcel had belonged to

DAVID GILPHIN GORDON
was born into a family of many genera-
tions in Harford County. He attended
Hosanna School and in his younger years
worked at the Berkley cannery. Like many
people in area, he began to work for
the Pennsylvania Railroad and, later,
with the build up for World War II, he
worked at Aberdeen Proving Ground
and Edgewood Arsenal. He was a con-
struction worker for most of his work-
ing life and his last job was with the
Wickersham Construction Company,
the firm that built the new Darlington
Volunteer Fire Department building.
David has always been a vital par-
ticipant and respected leader in the
Darlington and Berkley communities.
A political activist, he has campaigned
for and offered political advice to can-
didates to make certain that black voices
and concerns were heard in the demo-
cratic process. A World War II veteran,
he used his construction skills to provide
a comfortable home for his family and
college educations for his children. His
interview captures his love of his school
years being taught by Kenton Presberry
and his love of learning. David Gordon
died on March 15, 2003.

Interviewed 27 February 2000

Rosa Peco (Paca), the widow of Robert Peco, and one of their daughters, Minty Margaret Norton. The other daughter, Mary H. Peco was never part of the negotiations with the Cemetery committee and, as fate would have it, all members of the family died except Mary who inherited all of her father's lands. Mary never conveyed any parts of these lands during her lifetime so the land title was still vested in her at the time of her death. She did not leave a will and the title to these lands became vested in her many heirs of which there were more than seventy-five in 1917. Meanwhile, the cemetery corporation, chartered for only forty years from the date of its formation, had actually ceased to function before that time. The cemetery was neglected and management of the finances, records of lot sales, supervision of burials, and maintenance of the cemetery declined and, finally ceased entirely.

In 1949, confronted with this abysmal situation, a group interested in the Hosanna Cemetery joined together to clean up the grounds and place markers to guide in the identification of lots—but there was still the unsettled ownership.

Faced with the problem of obtaining clear title to the property, the Hosanna Cemetery Committee obtained legal counsel in 1951. Interestingly the counsel they chose was John Clark who was to purchase the Rigbie farm nine years later. A new corporation was formed to succeed the defunct Hosanna Cemetery Company, Inc. As counsel, Clark advised the new company, Berkley Cemetery Company, Inc. to get a clear title through a tax sale. At a tax sale in December 1952, the newly formed company purchased the part of Mary H. Peco's land that was the cemetery site, plus approximately four acres of woodland that adjoined it. A little more than a year later a clear title was issued and the property was deeded to the Berkley Cemetery Company, Inc.

John Clark remembered his efforts on behalf of the cemetery committee, *"But, anyway, I got into it and, without going into the details of how we worked it out, I did work it out ... I had handled the tax sales here in the county for many years, and I knew that you could use the tax sale to, if nobody paid the taxes on it, put it up and sell it, and then I could have them buy it again, you see. So that's the proce-dure we used, and so they bought it and I worked, did all the legal work for them, and*

Early 1970s Members of the Berkley Cemetery Committee
Officers: President, Irvin Smith; Vice President, Thomas Presberry; Recording Secretary, Esther Fennel; Financial Secretary, Evangeline Ford; Treasurer, Edward Presberry. Members: Judge John Clark, Nicolas Smith, Genevieve Jones, Pauline Bond, Mabel Smith, Milton Smith, Howard Presberry, John Webster, Louisa Presberry, Leo Webster and Jean Shannan.
100th Anniversary Booklet—Hosanna A.M.E. Church

helped them with the cemetery. And the corporation, and so forth, and they got a real nice growing operation."[229]

The Company and friends continued to clean up the cemetery behind the Hosanna Church and clear the new land. Eventually, the land was surveyed, lots marked out, and an access road was built. The Berkley Cemetery Company is still managed by a volunteer board of directors and remains a source of pride in Berkley as the board members work to maintain a well-kept resting place for loved ones.

The Watering Trough

The general humility of the Quaker faith is reflected in the modest grave markers one finds in a Quaker cemetery. Joshua Cowgill Smith died in 1911. His widow, Edith Smith, abiding by the principles of her faith, placed a modest marker on her husband's grave. She did, however, wish to honor his life through something permanent, and, one can assume, functional. To that end, after some time had passed, she commissioned a watering trough to be carved from a solid block of granite. She had it placed between the Towpath Tea House and the entrance to the Conowingo Bridge for the refreshment of the many horses traveling the route. Chiseled into the granite was:

Joshua Cowgill Smith 1857–1911. John Cooley recalled, *"... there was a water trough there where you could stop and water the horses before you went over the bridge."*[230]

The trough remained in use at this spot until the bridge was destroyed and the road over the Susquehanna Dam was completed in 1927. Yet it continued to serve. It was dragged half way up the road to Berkley, placed at the side of the road, and re-invigorated many a thirsty horse until that mode of travel faded from the landscape.

Many years later, Joshua's daughter brought it to Swallowfield where it remained until it was donated to the Susquehanna State Park at the Rock Run Mill. Moving it to a new location was a monumental endeavor. Spurgeon Lentz had heard that the first attempt to relocate the heavy water trough had ended in failure "when the truck's front wheels raised up in the air."[231] He volunteered his tow truck and successfully hauled it to its present resting place at the Mill. It sits beside the dirt road just south of the Rock Run Mill on the opposite side of the road.

Edith Smith's desire for a permanent memorial to her husband is still being fulfilled. The trough continues to refresh the horses as they travel the bridle trails throughout the Susquehanna State Park.

Joshua Smith Memorial Watering Trough at Susquehanna State Park

PART IV

The Open Road Beckons

"The biggest dam anyone had ever seen"

The Conowingo Dam Changed Berkley
Stone-Webster, Conowingo, 1928

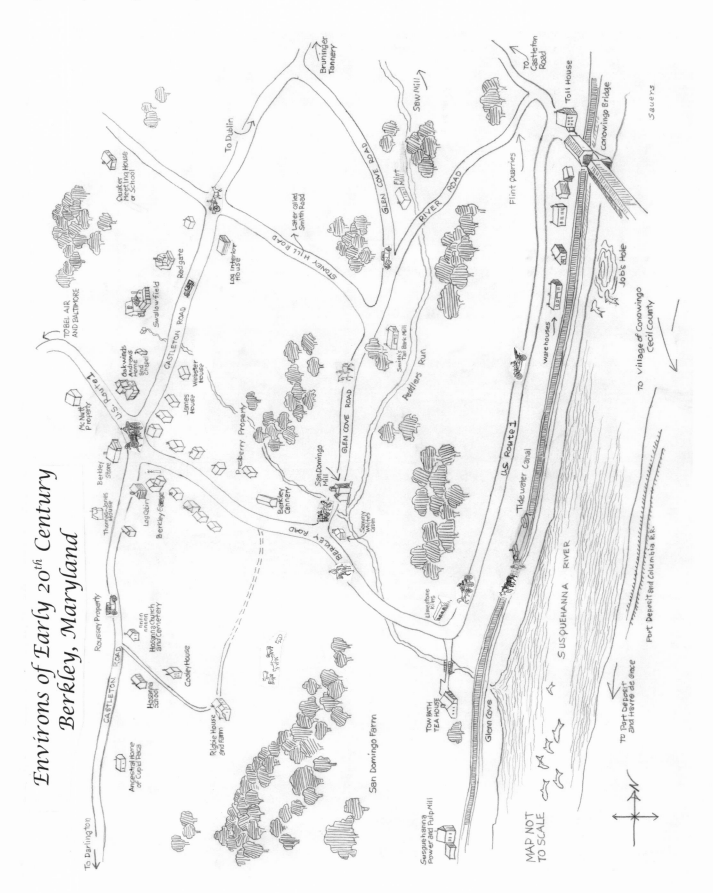

Environs of Early 20th Century Berkley, Maryland

The Open Road Beckons

With the demise of the Tidewater Canal, the major industries along the river began to decline. Just after the turn of the century, Berkley's focus was shifting from manufacturing, milling, and mining back to its agricultural roots and its service to the travelers, both commercial and private, who would pass through Berkley on the Monumental Trail.

While the Berkley journey thus far relied heavily on texts, maps, land records, journals, diaries, letters, and some voices, the last part of the journey, through the twentieth century, will be the voices of the travelers, in their own words and stories. It is a voyage of great change—of a dam being built, of the country at war, of "separate but equal" no longer the law of the land, of technological marvels and woes, of strong urbanization and disappearing farmland, and of life in a small hamlet.

Today, the intersecting roads in Berkley are referred to as the "crossroads" but the intersection was actually a three-corner road until late in the nineteenth century. The 1878 Martinet map shows a three-cornered road with travelers and commodities coming south toward Berkley from Castleton or west from Bel Air to make a left on the Berkley Road leading to the Conowingo Bridge. The road coming from Darlington was called Berkley Road and upon coming to the Berkley intersection one would make a right, continuing on Berkley road to the bridge. By 1902, according to the U.S. Geological Survey Map, the configuration had changed and the intersection and roads leading to it appear as they are today—a true crossroads—with Berkley Road coming up from the Susquehanna River and crossing the Castleton Road intersection and continuing to today's U.S. Route 1. This newly configured road became a major corridor for interstate travel throughout the first part of the twentieth century.

And a new and exciting phenomenon was occurring—motoring and touring. Most of the nineteenth century population traveled no more than twenty miles from their homes and business in their lifetimes. But here came the horseless carriage, the "Tin Lizzy," the flivver, the automobile! Joshua Smith owned one of the first cars to venture through Berkley—a Stanley Steamer. As Fred C. Jones described it:

> It was a good machine but it required a lot of water so that the steam could be made and give it the power on steep hills. It was not unusual for the passengers to walk up the hill because the power was not sufficient to pull the machine with its load up the hill. Mr. Smith was a very ardent coon-hunter ... on one of our coon hunts we visited a branch on Green Coat Hill and let down the hose between the planks on a bridge over the branch. We pumped up a good lot of water to make steam so to give the automobile more power.[232]

By 1913, Berkley had caravans of cars and trucks traversing the landscape, mainly on dirt or gravel roads, many reinforced with timbers and, in Berkley's case, one macadam road—the Monumental Trail, also known in Maryland as State Route 275 and in Pennsylvania as State Route 647.

These route numbers continued until the Berkley Road was designated as U.S. Route 1 in 1926. According to the Maryland Roads Committee, "It should be noted that that U.S. Route 1 was not the first road to be designated as a U.S. highway, as the whole system came into being at the same time. Per the numbering system, the '1' designation only indicates that it is the easternmost main north-south route ... Before the advent of numbered U.S. highways these were the marked auto trails and each of these roads was marked with a distinctive colored sign."[233] The American Association of State Highway Officials (AASHO) "laid out the U.S. highway system along primary intercity roads of the day. The final list of U.S. highways was agreed upon on November 11, 1926."[234]

The sign color for the Monumental Trail has not been rediscovered but the American Automobile Association (AAA) Blue Book of 1913 gave such explicit and detailed definitions and directions along this "Trail" that very likely the driver required a navigator and a backseat driver as well.

The book's explanation of terms probably made it possible for the traveler to rumble and bump successfully to the desired destination:

Explanation of Terms Used in Text of Routes

A fork—where two roads diverge at less that a right angle
Cross-roads—where two roads cross. **3-corners**—where three roads join at
   about equal angles.
A right- or left-hand road—meets but does not cross the straight road
Keep right—avoid fork or branch road to left.
Bear Right—turn slightly to right, as at a fork.
Turn square right—to turn, a right angle (90 degrees) to right.
Turn sharp right—to turn more than a right angle to right.
Jog right and left—turn to right and an immediate turn to left.
Cross RR.—cross tracks at same level with road.
Over RR. Bridge—above tracks on bridge, sometimes called "overhead
   crossing."
Under RR.—railroad is above highway on bridge. Sometimes called "RR.
   Underpass."[235]

The AAA directions from Bel Air to Coatesville, Pennsylvania, and beyond took the tourists and travelers along an old winding, narrow, and wonderfully scenic route, part of which remains today as Forge Hill Road, continuing through Berkley, over the Conowingo Bridge and to points beyond:

Route 647—BelAir, Md. To Coatesville, Pa.—54.3 m.

A connecting link for motorists going north and east wishing to avoid Philadelphia.
Fair-to-good dirt; some macadam.

Mileages

Total	Intermediate	
0.0	0.0	**Bel Air,** 3-corners at stone church. Start northeast in front of church on macadam. (A left turn, coming from Baltimore.) Thru cross-roads and across iron bridge 0.8, thru small hamlet 3.2 Avoid left fork 4.7, down easy grade on winding macadam across cement bridge 7.5. Caution—avoid right fork just beyond. Ascend easy grade on macadam, curving left to
9-7	9.7	3-corners, turn right with travel through cross-roads ll.1 on macadam to
12.8	3.1	3-corners; turn left thru cross-roads at **Berkeley** (P.O. on left—13.7) downgrade over cement bridge 14.6 and up grade to
15.2	2.5	3-corners; turn square right over long iron bridge (Susquehanna River) and past toll-gate 15.6, crossing RR into
15.9	0.6	**Conowingo,** end of road

Turn left, up steep grade with water-bars, thru cross-roads at **Pilot, Md.** On fair dirt to ... [236]

One page of directions later after making many "square" and "sharp" turns while motoring along over more dirt, gravel, and a few more macadam roads for another 38.4 miles one would arrive at Coatesville with the "Speakman Hotel on the left" and "Straight ahead with trolley is Route 460 to Philadelphia."[237] The return trip iterates the same directions, "on macadam thru Berkeley"[238] and ending in Bel Air at the stone church with "Kenmore Inn, to left" and "Square right is Route 274 to Baltimore."[239] Jean Ewing, who traveled frequently between Philadelphia and Berkley recalled the route well, as she remarked in her interview, *"... the road running east and west from the river inland was paved—was a high crown asphalt road and narrow. It was quite treacherous to drive on and it still is. From Berkley east it is the way it used to be. That was the best road there was between New York and Washington."*[240]

The Speakman Hotel in Coatesville and the Kenmore Inn in Bel Air may have been the premier lodgings of the day but scattered along the route were cabins for

The new motoring public found a welcome respite at the many tourist cabins along U.S. Route 1. Located just south of Berkley, the Glen Echo Store remains but the cabins stand no more.

Historical Society of Harford County
(Photograph ref. 459)

GENTRY PHIPPS

was born in North Carolina in 1908. He moved to the Berkley-Castleton area as a young child and still resides on Glen Cove Road with his sister, Bertha Davis. He attended Franklin Church School in Upper Castleton. As a young teenager, he had already begun to seek employment by working on the dirt, but mostly mud, roads in Castleton and Berkley, hauling boulders and logs to make the roads passable for the new horseless carriages. Gentry also, during this same period, worked as the chicken plucker at the Towpath Tea House where he was befriended by the cook, Dinah Washington. Still in his youth he got a job at the Conowingo Dam during its early construction. He started by hauling coal to the steam shovels and learned to fire the boilers. He then became a boiler fireman on the dam—a job that led to a career with the Federal Government at Edgewood Arsenal where he was given a meritorious award for his valor during a phosphorous explosion in a bomb factory during World War II. His living room walls are filled with pictures of his six children, 22 grandchildren and seven great-grandchildren.

Interviewed 26 February 2002

overnight respite. It is not documented that there were tourist homes in Berkley but along Conowingo Road (U.S. Route #1) just outside of Berkley were several early "motels" for the weary travelers. These overnight stops were inns, ordinaries, tourist homes and, later, individual small cabins. Remnants of the Iris Cabins enterprise still stand today, located at the corner of Smith Road and Conowingo Road just outside of Berkley. Remains of another cluster of cabins are on the left just south of the Smith and Conowingo Road intersection and a short distance beyond were the Glen Echo Cabins.

When Gentry Phipps was 14 years old, he was hired to help make Castleton and Glen Cove Roads passable. These dirt, and many times muddy, roads required regular upkeep involving rather intensive manual labor. He recalled, *"… we got the stones out of the fields. It's on this road from here toward Dublin, Glen Cove … It was a dirt road. We put stone in—a whole layer of stone. Martin Smith got the money from the county, and I was asking him for a job and he give me a job too, but I just got half pay. But I picked up as many rocks as them 'cause I was wantin' a job, you know … it was raining and muddy, the ruts was so deep your wheel'd get in and you couldn't hardly get out of that rut. You just had to run in the ruts."*[241] According to John Lamb, this old route was still in use during the Ford Model-T era and *"the mud was so bad in the spring that the Model Ts had to back up the hills due to the lack of power in the forward gears."*[242]

After Gentry Phipps got his first car, a Model T Ford, he traveled these roads and recalled the "breakers," *"Breakers, you know, they had 'em placed and routed out so often down the hill, so the water'd run across and not cut the road off, see? They put breakers and bulges in it. They [the water] would run off, over to the ditch all the time. They got a ditch on each side, but the breaker would keep it from going down the middle. See, there wasn't no crown in a dirt road, and then when they blacktopped it, they just blacktopped it with the bumps in it."*[243]

Berkley and Castleton Roads today still contain the blacktopped breakers and bulges. Phipps also remembered traveling on U.S. Route 1 through Berkley, *"You got on Route One at Berkley from here … through Berkley, out to where it goes to hit*

Route 1 now. And it used to be real crooked out there in Rabbit Valley, a lot of wrecks."
Rabbit Valley is located at the intersection of today's U.S. Route 1 and Maryland
Route 440.

What and Who Were Where

Charles Cooley's eyes and memory capture the look, feel, and flavor of Berkley
during the early part of the twentieth century, *"I was approximately two years old, my
first recollection of Berkley Intersection. My father used to let me ride the wagon when
he took milk to the milk-stand behind McNutt's store. The milk-stand faced Wilton Mc-
Nutt's house, which the Howards live in now. There was a blacksmith shop on the right
going from McNutt's toward the river, which Mr. Oliver owned and ran the blacksmith
shop and a buggy shop. They built buggies, which later became a Ford dealership when the
buggy trade went down. But, my trips up there was normally early in the morning, when
my father took his six or eight cans of milk up to the milk-stand in a little yellow wagon.
I came out our lane to hit the Massey Lane in which a Sarah and Charlie Webster, a
colored family, lived there which I later on called them Aunt Sarah and Uncle Charlie.
In fact, my mother and father and I and sister went to their funerals at Hosanna in later
years. At the end of the lane was a pavilion that belonged to the colored people, where they
had cookouts and dances—beef cookouts and pork.*

*"And if you turn left going up Berkley Road, which
is now Castleton ... you went up past the principal of
Hosanna School, which was Kenton Presberry, and he
lived in the little gray house that sits over the bank that
John Clark owns now, with a spring below it. Then you
had, on the left, was a people by the name of Roussey,
Grafton and Mary Roussey. Grafton had a cider mill
that he made and sold to all the local people. Then you
had the schoolhouse, the lane that went in to where I live
now. And the Jones farm [Rigbie] was next. Further
back was a farm that belonged to a Davis which disappeared when they bought the land up for Conowingo
Dam in the late twenties. As you proceed up the road,
the first place on the left belonged to Oliver and Carrie
Thomas, which they had three children—two boys and
a girl. And he was the one that had the blacksmith shop
and the buggy shop in Berkley.*

*The Roussey House, later owned by the
Thomas-Jones family, the McNutt Family,
and currently owned by Warren and
Barbara Baity, whose families have a long
history in northern Harford County.*

Photograph by Scott Prettyman

*"Across the street was a house that I don't remember the name of the people that lived
there in those early days. But, later on, a people by the name of Sid Dow and family moved
in there. Also on the same side were ... a barn and a gate that belonged to a Wilton Mc-
Nutt that lived right on the corner where the Howards live now. The store belonged to a
McNutt and they in turn live where Chance lives now—his name was Nelson McNutt.
My grandfather worked for them once in a while, when he was out of a job wallpapering*

or painting … The blacksmith shop was visited by my father, because they had a horse that needed shoes reset every six to eight weeks.

This 1950s photograph of a house at the crossroads has a preserved log cabin in its interior. The African-American James family owned this house until the late 1800s. Later owned by the McNutt family, it is currently under the stewardship of Stephen and Gwyneth Howard.

Private collection of Lois Steele Jones

Originally the McNutt house, it was owned in early to mid-1900s by Clifford and Marian Trott and owned now by Robert and Mary Chance.

"But going towards the river from Berkley, when it was Route 1, the first house on the left at the intersection, the opposite corner of the store, was a lady by the name of Annie Stewart. She was a seamstress. Everybody went there to get their clothes sewed. The next house, in later years was a Burkentine, and he came in there during the construction of the Conowingo Dam, moved in that house. He had two boys. The next place was a Norman Gorrell … he was a painter and paperhanger, and his sister married Cliff Trott, Marian. But on the other side, below the garage was Robert Oliver Thomas' house, and he was married to Lucy Jones, which was my grandmother's niece from up at the farm behind me [Rigbie Farm] and they had two boys and a girl—Robert Oliver, Dorothy and Harold T. … The four houses in a row below Berkley Store were owned by Oliver Thomas. He either rented them out or let the son have one … but the colored people had a parsonage in one of the houses at the time. But after you passed Norman Gorrell house, there was another colored family. He was a single man, lived in a little house that was set back, but very narrow … then the people by the name of Taylor lived there, and she ran a beauty shop in later years, a colored beauty shop. The lane went into the Berkley farm, which Charlie Andrew owned, which was sold in the thirties to a southern family by the name of Dwight Henderson.*

"But going down the [Berkley] road, you had the opposite side, was a Weaver, Oscar Weaver, he was a stone mason. The next one was a Tom Presberry, which I know as Bunny Presberry, also, a Pete Cain, and I used to visit them when they were digging graves as kids. The next place was another Presberry … and then people by the name of Bailey come down from up around Highland and bought a place there right behind the old canning house. … Along the road was the foundation and the canning house still existed up into the thirties. That Charlie Andrew run the canning house, and people come in, migrant* *workers come and canned tomatoes in the canning house. If you go down the road on the curve another colored family lived there by the name of Presberry, but everybody called*

The Robert Oliver Thomas House located just east of the crossroads was home to the owners of the Berkley Garage and the new Berkley Store.
Photograph by Scott Prettyman

The James property since early 1800s. Now owned by descendant, Genevieve Jones.
Photograph by Scott Prettyman

him 'Whiskey Bill,' I guess that's because he drank. The next place down on the corner, was Berdell Presberry's house on the left ...

"... if you come back up to Berkley and go straight through, going north toward Castleton, you have Charlie Andrew's house on the left, Stewarts' on the right, then Pomraning on your right, then another house that I don't know who lived in it, or don't remember [Ancestral home of Genevieve Jones]. Across the street [Castleton Road] was the chapel, I think a Green lives there now, but it was Charlie Andrew's chapel for his own family's religious purposes. Across the street was Bud Webster. Beyond that was, where the Johnson's live now a Maurice Dorsey, who worked as caretaker for Stokes mill down on Deer Creek. That was the only house from there to the intersection of Stoneyhill, the road that goes back down to the river. It was called Stoneyhill in my day. It's called Smith Road now. After you left Charlie Andrew's chapel, the next place was called Swallow-field. It was a very refined place, somebody there during the summer months and the names Ewing and Waring ring a bell as who were there. The next place Red Gate Turkey Farm which was a Mason girl that ran the Tea House down Old Conowingo, according to my parents and my grandparents. But when they flooded that [the Conowingo Lake] that put her out of business. She in turn went with her family to Jamaica, and it was the talk of the town when she came back, she was married to this Englishman in Jamaica. They bought Red Gate Turkey Farm, and they raised turkeys and he was pretty handy with the wood work and as a kid, Bill Bostic and I would go over there and watch him make pipes, smoking pipes on the lathe out of cherry root and walnut root."[244]

Cooley's recollections provide a foundation for exploring other memories, events, and daily life in the first half of the 20th century.

You Can Get It at the Country Store

C. Milton Wright memorialized the country store when he wrote, "At almost every crossroads in 1850 there was a center of barter and exchange which revolutionized the lives of a people who had thus far relied almost entirely upon their own ability and re-sourcefulness. The country store was a unique institution in those early days."[245]

Senator Charles Andrew in front of his general store and post office in Berkley, located at the crossroads.

Harford County Historical Society (ref. 895-4)

The Berkley general store, built by Charles Andrew in the 1890s, was located on Andrew's property at the corner of Berkley and Castleton Roads and also served as the Berkley Post Office. This store, like other country stores in rural America, was the place everyone in the community came to get everything—at least almost everything. Country folk looked to the store to stock everything they could not grow or build or make on their own. This variety store provided everything from work clothes and light farm equipment, to food staples and the occasional treat.

If a family owned enough land they were almost self-sufficient. Christine Tolbert's maternal grandparents, Carroll and Annie Webster were a good example. They raised their own meats, vegetables, apples, pears, grapes, and berries along with milk, eggs, and butter. Her grandmother made soap from lye and lard, quite harsh and not very fragrant. Store-bought soap was a luxury as was store-bought milk and bread. Homemade root beer took the place of sodas and was made only on special feast days like Christmas. Supplies they could not produce were bought from the store, such as lye for the soap, washing powder, confections, sugar, patent medicines, sewing supplies, and farm tools. Kerosene was available at the store for oil-burning lamps. Prior to the automobile's arrival, the country store provided supplies for buggies and harnesses and other supplies for the horses.

Jean Ewing spoke about her familiarity with the store, *"... It was a funny, musty old place with a great high porch and a high floor and it had all kinds of dried foods in it. And a great big bin full of all kinds of soda in it. I remember I used to get a different one everyday, chocolate, lime, and coffee soda, and ginger ale and root beer and all. But that was a great attraction. Then Charlie Andrew got tired of having the store on his place and he built a store across the road. And that was someplace I wasn't allowed to go, couldn't cross U.S. Route 1."[246]*

The store remained on Andrew's property at the corner until about 1918 when he lost interest in running it. A new store was built and located on the other side of the Monumental Trail. Owned by Nelson McNutt[247] it continued to provide similar goods and wares for the crossroads community and gave brief respite for the travelers passing through the crossroads. McNutt also acquired the right to maintain the Berkley Post Office in the new store. He sold picture postcards featuring the Berkley

The New Berkley Store opened in the early 1900s after Charles Andrew closed his store across the road. This store stayed in operation as a general store until the early 1960s although postal service was not available after 1928.

Private collection of Lois Steele Jones

Crossroads and other local points of interest for travelers to mail back home to those envious stay-at-homes with a postmark of Berkley, Maryland. The Berkley Post Office continued to operate in the store until 1928 when Rural Free Delivery (RFD) began. Until that time, the Berkley Post Office provided an important service to the rural community because many were within walking distance of the crossroads for, as Laura Bradford said, *"we all traveled by shank's mare,"*[248] or as others said, "hoofing it."

McNutt continued serving the local residents and travelers until at least 1926. Marvin Cooley, Charles Cooley's grandfather, worked briefly for McNutt. Cooley said, *"My grandfather on my father's side was a painter and a wallpaperer. He wasn't doing anything one winter and McNutt needed somebody to help out in the store. So he helped out in the store, in turn he cut his finger on the metal band of the meat barrel. Which he got blood poison and he didn't say anything to my father or his wife for three days. But his hand swelled up and Dad took him down to Johns Hopkins and he died the next day from blood poisoning."*[249]

Isaac Washington, descendant of Isaac and Frances Washington, worked at Swallowfield as did the earlier Isaac. Loved those Koester pies!

Private collection of Doris Toliver Presberry

Sometime after that McNutt sold the store and the adjoining property to Oliver Thomas, who had owned the blacksmith and buggy shop in Berkley. Thomas built a house for his son, Robert, on the adjoining property located on Castleton Road toward Darlington. Robert had married Lucy Jones, who lived at Rigbie farm. Eventually, Robert took over the Berkley Garage from his father and his wife and daughter, Dorothy, ran the store. Thus the Thomases held the two major service centers in Berkley during the 1920s.

People had special memories of the happenings at the store. According to Cooley, Isaac Washington loved Pepsi Cola and French apple pie. Isaac Washington, he said, had a ritual. *"He would come to Berkley Store every noontime and buy a Pepsi Cola and a French apple pie, a Koester French apple pie. [Koester was the primary commercial bakery that delivered at Berkley store in the 1940s.] That was his*

89

lunch. But you could set your clock by him he was there ..."[250] One resident recalls going to the Berkley store in the '30s and '40s and buying orange pineapple ice cream for her mother—for which she had to take her own bowl. This same resident declares Berkley Store had the "absolute best" hot dogs available.

Evangeline Ford recalls the store but also the huckster served the needs of the Berkley families, *"As far as food is concerned, hucksters came around. What we called hucksters. They came around in their wagons, and some of them apparently had some kind of a motor vehicle, like a truck ... The iceman came around in the ice wagon. The ice was gotten from the river and you bought your ice from a man who came along. People would come with meat. I can remember my mother and grandmother loving beef, and she would buy a piece of beef from the huckster. They came around with vegetables and staples. But there was a store at the corner at Berkley, Thomas' Grocery Store ... you walked to get things from there but when the hucksters came, anything special, like fish on Fridays, the fish people would come because they got the fish out of the river."*[251]

Dorothy and Lucy Thomas developed a very personal relationship with their clientele. They knew everyone by name. During those times of segregated facilities people who established a record of paying their store bill on time were permitted to run a tab—black or white.

Richard Presberry, who grew up in the community, told how as children they would go to Berkley Store. When they tried to buy candy or something their parents did not want them to charge, Dorothy and Lucy Thomas would say, "You may not have that. Your parents do not want you to have it." Lois Steele Jones remembered, *"I know that the Thomases kept a little book over there so that people in the community, if they wanted to run an account, they could, and whatever agreement they made with the Thomases, whether they paid weekly or paid monthly ... but I can remember we would get bread or milk or things like that over at the store, and often Dot would write in the book, you know, what we got ... I think sometimes we even had a little book there for a while."*[252]

But Lois' fondest memory is of the gas pumps outside the store, *"Up at the Thomas' store, they had this gas pump that always fascinated, and you had to pump the liquid up into the top of the tank before you could pump it into the car*

EVANGELINE JAMES FORD, born in 1915, can trace her family's roots in Berkley to the early 1800s when her ancestor, Abraham James, owned properties on Castleton and Berkley roads. Her grandparents lived on Castleton Road opposite Hosanna School. As a child she lived with her mother and grandmother, India Anna James, who took in washing for other families in the community, particularly the white residents. Evangeline attended Hosanna School and later attended Downington Industrial and Agricultural School and Hampton Institute. After college she worked as a secretary to a professor at Howard University, then spent the majority of her work life in the employ of the Federal government. Now retired and living in Pennsylvania, she is still connected to Berkley as a long-time member of the Berkley Cemetery Board of Trustees and currently serves as the financial secretary for the Board. Her mother attended Hosanna School and her great-grandmother is buried in the old section of the cemetery behind Hosanna Church. Her mother, Ethel Taylor, had Ethel's Beauty Shop on Berkley Road for many years providing hair care services to the black community in and around Berkley.

Interviewed 6 April 2000

Dot Thomas, owner at of the Berkley Store, ran accounts for her customers but was quick to determine if the children coming to store really did have permission to "charge" candy and sodas.

Private collection of Jeanne Thomas

and, to me, that was fascinating, to a kid. I always watched while they did that."[253]

Richard Presberry also recalled the '50s when he and other black children would be allowed to come into the vestibule of the store and keep warm while waiting for their school bus.

The store belonged to the Thomases until the late 1960s. Lucy Thomas died and Dot went to work at the Bata Shoe Factory shortly after. The store was sold to John Delp and Martin Black. And as Gwyneth Howard related the story: "The store was bought and the owner moved into a silver bullet mobile home with his brother behind the store. The store itself was forever for sale, with no takers. In 1976 it finally re-opened as The Twice Blessed Thrift Shop. Primarily run by Esther Yeager, it was an outreach of the Episcopal Church in Darlington. It was a second hand store and was open three days a week. I was home then, with my daughter, Lucy, a year old, and I worked as a volunteer with Esther—sorting used clothes, tagging items, selling. Inside the store was pretty much as it has been described. There was a long, very solid counter in front of the shelves. There were shelves on the other walls, too, and, in the spaces between racks, room for clothes and a table for the smaller items Esther had managed to rummage together for sale. The place was always dark and always cold."[254]

The thrift shop continued in operation for many years until the early '80s when the store was sold and converted into a private residence. Because people continued to believe there was a store at the location, the new residents named their home "Store No More," and proclaimed it as such by an attractive wooden sign in the yard. Sold again in the '90s, the dwelling remains a private residence now owned by the Waugh family. Berkley and Darlington residents continue to view "Store No More" as a place of warmth and memories, standing as it does at the crossroads—a visible link to Berkley's bustling past.

The Blacksmith, the Carriage Shop, And the Berkley Garage

Oliver Thomas was known throughout the area for his carriage and buggy shop. He also was known for his sleighs. "His buggy was known as a good buggy all around here. When the model T come out he got a Ford dealership."[255] So, the Thomas' Blacksmith and Carriage Shop gave way to Thomas' Berkley Garage providing gas,

The Berkley Garage
Private collection of Jeanne Thomas

oil, and other motoring needs. The senior Sam Sauers who served the community as the village blacksmith handed over the "reins" to his son, Sam, Jr., who then became the mechanic for the garage. The Thomas garage then became the Berkley Ford Garage. The early Fords arrived partially assembled and the mechanics were responsible for completing the assembly before sale. According to Shirley Thompson, *"The Ford Motor Company had like a stopping point there where they built cars and they came down through Philly and on their way to Washington and, on south, they stopped in Berkley to do certain things to them on the shipment before they went to the next shipping station … it was like a processing plant … It wasn't really a plant plant, but they did certain things to the cars before they went any further. I don't know exactly if they put the seats in them or what they did to them … but one of the processing places was right there in Berkley."*[256]

Many people remembered purchasing their first cars in Berkley. Laura Bradford recalled her first car, *"I bought my first car in Berkley. Robert Thomas sold it to me. And he taught me how to drive. It was a Ford Touring Car, and it was half of my year's salary. It was four hundred and fifty dollars. I remember that because I didn't pay it all at once."*[257] She bought that car in 1924. Gentry Phipps also bought his first car there but with a less than happy experience, *"Mom wouldn't sign for it, so he sold it to me and I paid him and he paid the finance company, Robinson Finance Company … he went broke later and they kept trying to collect it off me, years after the car had wore out … But I had paid him and gotten my receipts … I don't know how come Bob Thomas go broke, but he had a thriving business in that garage for a long time."*[258]

John Sauers, the son of the well-respected mechanic at the Berkley Garage and grandson of Sam Sauer, Sr., the village blacksmith, captured a rather regular night-time occurrence at the Berkley Garage in his writings about Berkley:

> In the hour of a clear, cold winter's night the thump-thump from the wooden floor of Conowingo Bridge—sounds of a speeding vehicle roaring down the river road reverberated into the quiet of a Berkley village night. Just minutes later a fast moving long-nosed black sedan blew through the intersection—a night run of bootleg to Baltimore City. During prohibition the quiet of the Berkley nights were often interrupted by such incidents. This imagery was conveyed to my brother, Jimmy, and me by our father, Samuel Souers (Sauers), Jr. many years ago.
>
> As a young man, our father, along with our grandfather Souers worked at Bob Thomas' Garage. In those days (the '20s) the garage remained open at night. Our father attended the gas pumps. On nights when revenuers weren't in pursuit, the bootleggers would stop at the garage for gas and a stretch. My recall is that our father stated that when the bootleggers stopped for gas several men would alight from the late model sedan. He said they did not have much to say but were courteous, well dressed, and wore long coats. The weight of the bootleg made the car low to the ground. The back window curtain was pulled down. If I understood my father correctly he said the "customers" would give him a gratuity. Quickly they would be on their way—another night run from Philadelphia to Baltimore City. These incidents ceased when Route 1 was diverted over the Conowingo Dam in 1927.[259]

Not all of the bootleg just passed through Berkley; sometimes it was brewed and drunk locally, and sometimes the bootlegging started here. As Charles Cooley said, *"Now Darlington's changed a good bit since my day and time. There were three grocery stores ... a movie theater, a post office, a pavilion hall where they held minstrels. But that all changed when the money man in Darlington got killed. He was a bootlegger by the name of Mick ... made bootleg whiskey and peddled, drove it to New York and Philadelphia ... He got caught three times in a row ... local talent in Darlington served the time for him, and this guy Mick paid his wages right on ... Anyway he always give five hundred dollars to this church, a thousand dollars to that church, or a thousand for this. He owned the post office building and the movie hall. He donated the money to the people, so nobody said anything about him bootlegging. But in my time, I can name ten or twelve bootleggers that I knew as a kid growing up living around here and where their stills were. From walking around in these woods, you know them."[260]* Mick was done in by his wife and her Swedish lover who had jumped ship to work on the Conowingo Dam. But according to Cooley, *"She was a good looking woman and she got off with killing him."[261]*

According to Cooley, Austin Roussey who lived across from the Hosanna School made the local hard cider. Having reached the age of seventeen, Cooley made many a purchase from him, and so did most of the locals. People came some distance for the hard cider in Berkley. So not all of the purveyors of hard drink wore long coats and drove black sedans with dark glass in the windows—just passing through!

At some point, the Thomas garage switched loyalty because its later advertisements featured Chevrolets. Oliver Thomas later entrusted the business to his son, Robert, who subsequently lost the car dealership and the service garage closed not long after the completion of the Conowingo Dam.

Winding down toward the river to the bridge's approach, there stood another stop for the traveler, a place that had a reputation as far away as Philadelphia, Baltimore, and Washington, D.C.—the Towpath Tea House.

The Towpath Tea House

The Towpath Tea House nourished and comforted many travelers from 1920 to 1926. Located on the banks of the Susquehanna, it became a cherished traveler's stop and, for many in Philadelphia and Baltimore, it became the destination for a weekend lunch or tea.

Ann Gregory, the daughter-in-law of the owner of the Tea House, interviewed Jean Ewing in 1998 and recorded her memories of the Tea House. She coupled her knowledge of the family with her delightful record of that interview:

> After graduation from Vassar College in 1918, Evelyn Mason moved from Germantown, Pennsylvania, to Harford County. Her parents, Samuel and Katherine Stokes Mason "set her up" at Red Gate Farm in Berkley. At that time there was no place in the area for a traveler on Route l to buy refreshment, so the owners of the Berkley Store placed an ice chest on their porch to hold cold drinks. Perhaps this inspired Evelyn to establish the Towpath Tea House.
>
> She employed several local men to help with the construction of her restaurant but worked along side of them, shingling the roof herself. Will Cleary, "a quaint gentleman who smoked a corncob pipe," was very handy, so she hired him. At one point in his career, he is known to have modestly insisted that he couldn't accept a raise because he "wasn't worth $.75 an hour."
>
> The Towpath Tea House sat near U. S. Route 1 which was a macadam road that crossed the Susquehanna on a long narrow bridge north of Glen Cove. Intriguing little green signs were erected a mile apart to "count down" the distance for the prospective diners traveling toward the Tea House. Other billboards were posted as far north as Media and Kennett Square, Pennsylvania.
>
> The Tea House was open for tea and lunches from May through October. Over 6750 signatures were listed in the guest book between May 18, 1920, and October 26, 1926, when the Tea House was torn down to clear land for the construction of the Conowingo Dam. Visitors from thirty-four states as well as Denmark, London, Paris, Spain, Panama Canal Zone, and Sidney, Australia stopped. On June 4, 1921, President Warren G. Harding and his wife, Florence Kling Harding, and their

entourage had lunch there. Samuel Mason included a brief account of their visit in his book *Historical Sketches of Harford County Maryland*. "Between 1920 and 1927, my sister operated one of the first tea houses in the East. It was called the Towpath Tea House; and was situated on the land side of the canal just below Glen Cove, now under water. Here she and her helpers served many people including President Harding and his staff. Shortly after their arrival, two of his henchmen came to my sister and inquired about liquor, but were told that no liquor was sold on the premises, the only exception being in the case of snakebite. The men crossed to the towpath where they were soon forgotten. Presently back they hurried, went to my sister, and in the most agitated tone said 'Get the liquor quick, we have both been bitten by copperheads.'"[262]

Soon after the closure of the Towpath Tea House, Evelyn Mason accompanied her parents on a trip to Jamaica. There she met Basil Monro Gregory, a banker from Barbados, B.W.I. This was the beginning of a courtship that led to their wedding on March 15, 1929. After their marriage, Basil Gregory moved to Red Gate Farm where they owned and managed a turkey farm until his death in 1938 at the age of 42.[263]

Jean Ewing also remembered Dinah Washington, a member of a well-respected black family in the community, who served as the cook at the Tea House—and judging from the menu, in today's world, she would have been called a master chef.

The Towpath Tea House
Private Collection of Ann Hopkins Gregory

As a youngster, Gentry Phipps worked for Dinah Washington at the Towpath Tea House. He remembered his job as the chicken picker for the Tea House, *"I'd pick them every morning. On Saturdays, three or four 'cause Sunday's coming up, see? She had a pretty good business off of U.S. Route 1 ... I just went there for an hour and picked. The chickens had a little building where I picked them, killed them, and, of course, I didn't get inside. I just took the chickens to the back door and Dinah washed them. If I picked 'em real good I got a big cone of ice cream. And I got three dollar and a half a week."*[264]

Jean Ewing was a frequent diner at the Teahouse and shared these additional memories, *"Evelyn was a very attractive and very efficient innkeeper and the little Towpath Tea House was a thriving business all summer long. And she had wonderful help in preparing a small menu of excellent food and people came up the Susquehanna. It was right along the river, right along the tow-path, right along the canal. And people made a special trip up here and turned around and went back to Baltimore or Washington. Or back to Philadelphia sometimes ... the creamed chicken was the best.*"[265]

In addition to serving a President of the United States, Cooley remembered United States Senator Millard Tydings, a resident of Harford County, was a regular diner at the teahouse.[266] Ann Gregory still has the teahouse guest book listing more than 6000 people from many countries who dined there during its six years of service.

Burkleyville, Berkleyville, Berkeley, Berkley, Santo Domingo?

Early writings about Berkley refer to its name as Berkley, Burkleyville, Berkleyville, or Berkley Village and "It is highly likely that Abingdon, Darlington, Stafford, and Berkeley were named for towns in England."[267] By the late 1800s, the hamlet bore the name it has today—Berkley. But something happened along the way between 1911 and 1920.

In 1910 the Chesapeake and Potomac Telephone Company listed the names and telephone numbers of several individuals placing their residence in Berkley, so it is known that Berkley was still carrying the same name in 1910:

> *Andrew C A—res* . . . . *Berkley, Md.*
> *Andrew C. A. office* . . . . *Berkley, Md.*
> *Brown Chas. res* . . . . *Berkley, Md.*
> *Carr Everett—Roller Mill* . . . . *Berkley, Md.*
> *Carr Everett—res* . . . . *Berkley, Md.*
> *James, Wm.—res* . . . . *Berkley, Md.*
> *Racine S. F—res* . . . . *Berkley, Md.*
> *Schenck Jas C—res* . . . . *Berkley, Md.*
> *Smith N N—res* . . . . *Berkley, Md.*
> *Smith V. Gilpin—res* . . . . *Berkley, Md.*
> *Stabker & Son Geo L—res* . . . . *Berkley, Md.*
> *Thomas Chas Y—res* . . . . *Berkley, Md.*
> *Thomas R. O.—carriage builder* . . . *Berkley, Md.*
> *Tobias J. H.—physician* . . . . *Berkley, Md.*[268]

Around 1920, Jean Ewing remembered, there were heated discussions and concerns within her family that "someone" was changing the name of Berkley. She spoke of the turmoil in the family about this audacious possibility that motivated her mother and her aunts to take action, "*They found that the town was going to be called something else and mother never would tell me what it was going to be called, but she said she and her sisters took four signs and put them at the four roads coming into Berkley to say 'You are entering Berkley.' And it took!"*[269]

There was no other evidence to substantiate the fact that change was in the wind, until, in searching her family's genealogy, Christine Tolbert found an enigma in the 1920 census for Berkley. Interestingly, this puzzle provided corroborating documentation that change was afoot. Whereas the 1910 census tract for Berkley and the 1930 census show no changes in the name of Berkley, the 1920 census lists Berkley residents as residing in the "Village of Santo Domingo."[270]

DEPARTMENT OF COMMERCE—BUREAU OF THE CENSUS

FOURTEENTH CENSUS OF THE UNITED STATES: 1920—POPULATION

U.S. Census 1920

Further evidence appeared when a photograph labeled "flour mill—San Domingo Mill" was found.[271] It was one of four pictures of Berkley owned by Mr. and Mrs. Edwin Kirkwood. All four photographs were thought to be pictures of Berkley, but no one had any memories of the mill. Thanks to a land records search, John Lamb discovered a reference to a San Domingo farm located near the river on the east side of Berkley Road. The earliest reference to this farm is in 1853 when Caleb Cope and wife purchased 181 acres from Charity Silver and others. The property at that time was referred to as the "St. Domingo" farm.[272]

The farm was located at the intersection of Berkley and Glen Cove roads along Peddlers Run. Today, on that site, are the remains of the foundation of a large structure and upstream are the remnants of a weir dam at the right angle and length for a flume. Fred Graybeal of Smith Road, a lifetime resident of Berkley, remembered a large round wooden enclosure that carried the water to the wheel. He recalled not only his visits to the mill to purchase flour for his mother, but also the fire that destroyed it. The size and dimensions of the foundation remains correspond to the base of the mill in the photograph. Therefore, without certainty, but with great probability, the site of the San Domingo Mill may have been found.

San Domingo Flour Mill. Located at Berkley and Glen Cove Roads, the mill ground wheat for flour that was sold locally and regionally.

Private Collection of Edwin and Emalyn Kirkwood

Why this name in a community settled by English, Welsh, Scots, African-Americans, Germans,

97

French, and others? There was another snippet of the past that drew interest. On July 10, 1793, "the citizens of Baltimore were surprised to learn that during the afternoon and night of the previous day a fleet of twenty-two vessels from St. Domingo had cast anchor off Fells point. More than five hundred whites and Negroes lay aboard the ships."[273] Plantations in St. Domingo had been taken over by slaves and "the surviving whites [Creoles] and those servants who had remained faithful to them had been forced into the harbor and had thrown themselves on the mercy of ships' captains and sailors. At midnight of June 23, 1793, a flotilla of one hundred and thirty merchantmen crowded with five thousand refugees had put to sea, its path lighted by the glow from the burning city."[274]

Baltimore welcomed these refugees and organized efforts to support and aid them by providing housing and clothing, and called for help across the state and country to assist this monumental undertaking either financially or to help in their relocation. Early contributions came from Philadelphia. "Some benevolent inhabitants of Philadelphia … had opened already a correspondence with the Baltimore committee and had intimated that they would be large contributors."[275] Knowing of the strong linkage between Berkley and Philadelphia, particularly with the Cope family, was it possible that the St. Domingo connection came through this or other Philadelphia Quakers in Berkley?

The St. Dominican influence did reach as far as Deer Creek. According to Hartridge, "The refugees for St. Domingo greatly strengthened the Catholic Church in Maryland, for there were clerics and hundreds of zealous laymen in the emigration. Several Creole priests were assigned to country parishes … Marcel-Guillaume Pasquet de Leyde, former almoner of the government and the general hospital of Port-au-Prince was assigned to Deer Creek."[276] Priest Neal's Mass House, as the chapel and house were

Ruins of the San Domingo Mill (pen and ink)

called, still stands on a knoll overlooking Deer Creek along Priestford Road, known more today as State Route 136.

The San Domingo farm and abutting properties were owned later by D. C. Wharton Smith and his wife. They were sold to Charles A. Andrew on January 11, 1906. The land transfer in 1906 contained "one hundred and sixty acres … comprised of part of a tract called 'Phillip's Purchase' … and frequently called 'San Domingo Farm.'"[277] This conglomeration of properties included the lime kilns over which Charles Andrew housed his offices. In other parts of this land record the San Domingo Farm was also referred to as Santa Domingo Farm and in the deed Berkley was called "Berkley Village." By 1907, Charles Andrew owned a significant amount of acreage and improved properties in Berkley—enough, actually, to almost own the village. Considering his influence throughout the state, could he have been the leading proponent of the name change in the 1920 census?

So, for mystery lovers, the 1920 episode remains unsolved. When and where have been answered, who and why remain undiscovered. But Berkley it is now—and Berkley it shall be.

Agriculture and More

According to the 1900 U.S. Census, farmers made up forty-two percent of the population. Most people worked an average of 52 hours per week, but for farmers, the average work week was much longer. Like the rest of rural America, farming was the primary occupation in Berkley. The rich fertile soil of the Piedmont plateau and the rather temperate climate permitted farmers to grow crops for about 170 to 209 days per season. Diverse farming was prevalent in Berkley and included dairy and turkey farms. Its vegetable farms produced particularly large crops of tomatoes and corn to supply the canneries. Field corn was grown to provide food for the horses and pigs that enjoyed their feed right off the cobs. The corn for the cattle was transported to the gristmill to be ground into feed. Wheat, buckwheat, barley, and other grain crops were transported to local mills for grinding thus providing a staple for family meals and for market. Harvested hay had two purposes—it was stored in the barn to be fed to the horses and cows but, once stored, it also became the playground of many farm children. Riding the wagons piled high with freshly harvested hay was a favorite pastime for the children.

Farming was an integral part of the lives of everyone in Berkley. A few planters owned and farmed hundreds of acres of land; many others owned fifty acres or less. The large farms operated like businesses and employed several people. There were workers who plowed the fields, toiled during growing

Presberry Men Gathering Hay
Private collection of Doris Tolliver Presberry

EDWARD JAMES PRESBERRY, was born in Darlington in 1920. He attended Hosanna School and did farm work on many of the farms in Berkley and Darlington and took produce to Baltimore to sell. He is a veteran of World War II and from 1936 to 1980 was an employee of the Pennsylvania Railroad. Mr. Presberry is one of the beloved residents of the Berkley community particularly for his extraordinary efforts to save the Hosanna School by paying the taxes on the property so it could be preserved. He served for many years as the Chairman of the Hosanna Community House Board of Directors. He is active in the Darlington Community Association and received Darlington's "Apple of Our Eye" annual award for his many contributions to the community. Mr. Presberry continues to welcome his children, grandchildren, and great-grandchildren to his Berkley home.

Interviewed 4 March 2000

season, harvested the crops, milked the cows, cared for the farm animals, kept the domestic chores done, and transported goods to market. In the 1930s, there were also the hucksters like Edward Presberry, *"I worked farms some and I worked on a huckster truck … My cousin [Thomas Presberry] had a route so we used to pick up green vegetables and all kinds of fruit and stuff. And you would come along the road and we used to sell, around Bel Air, all through the county."*[278]

More often than not in the early days the horse and wagon or horse and buggy were the main modes of transport over the dirt roads. Jean Ewing had fond memories of a favorite horse, *"There were farms all around us here and we had no car … If we wanted to get any groceries or anything that we couldn't get at the Berkley store we went into Darlington with the spring wagon or carriage. It was pulled by a very nice horse named Missy. And Missy looked like a little Morgan horse, she could do everything. She could jump three feet and she could go under saddle all day long, first under one then the other, then another, of us three children. Or else sometimes Isaac Washington would come in and say, 'Now Mrs. Ewing, the children can't have Missy today, she has to work in the garden.' And Missy was happy as a clam. She adored Isaac Washington. When he showed up with his bridle with blinders on it, she was in seventh heaven because she was going to work for him."*[279] Transporting goods to market was no easy task. Jean vividly described the method of transporting the milk from the Swallowfield dairy farm to market, *"It was a strenuous operation … The mules had to carry the milk down to the river and then transfer it to the Old Pennsylvania Railroad at Conowingo and transfer again in Perryville. I don't know how they managed to make it work at all."*[280]

Before the advent of the threshing machine the crops were cut by men with scythes, then beaten to separate the wheat seed from the straw. Roland Dorsey described the early process of harvesting wheat, *"They used to have old threshers to thresh wheat. It sat still and you had to take a horse or a tractor to blow it in a stack. Then you had a bailer, put it in the bailer part and bail it. The tractor had a pulley on it and you had to get in this pile of straw, dig it out with a pitchfork, throw it in the bailer."* Roland moved his hands around in a circular motion as he made a whirring sound, and continued, *"it drum, drum, drum, and then as the bailer got full, they had wire twine; they'd wire it up. And then they would kick it out and go for another one. It took a man on the stack, a man to put it in the bailer part, and then a man ties it, so that's three men back in those days."*[281]

Then there were the "truck" farmers who, in addition to farming their own small parcels of land, rented additional space to grow crops to sell. The small farmer often used his children, grandchildren and other family members to help on the farm. Genevieve Jones whose father was a truck farmer, said, *"I'd help him [my father] with his farm work … pick tomatoes, bring corn in. Now I could do all right until he went to husk the corn,"* she said squeamishly. *"And started talking about them mice running up your pants' leg." I said, "I've got to leave you now, cause I can't take them mice."*[282]

Taking care of the chickens and other poultry was usually the job of the women and children. They gathered eggs, fed, killed, plucked, cleaned, and cooked the poultry. There was almost always a great variety of poultry. Carroll Webster raised chickens, guineas, ducks, and turkeys primarily for consumption by family and friends. Although some women and girls had the job of milking, most of the time men milked cows twice a day. When they were done, the girls and women separated the cream from the milk, letting it stand in a container, often a crock, until the cream came to the top. Using a spoon, they would carefully skim the cream from the top and would place it into another container. Some farmers had milk separators; the milk was poured into the separator and as the handle was turned rapidly the milk passed through several disks and the milk and cream were separated and emerged through two different spouts. The cream was used for cereal, making ice cream, and making butter. For small amounts of butter, one could simply shake some cream in a jar until it turned to butter. For larger quantities, the cream was placed into a butter churn. It would be divided into one-pound sections, wrapped, and placed in a cool space, most likely the springhouse. It was then ready for home use or sale. The by-product of butter making was a desired drink—buttermilk. Christine Tolbert's grandmother made and sold butter and buttermilk along with other farm products. She recalled that, *"My grandmother raised chickens, ducks, guineas, and turkeys. They [my grandparents] also raised lambs, cows, horses, and pigs. My grandmother's job was to get the chickens from the yard, wring their little necks, ugh! My mother, her sister, and I would help scald, pluck, and clean the chickens. The same process was used in preparing the guineas, ducks, and turkeys. The guineas were the most difficult to pluck, so I often opted out on that job."*[283]

The larger animals were usually saved until butchering time. Butchering day was like a big neighborhood party. All year the farmers fed, nurtured, and groomed their animals preparing them for slaughter. There was great competition among the men trying to see who had the fattest hogs while the women competed to see who could hang the whitest sheets on the clothesline. Women with gray looking sheets on the clothesline and men with skinny hogs at butchering time were fuel for the gossip mill. Charles Cooley remembered the butchering, *"all the farmers got together to kill hogs and grind sausage, make lard. … That was the big thing in the fall of those years. Butchering, turning the sausage grinder, turning the lard press, that was the kid's job. … Like turning the ice cream mixer for making ice cream."*[284]

Evangeline Ford remembers subsistence on the family farm, *"Everybody had chickens and geese and ducks and cows and all things like that, and you lived off of your own produce. They had gardens and they butchered … I can remember people butchering. I always dreaded hearing the poor pigs squealing when they were stuck and drained, and then they would skin them, you know, take the hair and all that. And then the various parts* were cut up. You made sausage and scrapple and liver pudding, which I loved. There's a smokehouse where the hams were smoked and hung … We always had smoked meat that you kept all winter. You know, it was cold in those days and things were preserved so they kept. And for vegetables, you canned and those things were kept on shelves and the root foods were kept in root cellars. Now, we had a spring house where you kept your milk and your butter and your cheese and your cream … so that's what you did."²⁸⁵

Lois Steele Jones described the butchering activities she obviously enjoyed at the James/Webster farm, *"One of the stories that I remember, and it connects a little bit with the black family. When I was a youngster, I remember late November or early December hearing a lot of loud talking and squealing noises going on, and it seemed like it was coming from the direction of the Dorsey home [James/Webster home at that time], and they just lived three houses down from where we lived on the corner. Mother apparently knew what was going on because she told me to stay in my own yard. But with all the yelling and squealing that was going on my curiosity just got the best of me and, of course, I had to see what all the commotion was about. So, I slipped down to the Dorsey home and I stayed there in the field beside their house, and what they were doing, they were setting up getting ready to butcher hogs. They said I could watch, but I had to stay out of the way. And there were people running around after the hogs in the pen, and only later did I realize that they were killing the hogs, and they did that by cutting their throats, and this is what all the squealing, this commotion was about. And they would hang the hogs up by their hind feet on this wooden trestle, and then they also had these barrels of water that they were heating with an outdoor fire and when the water was scalding hot, then they placed the dead hog in the barrels and swished them back and forth a number of times and then they would hang them back on the trestle and then they would scrape the hair off the pigs or hogs. It sort of left me speechless."²⁸⁶*

Many women, especially black women, worked as domestics for families, cooking, cleaning, and taking care of children. Some women worked for several families each week; these employees performed what was known as "days work." Other women laundered for customers in their own homes. Customers would take their laundry to the home of the laundress usually weekly, and come back in a couple of days and pick it up. At some houses, domestic training helped black women acquire good paying jobs outside of the community. According to Jean Ewing, *"Swallowfield employed as many Negroes as they could. I remember Aunt Becky [Gould] was the last of my grandfather's family to live here. She used to train the young girls to be housekeepers and then she'd find them a job in Philadelphia among her friends. And a good many of them went through to Philadelphia to work that way … just teaching them to cook and wait on tables and clean."²⁸⁷*

Letter of recommendation for Ethel James by Rebecca Gould, owner of Swallowfield.

Private collection of Evangeline James Ford

Many times, interestingly, jobs were not gender specific. Women might work as chauffeurs as Genevieve Jones and Alverta Presberry did; some men were domestic workers like William Presberry, Sr. Speaking about the late 1930s William Presberry, Jr. recalled, *"Back then the only place you could get work was house work, cleaning people's homes. I remember back in 1938 she [my mother] worked for a family that had a horse farm in Darlington and she was a chauffeur. Well, my father did the same thing. He did 'days work' … He was like a chauffeur plus doing housework too in the late 1930s and early 1940s. He worked for a family up here at Deer Creek. In the summertime they moved to Rhode Island for a summer home, he would go up there and stay all summer."*[288]

Going away from Berkley to work was not unusual. Genevieve Jones, who worked for the Waring family, recalled, *"I went to Philadelphia to work in the early fifties … I would come home every weekend. The most I did was cook and chauffeur them around … I worked for them for thirty-seven years … Before Philadelphia I worked for them down here [Swallowfield] for fifteen years and was up there for twenty-two years. I lived with them. When I came home I stayed with my sister. That's how I could save money to keep Christine in college."*[289]

After the turn of the century, very few employment opportunities were available locally, unless one was in farming or provided a service. The "Industrial Revolution" that had taken place along the river's edge over the past century was coming to a sad and grinding halt. The paper mill had closed; some mills were functioning but the close of the Canal stymied their productivity and profitability. The canneries in the area, including Andrew's Canning House in Berkley, continued to be prosperous but provided only seasonal work, and the Red Gate Turkey Farm, while a commercial enterprise, produced very little opportunity for employment in the crossroads community. Berkley continued to thrive, but the previously close knit and interdependent community that heretofore had operated as a unit with minimal contact with the wider world, began to extend its contacts beyond the farm, the mills, the canneries, the blacksmith shop, and the stores.

*WILLIAM MARSHALL
PRESBERRY, JR.,*
a descendent of the Presberry family tree whose roots reach deep into Berkley's history, was born in Berkley in 1933. He attended Hosanna School, the Havre de Grace Colored High School and was graduated from the Central Consolidated School in 1951. He worked his first summer on the Conowingo Dam before attending Maryland State College for two years. He was drafted into the army and served a tour of duty of two years during the Korean War. William is a member of the Deer Creek Harmony Presbyterian Church serving in many leadership roles for the church. He worked on the Pennsylvania Railroad but found his career with the Federal Government working at the Perry Point Veterans Administration Hospital for over thirty years as a carpenter. In his interview, he recounted his many efforts to get fair employment for himself and others. He continues to reside with his family in Berkley.
Interviewed 4 March 2000

The Gregory children at their turkey farm at Red Gate in Berkley.

Private collection of Ann Hopkins Gregory

Can't Keep 'em Down on the Farm

During the late nineteenth century through the twentieth century mechanization began to change the lives of the farmers, altering farming practices in order to use fewer hands and, in most cases, increase production. Roland Dorsey worked for Walter Jourdan who owned a tomato cannery. Roland detailed his experiences, *"I started working for Walter Jourdan when I was twelve years old setting tomatoes. It would be five or six of us, and they [the other workers] would make the rows out, they marked the rows, and I would have a row [of tomatoes to set] and [when] I got to the end I'd start back again. Now, today they got a planter that plants its own tomatoes."* He continues shaking his head in amazement, *"Put them in a machine, every time that thing clicks, water drops in the hole and covers the plant right up, keeps right on going. One-man operation. One man."* he repeats plaintively.[290]

The seeds of the American labor movement—providing fair wages and safety for workers—had been planted by the twentieth century. The early twentieth century Progressive Movement challenged child labor and laid the groundwork for today's educational practices. Access to education was more widespread and everyone was becoming aware of the importance of education in this new economy and social environment. They were beginning to see that more opportunities were available in manufacturing, service, and transportation than in farming and its rural way of life.

In 1917 the Selective Service Act became law. Consequently the military draft began taking more men from the farm for the war effort and exposing them to wider horizons of opportunity. Many of Berkley's young men left for their tours of duty, came back with new skills, and sought employment elsewhere. This same pattern was to repeat itself after World War II.

Also in 1917, with the establishment of the Aberdeen Proving Ground, the need for research and development in the U.S. Army came to Harford County. By World

War II, the Proving Ground's facilities made it the premier military research base in the United States. Located fifteen miles from Berkley in Aberdeen, Maryland, its mission was to test military weapons under various simulated conditions. Another military research facility was located in Edgewood, Maryland, about twenty miles from Berkley. Edgewood Arsenal conducted cutting edge research in biological and chemical warfare, At these facilities, Harford County residents were given the possibility of lifetime employment with interesting work, good pay, regular working hours, and benefits. Bainbridge Naval Training Center was established in 1942 in response to the need to strengthen America's armed forces and to support World War II. Bainbridge was at least five miles closer to Berkley than the other military facilities and attracted a substantial number of workers from the area. Bainbridge was a training center for new recruits and for certain advanced service schools, as well as a Naval Academy Preparatory School. Like Bernice Bond Glover, more than one Berkley citizen found a lifelong mate at Bainbridge. *"I met him [my husband] at Bainbridge ... and we have been married ... forty-five years."*[291] Many residents of Berkley today continue to work for the Federal Government or are retired Federal employees.

David Gordon had the strong work ethic that was quite typical of people growing up in rural America. David's first job was at the Berkley Cannery, and said, *"I'll never forget the first job I got working in the canning factory. They had a canning house in Berkley and I used to work at the canning house. But the thing of it is, what happens, you know, they had laws. You couldn't work until you were a certain age. I was underage ... I was kind of small in stature, I used to have to hide every time inspectors came. And I'd go over to the part where they had the empty cans, sat back there in the boxes, and I'd hide back in there until after the inspectors come, then I'd come back out and go to work ... You could work on farms at sixteen but not on public works, cause most of those required you to be twenty-one. At sixteen I set my age up and got my first public job on the Pennsylvania Railroad. I was fortunate enough to get a pair of big pants and a cap, you know, kind of spruced myself up a bit. The railroad was a big thing, ... The biggest majority of people [men] worked on the railroad. That was the main source of income for people of color, until they started preparing for WWII at Aberdeen Proving Ground and Edgewood Arsenal."*[292]

As Gordon had observed, the railroad hired many blacks in the area, albeit they started out as laborers with only day rates. But many stayed on and became career employees of the Pennsylvania Railroad, taking courses to learn new skills and rising to supervisory positions. One, in particular, was Edward Presberry, who was railroading in the early years, *"They did not allow a black person to have anything more than a pick in their hand, a hammer. You wasn't able to use anything mechanically ... Later they'd let you use it, but you maybe get paid for it, maybe you wouldn't, but you wouldn't collect no service out of it ... no promotions ... one time railroad was mostly all white people. During the war [World War II], the white people got a better job. They left the railroad and we had the railroad. Anyway, my buddies, 'cause it was the three of us, we used to work together all the time ... they moved on, got a better job, here I stayed. Well, anyway, the boss, not the supervisor, the bigger boss, he seen me and he said 'I want to send him to school' which was to be an electric welder. My supervisor said, 'No, I don't want him to go, I want him to be a foreman.' They sent me ... I got qualified and learned, got qualified."*[293]

Edward Presberry went on to be a supervisor and retired from the Pennsylvania Railroad after 44 years of service.

As the years passed, fewer and fewer people actually worked within the boundaries of the hamlet of Berkley. The paper mill had closed, work at the various mills along Peddler's Run was waning, and the canning house, while still open, provided only seasonal employment. Fortunately, with the advent of the automobile, the railroads, and some public transportation, people could venture further away to seek work. Only one local construction project in the early part of the century made it possible for Berkley residents to work close to home—the Conowingo Dam. Ironically, this project would close the chapter on Berkley's role as a major transportation corridor.

Changing the River, Changing Berkley

Throughout the nineteenth century there had been visions, discussions, and even aborted plans to dam the Susquehanna River at various points in New York, Pennsylvania, and Maryland. Frustrated by damaged and destroyed bridges, discouraged by the springtime freshets washing out canal banks, and needing to produce electricity for the newly "wired" economy, government and industry would make these old dreams and plans a reality.

When the paper mill owned by the Susquehanna Power and Pulp Company began to fail, it was sold to another corporation that later became the Susquehanna Power Company, carrying with it the properties, rights, and authority that had been granted to the Susquehanna Power and Pulp Company. According to a Philadelphia Electric's treatise, "In 1905, this enterprise [the Susquehanna Power Company] decided to build a hydroelectric plant and, while in the development phase of the project, came into conflict with the Susquehanna Electric Power Company and the Mc Call Ferry Power Company, which also had hydroelectric rights on the lower Susquehanna."[294] These three companies consolidated to form the Susquehanna Power Company but did not have a market large enough to make the production of electricity profitable. Pennsylvania's Holtwood dam, built across the Susquehanna in 1910, had been the only successful prior effort. In 1922, the Susquehanna Power Company offered an option on its rights and properties to Philadelphia Electric. While it rejected the option because of too many restrictions, Philadelphia Electric was still interested in a dependable and comparatively inexpensive source of electricity for West Philadelphia. In 1926, with the assistance of Drexel & Company, a prominent Philadelphia financial institution, Philadelphia Electric negotiated a new option that was accepted. Drexel & Company continued its affiliation with the project and led the group that floated the bond issue to finance the construction of the Conowingo Dam, a project funded completely by private investment.

There were two other hurdles to cross that required governmental involvement before construction could begin. First, the utility commissions of Pennsylvania and Maryland had to approve the project because it involved land and the distribution of electricity in both states. Secondly, the Federal Power Commission had to license the venture because, since the early 1800s, the Susquehanna River had been designated as a navigable river. With these two approvals, private financing of $52,200,000, and the prestigious Boston firm of Stone and Webster hired for the construction, this monumental undertaking was ready to begin.

This period of regulatory fine-tuning and licensing had not stopped the preliminary site preparation. Philadelphia Electric had begun to prepare aggressively for immediate construction once these hurdles were crossed. The forestlands on the granite outcroppings on either side of the river were harvested by George W. Bagley who cut 700,000 feet of timber.[295] Sixteen miles of the Columbia & Port Deposit branch of Pennsylvania Railroad were relocated above flood levels and changed from a single to a double track line to accommodate both regular freight and passenger traffic and the transportation demands made by the project dam construction. The 200 residents of the town of Conowingo were already being relocated. E. Savage Shure, self-described as the "oldest resident hereabouts," sold his farm, 1600 acres of land, to be the site of the Conowingo Dam's hydroelectric plant. According to Shure, "kited property values" as he described them, enabled him "to sell all his holding and take himself to Florida." As a parting shot, he announced the dam would never succeed because it was "tampering with nature."[296] The name Conowingo was selected very early in the process. It could not be determined if it was to honor the town of Conowingo in Cecil County that was to be submerged in the new lake behind the dam or if it was named to honor the Susquehannocks whose word Conowingo meant "at the rapids." Regardless, both reasons are worthy because the name continues to conjure up memories of the old town and a reminder of the Native American presence of the past.

To provide access to the site for supplies and workers, a spur line of the Pennsylvania Railroad was constructed along the west bank on the old Susquehanna and Tidewater Canal towpath. During the life of the project, it handled 13,000 cars and carried half a million passengers over the 10-mile course.[297] These passengers included workers living in Havre de Grace and beyond who boarded the trains daily for their 12-hour shifts. Land continued to be purchased on either side of the river in Maryland and Pennsylvania to make way for the 14 square mile lake that would be formed behind the dam impounding 150 billion gallons of water. A 58-mile electric transmission line to Philadelphia had been designed and erected. Also included in the plans for the dam was the realignment of U.S. Route 1 over a roadway to be built on the crest of the dam. This realignment meant the end of the Conowingo Bridge, which was scheduled for implosion upon the completion of the dam, and the decommissioning of the Berkley Road as U.S. Route 1, known as Baltimore Pike. The license authorizing the construction of the dam and power plant was issued on January 25, 1925.[298]

On both sides of the river, worker housing was finished on March 9, 1926, complete with mess halls, commissaries, and a hospital. A limited number of 2-room and 5-room cottages were built at each camp for those supervisory employees with families and segregated shanties were constructed for black workers. Electricity for the camps came from Holtwood. The water supply from the river was filtered, chlorinated, and pumped to a 100,000 gallon steel tank from which it was piped to the dam's construction sites and to the camps. Sewage treatment plants chlorinated waste before

Pauline Gahagan in front of the living quarters at the construction site of the Conowingo Dam.

Private collection of Joyce Gahagan Crothers

discharging it into the river. Uniformed guards vested with the powers of deputy sheriffs policed the camps.

With heavy media coverage from Virginia to New York and salaries guaranteed by private investors, an eager and prepared-to-work labor force had begun to arrive even before construction began. Gentry Phipps remembered the black laborers, *"Don't you know that there were many colored people working over there on that dam? Down below the dam … built up a place called Black Bottom. A lot of black people in there that worked on the dam, and some white. I remember going down there a couple of times. I don't know what they were doing but I remember it was on the Cecil County side, down below the road now. See, they'd bring 'em up from Baltimore about a week, the bus'd bring 'em. Whenever they didn't work no good, they'd bring another load. That's how they got a lot of their help out of Baltimore. Bus them up here."*[299]

Cloy Gahagan, one of the first trained construction engineers at the dam, brought his bride, Pauline, down from Holtwood, established an apartment above a millinery in Havre de Grace, and initially commuted to the dam construction site by train. Unhappy with the "fast life" in Havre de Grace, the Gahagans occupied one of the newly slapped together shanties intended for black workers on the Harford side of the river. The Gahagans may have been the only white family ever to live in the shanties.

CLIFFORD TROTT
and his wife, Marian, were long-time residents of Berkley. Born in 1908 in Wales, he immigrated to the United States, and as the story goes, was here illegally for some time. Working on a ship traveling from Europe, Mr. Trott jumped ship in Baltimore in 1919, and was walking to Philadelphia when he got a ride as far as Darlington "where there was work." He began as a water boy working on the Conowingo Dam and worked his way up to rigging the towers. He then worked for three years for DuPont; then he worked at Bethlehem Steel at Sparrows Point until he retired. He resided in the McNutt house built in the 1890s located on Berkley Road next to the Berkley general store. Cliff's grandfather was the Deputy Lord Mayor of Cardiff, Wales, and his interview takes one from Wales to his efforts to become a United States citizen. His interview was also replete with early 20th century Berkley stories. His wife, Marian, whose voice and memories may be heard in this interview, died in 2002.

Interviewed 30 June 2000

The impact of the population influx on the immediate communities was enormous. The construction firm had built temporary housing for 1500 workers, but

108

3800 workers were employed. Since construction began on schedule, jobs were quickly available and living facilities sparse. Homes in the Berkley and Darlington areas became "roomer havens." It became very profitable for those local families with empty rooms or start up money to establish lunchrooms and other service businesses. Rooms in Berkley were available for both black and white workers and everyone who could offered a room for rent. Former Berkley resident, Clifford Trott, "jumped ship at Sparrow's Point" in 1926 and, picked up by a Darlington trucker, was working on the dam within a week. Trott said the construction of the dam resulted in extra income potential in Berkley, *"Conowingo Dam had just started when I went to work there, and in those days everybody in Berkley that had room took in boarders, and I was water boy in the rigging gang at Conowingo and Marion's [Trott's wife] Aunt Elizabeth had four boarders—Germans, who had also jumped ships."*[300] Charles Cooley's grandmother *"rented part of her house … my grandfather would run a steam shovel down here when they were building the dam."*[301]

Genevieve Jones remembered a boarding house at the Berkley Crossroads, *"Up here on the corner, this woman [Edith McNutt], when they were building the dam, she had some boarders. And I would go up Saturdays and help her clean—scrub the kitchen floor and dining room floor. She had linoleum on both. And wash up her dishes some. She was an awful nice woman. And she always, oh, she could make the best lemon pies. And she always saved me a great big hunk of lemon pie, lemon meringue pie."*[302]

The owners of the Thomas house, next to the Berkley Garage, partitioned rooms in their homes to provide room and board for the workers. So did many others. Shirley Dunsen remembered her home on Castleton Road packed full of workers, *"… My mom started taking in boarders and, at one time, there were twenty-three boarders in that house."*[303] Others, like the Burkins' family, opened a restaurant in Darlington, and still others began the legendary floating crap game that moved from back room to back room, business to business, throughout the construction period.

At the time, the Conowingo Dam was the biggest construction project of its kind, and like other epics-in-progress, it produced surprises. The first surprise was the probing done in Job's Hole in 1922 when the U.S. Corps of Engineers made soundings of the hole but stopped when their plumb line reached its limit at 850 feet. They never reached the bottom. Described in 1923 as "a surging, sucking monster that never loses its grasp upon its victim,"[304] this measurement continued to give credence to the old

SHIRLEY GITTINGS DUNSEN was born in Street, Maryland, but returned at an early age with her parents to their family farm on Castleton Road between Berkley and Darlington. A student at Hosanna School, she later attended the Bel Air Colored High School, central Consolidated School in Hickory, and was graduated from Bowie State Teachers College. Her parents, Herbert and Marie Gittings, were the owners of one of several black businesses along the U.S. Route 1 corridor. A retired schoolteacher, her interview captures the spirit of black businesses in the area during her childhood before integration, her determined pursuit of a college education and her early employment at the Scarborough Store in Darlington.

Interviewed 17 March 2000

109

colonial story that "anything sucked into it would never be seen again until it emerged some place in the James River in Virginia."[305] More importantly, routing the Susquehanna out of its bed and sending it through diversion tunnels led to a major discovery. The granite, which was assumed to be solid, was badly fractured in the riverbed. The granite cliffs were weathered and also prone to fracture. There was a lot of work for jack hammers and for small bore dynamiting, but with the Conowingo Bridge still in use, no dramatic high scaling or massive dynamiting projects were tried. Cars traveling the U.S. Route 1 corridor drove through crumbling rock and granite dust as they crossed the old bridge. The shattered granite, cleaned out of the riverbed by the black workers, was hauled out by train, crushed and mixed into the cement that later formed the sections of the dam.

The first concrete for the dam was poured on August 2, 1926. The powerhouse with its turbines was placed on the west, on the Harford County side of the river, with the gated spillways traversing the riverbed to the granite escarpments on the east bank in Cecil County. Stone and Webster Corporation concentrated on the energy-generation side of the project and the Arundel Corporation, as a sub-contractor, worked from the east bank. The turbine units came from Allis-Chalmers in Milwaukee, Wisconsin, the steel from the Otis Steel Company in Cleveland, Ohio, and the engine blocks from Wheeling Mold and Foundry Company in West Virginia. The Port Deposit and Columbia branch of the Pennsylvania Railroad hauled timber down from Maine and up from Tennessee. Oregon fir, also used in the construction of the cofferdams, was shipped by freighter from the Pacific coast to Baltimore and then to Havre de Grace to intersect with the Pennsylvania Railroad spur to the dam.[306] As described by R. G. Rincliffe, "To permit riverbed construction work, huge cofferdams, using nearly eight million feet of timber, were built, and over 660,000 cubic yards of concrete were poured before the project was completed."[307] All supplies were hauled to the work areas on temporary tracks built on the cofferdams. The cement was mixed in train cars, delivered to the dam site, and transported on the cofferdams to the current work area. Clifford Trott remembered when *"standard gauge and yard tracks ran through all the shops, or almost everywhere on the site."* And Gentry Phipps, employed by the Arundel Corporation on the Cecil side of the construction began working as a youngster. *"Started out I was just a boy, too little to get in the gang; my brother was in the gang. It was a labor gang, and he asked this man, the boss, for a job for me. He gave me a job carrying coal to the shovel. All I had to do was keep coal on it, and I learned how to fire the boiler while I was carrying coal. The fellow quit and they give me the job … I fired the boiler after I carried the coal about a year."*[308]

The physical work was intense and unceasing. The men worked twelve-hour days. They were paid twice a month with paydays which involved thousands of workers lined up to receive their paychecks, most of whom earned a base pay of seventy-seven cents an hour. The workers were allowed two days off without pay, Christmas and Easter. There was a large and predicted turnover of the less skilled workers who simply made their money and moved on to other jobs; therefore, no lists were ever kept of these employees. There were double shifts in place at all times, closely supervised by Dr. William C. L. Elgin of Stone and Webster, who died a few weeks before completion of the project, allegedly from overwork and compounded by a brain tumor.

The whole structure grew section by section, until the two sides reached the middle and the last spillway and gate crane were put in place. Already with an eye for managing the power once the dam was in operation, Stone and Webster saw to it that large water storage tanks, water treatment facilities, water pipe lines, a sewage treatment plant and power lines were laid to sustain not only the temporary "towns" adjacent to the construction sites, but also the projected Conowingo Village, a company town completed in 1929. Built of Maryland fieldstone and wood siding, the houses in the Village boasted of up-to-date appointments such as in-house plumbing with bathrooms on each floor, and full house wiring for electric stoves, refrigerators, and other appliances. Situated on a bluff overlooking the dam, these modern living quarters would provide permanent housing for the engineers and administrators responsible for the day-to-day operation of this big powerhouse. "It was the perfect place to grow up in," recalled Joyce Gahagan Crothers, who was the Gahagan's first child born in "the Village."[309] In 2001–02, except for the preservation of one of these exquisite houses, the entire village was condemned and razed.

Second only to the Niagara Falls Hydroelectric Dam in power production, the Conowingo Dam was described at its start-up as "the biggest dam any one had ever seen."[310] With a length of 4,648 feet, the dam and its generators were fully operational in the summer of 1928 when all seven state-of-the-art power-generating units with a total capacity of 378,000 horsepower began supplying the energy needed for the Philadelphia area.[311]

From the first concrete poured in 1926, the Conowingo Dam was the object of unflagging loyalty from the engineers who operated it, and the dam reflected the admiration and pride of the men who were involved in its construction. People came to sightsee during the construction years, to inhale the scent of primal ooze rising from the river basin, to witness the blowing up of the Conowingo Bridge, and, when the final unit was in place, to watch the 290-foot deep Conowingo Lake form behind the dam, slowly drowning the abandoned town of Conowingo and the remains of the industries, the canal, and the farmland in Harford County in its bed.

Cloy Gahagan, the first engineer at the Conowingo Dam throws the switches to begin the generation of power.
Private collection of Joyce Gahagan Crothers

The realigned U.S. Route 1 over the dam was opened on November 16, 1927 and the first car to pass over it was driven by Darlington resident, Earl Hopkins. Two weeks later the Conowingo Bridge was sent to its watery grave when forty-eight charges of nitrogelatin set off explosives that "snapped the beams like toothpicks and … seven twisted spans of the old steel structure lay at the bottom of the Susquehanna."[312] The old stone piers, however, did not falter. They continue to stand under 40 feet of

111

Susquehanna water. The town of Conowingo was vacated officially on January 18, 1928 and shortly afterwards the waters of the Susquehanna began to rise, covering the town in one day. The *Cecil Whig* reported that the water was "rising almost imperceptibly earlier in the day, the back flood gathered in force and by noon spread over flats and crawled up bluffs and back into creeks. By evening, all that was left of Conowingo was a half-submerged building, its roof jutting above the rising river."[313]

Hundreds of observers lined the Conowingo Lake to watch the Conowingo Bridge explode and slide into the waters of the lake.
Stone and Webster, *Conowingo* 1928

Some of the workers eventually settled in the area and married local girls. And those tapped to manage and run the dam were moved into the new Conowingo Village. Laura Bradford, who taught some of the children of the dam employees, said, *"The dam made a lot of changes ... Introduced new people in the community who married and stayed on. The dam work stayed on and gave jobs to new people in Darlington and Berkley."*[314]

For the new travel route, Jean Ewing lamented, *"We had to take a new approach to the river, because the Conowingo Dam was built south of the old bridge and I remember seeing the lake back up behind the dam, and thinking how dreadful that they had ruined that whole river valley, just by covering it solid with water. I never forgave them for ruining the old river."*[315]

No longer could travelers enjoy Berkley Road's beautiful scenery or dine at the Towpath Tea House. Old U.S. Route 1, with its paving lapped by the lake's water, disappeared beneath the surface to continue its route to the remains of the Conowingo Bridge underwater. To Berkley residents like Clifford Trott, the water's edge became a place *"where you parked the car and went for a swim."* Or, as his wife, Marian, said, *"You washed your car."* By 1930 the car dealership on Berkley Road was gone, the work at the dam shifted from construction to operation, the boarders who swelled Berkley's population had left for other jobs, and Berkley became the rural crossroads that exists today.

In his book Samuel Mason lamented the loss of the sound of the river:

> The ridge on which Darlington and Berkley stand, was undoubtedly covered with enormous white oaks, one grove blending into the next, with column like walnuts growing on sunny bottom lands and here and there through the forests, chestnuts of gigantic size. The silence of the woods at noon would be broken only by the intermittent rapping of the pileated woodpecker, or the distant sound of a solitary woodsman's axe; and if you paused to listen, the ever present roar of the old Susquehanna, which has been now unfortunately silenced.[316]

At The Water Edge. After the completion of the dam, old U.S. Route 1 stopped at the water's edge and became a recreational area for the community.
Private collection of Lois Steele Jones

PART V

Coming of Age

"No segregated feeling when it came to helping"

Childhood Playmates, Lifelong Friends
Christine and Megan
Private collection of Megan Evans

Sweet Memories of My Youth in Berkley

Sights

The blossoming locust tree in my grandmother's yard;
how we enjoyed these tidbits, sweet as honey.

At harvest time, neighbors helping each other to bring in the crops.

The gardeners and their helpers harvesting tomatoes in late summer.
The wagons loaded with baskets of tomatoes on their way to the cannery.

The rows of women at their benches in the cannery
preparing tomatoes for processing.

The beauty of the snow-covered land on moonlit nights
while riding with my grandfather in his sleigh.

The young children in all their finery at Easter,
when they presented their "pieces" during Sunday
school or at a special program.

Sounds

The plaintive song of the bobwhite far off in a hidden bush or tree.

The rippling water of the branch at the bottom of Grandma's yard.

The plop-plop of the hucksters' horses as they came hawking their wares.

Smells

The aroma of the varied goods in Thomas's store—
foods, dry goods, kerosene, paper products …

The tomatoes being processed in Andrew's cannery.

The various products of butchering being prepared for storage—
cooking sausage and packing in jars—for the winter table.

The barnyard!

—*Evangeline Ford*
Written after her interview
2000

Coming of Age

From 1929 to 1945, the pleasures and joys of Berkley's youth were tempered by the times. Some of the voices in this journey recalled the Depression of the 1930s and the nation at war in World War II. During the Depression, times were as hard in Berkley as they were throughout the country. Many people worked for the WPA while others continued at the railroads, the Aberdeen Proving Ground, Bethlehem Steel, the Chesapeake and Potomac Telephone Company, and Philadelphia Electric. Still others provided for themselves and their families doing any odd job that became available. Because of the rich farmland available to all of the residents of Berkley, the ability to grow, preserve, and store their own food gave assurance that no one would be hungry. Edward Presberry recalled, *"Well, we ate good. Don't misunderstand me, it was everything that if you ate it today they say'll kill you. We ate pork, never had too much beef. Had chickens, you had guineas, you had ducks, you had geese and you had fish. Opossum, people won't eat today ... but if it hadn't been for opossums, I'd have been dead. Coons, rabbits, squirrels. Had all kinds of vegetables ... peas, corn, string beans, dried beans, lima beans ... cornbread, biscuits, hotcakes ... We growed apples, pears, peaches, grapes, berries, blackberries, dewberries, wineberries, raspberries. Turnips, we used to eat turnips ... chitlins, pigsfeet ... you could go to most anybody's house they'd feed you."*[317] Almost every voice that recalled those depression years echoed the same refrain, "It was hard."

The war years touched everyone—some served their country militarily and others joined the civilian workforce that would support the war effort at home. By the late 1930s, Aberdeen Proving Ground and Edgewood Arsenal were strong and important resources for the coming war. Aberdeen Proving Ground was the home of the Army's Ordnance Training School and site of the premier research and development facilities for the army—the Ballistics Research Laboratory and the Development and Proof Services. Edgewood Arsenal, located just south of the Proving Ground, housed the chemical and biological research facilities. During the war bombs and other munitions were built for the military and testing continued to develop new delivery systems —better tanks, better guns, and better munitions. Many residents of Harford County worked at these facilities putting in seven-day weeks throughout the duration of the war to provide munitions and other military resources needed for the troops. During the war, three Berkley residents, Annabelle Dows Burkins, Wilson Ross Presberry, and Gantry Phipps worked in the munitions plant at Edgewood Arsenal under very hazardous conditions.

Burkins began working at Edgewood right out of high school. She worked the midnight shift in the "gas manufactory" building bombs, *"I built bombs. I did a little bit of everything. I even did some spray painting on the bomb. I worked on the part that fired the bombs ... It depends on phosphorous ... I was in an explosion, a very bad explosion that I think killed twelve people ... white phosphorous is what went up in the explosion. People just disintegrated ... That's where I got the scars on my face ... I wasn't even in the building where the explosion happened. I was in the other building, but it caught fire and I was blown off my stool really and found myself on the floor, and I sort of woke up and whatever was here,"* she gestured to her face, *"I pulled out a*

ANNABELLE DOW BURKINS moved to Berkley at an early age. The eldest of six children, her family settled in what is now the Yeager house on Castleton Road. With no electricity or indoor plumbing, she and her family experienced the hard times of the 1930's depression. She lived there until 1945 when she married Leonard Burkins, a Darlington boy, whom Annabelle "knew from the church." As an employee at Edgewood Arsenal during World War II she was injured in a phosphorus explosion and, in her interview, tells of that experience. Leonard and Annabelle Burkins were well known in the community for their efforts in the Civil Rights movement by working for equality and opportunities for black citizens.

7 December 1999

piece of shrapnel right here. My hair was burned. We were taken to the hospital in an ambulance.[318]

In that explosion, Wilson Presberry, who was Christine Tolbert's father, was taken to the hospital suffering from severe burns from mustard gas. And Gentry Phipps received a citation from the U.S. Government for his quick thinking. He was an engineer on the train lines that brought the chemicals and materiel to the bomb factories. When the explosion occurred, there was a trainload of white phosphorous sitting next to the building. Gentry took his engine, hooked it to the cars and pulled them away from the building, *"… The building blew up and it had a lot of hand grenades and they kept going off, and several people got killed. But we had had cars loaded with blow-ups ready to go in front of the building. And so me, I was running the locomotive, me and one of the brakemen pulled them cars out and there was so much trash on top of them burning, I got up, after we got 'em out, I got up and climbed up and kicked the fire off them. Then we got a big write up, but no money … got my name in 'The Aegis,' picture in 'The Aegis' and all."*[319]

Charles Cooley served his country from 1942–1946. He received his basic training at Fort Eustis, Virginia, had additional training at Fort Stuart, Georgia, in a heavy automotive maintenance company and then was shipped overseas. He said, *"I passed through London to Southampton, Omaha Beach, St. Lo, Paris. They were going to ship me to the Bulge; they broke out of that and I didn't have to go and then I was a half a point shy of getting home after the war was over in Europe. I had to go to Vienna from September through March. It was terrible duty up there, oh, that was tough—opera and beer gardens … But someplace over there, I wrote a letter to my mother, I guess it was before the Battle of the Bulge because they were taking all of us single guys and making us ready to ship us up to the Bulge, that if I got back to Darlington, Maryland, I wasn't leaving. And I haven't been too crazy to leave either."*[320]

Soldiers training at the APG were frequently in Berkley on maneuvers and bivouacked on the farms in the area. Phyllis Price would see them coming through, *"… They went up Castleton road and would bivouac somewhere up here. But I remember they would come down and they would stop there [at the crossroads]. They went into the store to get, you know, some soft drinks or some candy or something like that. And they would just be sitting around with comic books right there at the intersection wherever they could, you know, be off the road and wouldn't interfere with the traffic."*[321]

Annabelle Burkins vividly recalled one of the exercises, *"One time, they were marching up the road in Berkley and, the first thing you know, a plane went over and bags of flour just flew. I guess it was flour. I don't know what it was, some sort of white substance. And these fellas, they scattered over in our yard, under the trees and bushes ... They pitched their tents on the Henderson farm ... And, of course, I had to walk up and down the road."*[322] And Shirley Dunsen remembered that she *"used to always stand on the front porch and watch them march through."*[323]

The women in Berkley and Darlington did their part for the war effort also—volunteering for the Red Cross, "knittin for Britain," recycling tin and paper to contribute to the war effort, and, according to Phyllis Price, helping the war effort by shopping frugally—*"meat and sugar and butter were rationed. And you had a little coupon book that you would use when you bought some of these things."*[324]

It is often noted that women who had servants at home supported the war effort because they had time to do it. What must not be forgotten, however, was that the women who worked on the farm, in factories, and on the military bases found time to contribute volunteer hours to the cause—in addition to their jobs. Many women organized groups all over the county for the sole purpose of supporting the effort. One such group was organized at the Hosanna Church. The church had a women's organization that met regularly to make and assemble packages and medical supplies for the troops. These women wrapped bandages, prepared gift packages, and worked on any project necessary for the war effort. The membership included many of the family names mentioned throughout this journey: Mrs. E. N. Thomas, president, Mrs. E. N. Washington, Mrs. Dora E. Presberry, Miss Esther James, Miss Rachel Presberry, Miss Margaret Cain, Mrs. Sarah J. Parker, Mrs. Hannah Webster, Miss Addie Warfield, Mrs. Rachel Smith, Miss Pearl Warfield, Miss Myrtle McCall, Mrs. C. A. Hopkins, Mrs. Martha Presberry, Miss E. M. E. Davis, Mrs. Rachel McCall, Mrs. Cassie Archer, Mrs. India James, Miss Ruth Gordon, and Mrs. Annie Webster.

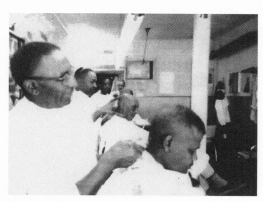

William Marshall Presberry, Sr. at his Berkley home barber shop in the early 1950s. Another Berkley resident, Ethel Taylor, provided the black women a fine coif at Ethel's Beauty Shop also established in her home in Berkley.

Private collection of Doris Tolliver Presberry

And there is one final story about the Conowingo Bridge demolished in 1927. The collection of scrap iron and metals was an important activity undertaken by everyone during the war including the U. S. Army Corps of Engineers. They had devised a salvage plan to retrieve the iron remains of the Conowingo Bridge from the depths of the Conowingo Lake but "problems arose, in part due to Job's hole. The bridge had spanned this whirlpool in the Susquehanna, but a good part of the bridge apparently slithered into the hole," so the bridge could not be called upon to serve the nation again.[325]

After World War II, Berkley settled back into the quiet hamlet it had become after the construction of the Conowingo Dam. In the 1950s there were still a few small businesses. Ethel's Beauty

Shop run by Ethel James Taylor, mother of Evangeline Ford, continued to provide salon services to the black women of Berkley and William M. Presberry's Barber Shop for black men was still operating out of the basement of his house. The Berkley Store continued to sell foodstuffs, various utensils for home and garden, and ice cream and candy to families in the area. In addition to the multigenerational names in Berkley, the mailboxes during this time included names such as Burkentine, Pomraning, Weaver, Joines, Trott, Andrews, Gorrell and Steele. The voices in Hosanna A.M.E. Church were raised in song and praise regularly but the Hosanna School no longer held the sound of children. By 1960, Swallowfield, which had been owned by various members of the same Quaker family for more than 100 years was sold; so was the Rigbie Farm, which had been in the Jones family for more than a century. The store changed hands and became a thrift shop. The children who had grown up through the Depression and World War II found employment and opportunities elsewhere, and the population began to age.

Shirley Thompson lamented a period of slow deterioration in the community, *"... Some of the houses have really went down. I mean, some of the houses used to be gorgeous ... I just thought that the Berkley intersection had the nicest houses, but I don't see it that way ... A lot of the properties changed hands. A lot of people either died or the children moved away and the homes were sold ... they couldn't use that big a house anymore so they moved away and then ... I think they've changed hands a lot of times. Continuity has not been a thing that has stayed there, whereas it used to be."*[326]

Twentieth Century Education in Black and White

Throughout the first part of the twentieth century, the schools in Maryland adhered strongly to the 1896 "separate but equal" decision of the U.S. Supreme Court. Educational facilities, from elementary school through college, were, indeed, separate, but, as the Hosanna School story illustrates, they were far from equal. Maryland schools did not begin to integrate until after the Supreme Court decision on Brown v. Board of Education in 1954. Although they lived as neighbors and childhood playmates, Berkley's children continued to be educated on separate paths.

The white children in Berkley continued to attend the Darlington Academy that had been rebuilt in 1896. Charles Cooley attended the Academy where his family was influential, *"First principal I had was a Tom Hackett ... and that used to be the old Darlington Academy where my great-grandfather, John Marchborn Cooley taught. My first teacher was Laura Bradford, and she's still living ... a music teacher and she had a little thing called a pitch pipe and she'd get up there in front of the class and tweet, tweet, tweet, sound your A or sound your E. I can remember that distinctly to this day. I couldn't get an E or an A because I wasn't musically inclined ... Tom Hackett was tough. He had a paddle with holes in it ... Later we had a superintendent by the name of Miss Nailer. She's a woman and she had the biggest feet of any person I ever saw in my life. But she come in there with those laced up shoes on and they must have been thirteens. But everybody walked the narrow when she come around. We had outhouses for bathrooms, boys and girls. Some*

The Darlington Academy School children—1921.

Personal collection of Mrs. E. W. Chambers

Darlington Elementary School 1966

Personal collection of Doris Toliver Presberry

of them ornery boys, I don't know who it was, but they grabbed a chicken and throwed it down the girls' toilet. So that was school life in the country. And every noontime, we go across from the school, behind the Methodist Church there was a hill, we took our sleds to school. Go sledding at recess and at noontime."[327]

In 1938, with the assistance of a public bond issue of $95,000, an eight-room brick building was erected on the site of the old Darlington Town Hall. This school building continues in use today. Many of the people interviewed for this book who attended the old Darlington Academy and the new Darlington Elementary School had fond memories of classmates and their daily learning routine. In addition, they remembered their first grade teacher, Laura Bradford—an icon in the community. She began teaching in a one-room school and she retired 46 years later, having taught generations of Berkley and Darlington children. Shirley Thompson's memories reflect those of many others who attended the Darlington schools, *"I think, the school started at eight-thirty. First, you had your homeroom opening, your homeroom Pledge of Allegiance and your Lord's Prayer and all that, because we said the Lord's Prayer when I went to school. We had an opening assembly for the whole school together in the auditorium and then you would go back to your classroom and you would be going to your specialties, you know, like your math, your spelling, or your reading. ..."* When asked if she had a favorite teacher she replied, *"I would say at Darlington it was probably Miss Bradford ... Miss Bradford was special to us because she knew all of us and ... she took an interest in us."*[328]

Before her remarkable career as a teacher in Darlington, Bradford was a student at the Darlington Academy where grades one through eleven were taught. Mr. A. F. Galbreath was one of her teachers, *"We had an opening exercise. He would read from the Bible, and I can always remember some of his readings that were familiar and he liked reading them. 'When I was a child, I spake as a child, I understood as a child. But now that I've become a man, I put away childish things.' He was very strict. And we'd sing. 'There's Music in the Air,' 'Hoe Your Row.' We'd have recess. And we didn't have a big school ground, we had a little back yard. And so, you could do what you wanted to do during recess, as long as you stayed out of trouble. And it was over very soon ... I think the older girls walked up town. We called it up town from the school—up to the candy store and ice cream store. And no supervised play but the boys would get together and play some kind of games. He just trusted everybody to be decent. And they were."*[329]

Schooling for the white children at the Darlington Elementary School has been well documented in many sources. The struggle for Berkley's black children to receive an education has not been preserved or recorded, so the stories of those residents who either taught at Hosanna or attended the School are especially interesting and important.

The black children of Berkley and Darlington continued to be educated in the two-room Hosanna School and other segregated schools until the 1960s. Grades one through seven were taught at the Hosanna School. From 1867 until about 1930 one teacher taught grades one through three upstairs and another taught grades four to seven on the first floor. From 1913 to 1933, Kenton Presberry, an influential teacher and mentor of many students, served as Hosanna's principal.

The daily schedule and curriculum at Hosanna School were similar to the schedule at the Darlington school, except for the fact that Hosanna students learned from secondhand books discarded by other schools, had sparse school supplies, and had no running water. All of the children at Hosanna walked to school. Roland Dorsey said, *"We walked, I say, about six or seven miles ... I don't mind walking, the hardest part was the winter time ... the snow was tough, snow and ice hitting you in the face is rough you know."*[330] Shirley Dunsen agreed, and said with a brrr, *"I remember how cold my hands used to get walking to school. We'd get to the school and the teacher would pour cold water over our hands because they would really ache."*[331] And as the students were quick to discover, placing their cold hands near the red-hot potbellied stove would result in cries of pain, and they learned that the teacher knew best—cold water for cold hands.

At nine o-clock on a typical Hosanna School day, the teacher rang a handheld brass bell beckoning the children inside to begin classes for the day. The children eagerly scurried to get in to start the day's activities. The boys hustled to see who could be first so they might stand a better chance of being chosen to bring in the wood or coal for the stove or to go to the spring to get the daily supply of water. Student William Presberry warmly remembered, *"We had to go up to Mr. Presberry's house to get water. He had a spring on his property and it was a big thing for us."*[332] After greeting the students the teacher conducted morning exercises, then explained the assignments for the day. Morning exercises included the salute to the flag, the Lord's Prayer, a patriotic song and, perhaps, the recitation of a poem. It was common practice to divide students into groups by grade or ability. The students alternated between working with the teacher, copying assignments from the blackboard, reading silently, answering questions in a book, and reciting their lessons in front of the room. This process permitted students to get exposure to each other's lessons and provided a great opportunity to use different ways of learning the same lesson. The teacher would walk around the room checking each student's work and offering assistance or giving new assignments to those who had completed earlier work.

Older students also assisted their younger schoolmates. *"When the teacher would leave my little section and go over to work with another section,"* Shirley Dunsen explained, *"you had plenty to keep you busy and you didn't have time to goof off 'cause you had to get it done. She would have seatwork all up on the board, then she would go over and work with the other children."*[333] David Gordon remembered the writing tools used by the upper grade students, particularly the pens, *"I distinctly remember, very distinctly, the first pens we had. We had a pen that had a point in it that you could take out. When it got bad you put another point in. And we had a little inkwell that set in this desk. You dip the pen in the ink and then you would write until that wrote out and then you would have to dip it back in again and write some more."*[334] Christine Tolbert remembered the condition of the books, *"When they were finished at the white schools with the books, they would hand them down to us ... We became the best context clue readers in the world because it wasn't unusual for you to get a book with part of the page gone, or the whole page gone. You had to read between the lines."*[335] And Shirley Dunsen lamented, *"we got a collection of books out there now [at the School Museum] that was really, really—they're ready to fall to pieces right now. And that's how some of them were when we got them, you know. We never got any new books. We had Tom, Dick, and Jane*

BERNICE BOND GLOVER, born in 1935, attended Hosanna School as did both of her parents. Born in Darlington, her earliest memories are of the gardens, cutting grass, and picking fruit. She lived with her parents in her grandmother's house on Castleton Road. Her grandmother was a stewardess at the Hosanna Church, responsible for communion and the famous Hosanna Church dinners. She attended Central Consolidated High School and worked in dietetics at Bainbridge where she met her husband. Later she worked at Perry Point Veteran's Hospital and Glen Eagle's Sewing Factory in Bel Air until she was 55 years old. She then attended Cecil Community College to study phlebotomy and worked at Harford Memorial Hospital. As a child in Berkley, she studied piano under Aurora Bransford and Alice Presberry, who was the organist at Hosanna Church. She belonged to 4-H and sang in the youth choir at Hosanna Church. Today she is a member of the Eastern Star and a trustee of the Hosanna Church.

Interviewed 10 June 2000

and those little things with pages were torn out of them, and everything—all hand-me-downs from the white schools. But we learned to read and write."[336]

Students had a recess in the morning at Hosanna. There was no playground or playground equipment, but the children found their pleasures. William Presberry remembered the cemetery, "*Right behind the school was a cemetery, that was our playground, back in the woods, the old cemetery.*" And David Gordon recalled, "*We could play dodge ball and baseball on a little section from the school to the road.*" Bernice Glover's playtime took her and her playmates to the woods behind the school to get sticks so they could "*break off a stick and we'd pull ourselves driving cars, pretending to drive.*"[337] Students also played hide and seek, tag games and, if weather kept them inside, checkers and dominoes. At lunch hour, the students ate their simple cold lunches often consisting of leftovers from last night's dinner, or peanut butter and jelly, scrapple or just plain lard. Sometimes in the winter the teacher would prepare hot soup or hot chocolate for the children on the potbellied stove that sat in the middle of the classroom. Other times a volunteer parent would bring something hot for the children. No one used paper bags. Some lunches were wrapped in newspaper but most children carried lunches in metal lunch boxes or old discarded lard or molasses cans. At the end of the school day the children cleaned the blackboards, swept the floor, and emptied the ashes in preparation for the next day of school.

Recitation and memorization went beyond the schoolroom and was reinforced in the programs the teachers sponsored for parents. Genevieve Jones, who began attending Hosanna School in 1923, recalled the Christmas presentations, "*We'd get up and read some poems or learn poems and speak 'em. They'd have what we called a little concert, and have parents come and listen to you. And the schoolroom has a little platform. I can remember red curtains. They'd pull across and they were holey and the teacher had us patching them.*"[338]

Discipline during these times was strict and corporal punishment was the rule rather than the exception. But the students, in retrospect, seem to have appreciated it. Kenton Presberry's daughter, Elva Presberry Cain, noted there was no advantage to being the principal's daughter where discipline was concerned, "*He had discipline. On his own children he was stricter than he was on others, because he didn't want any one to think he was showing favoritism.*"[339] Edward Presberry, a student at Hosanna School in the 1930s, agreed and contended, with a measure of pride, *"The teacher was in charge, now the boys got big and he had a strap to use for us. He'd get so mad that you would get the strap."*[340] According to David Gordon, Kenton Presberry was not only a disciplinarian, he was also a good and inspiring teacher who encouraged students to believe in themselves, *"I remember a lot, because he was a good teacher. He gave you just the plain facts ... I remember him saying to me ... 'It ain't no such word as can't, old can't is dead and buried.' He said, 'Don't worry about can't, you CAN.' And you would get it, because he would stay right there until you got it."* One could hear the enthusiasm in seventy-eight year old David Gordon's voice as he expressed his desire for an education, *"I loved to go to school even though it was a struggle for me to go to school and finish school, because of staying with my grandmother. I was able to go to school even after my grandmother remarried and moved out of the state of Maryland; I had enough uncles and aunts and everybody I could think of I bunked in with till I could finish school."*[341]

With all of his emphasis on discipline, Kenton Presberry could also be kind and compassionate. Genevieve Jones described him as "quiet and easy going." She talked about how he understood the great loss she felt about losing a precious Christmas gift. She had received a wonderful thick composition book for Christmas—it was the thickest one she had ever seen, and it was the most prized gift she had received from Santa. Even though she was happy to get the typical Christmas gifts of oranges and candies, the store-bought composition book was very special. Mrs. Smith, her first grade teacher, was leaving the school for good because of an illness and her students had to move downstairs for their classes. As she told the story, *"The teacher was getting ready to leave and they were moving us downstairs where the bigger children was ... she was giving us the things she had, papers you could color and things. And she was giving us time to go up and get them. When I came back down, I couldn't find my composition book. I looked and looked. Mrs. Cain's father was the teacher downstairs. And I look and looked, then commenced crying. 'Oh. What's the matter?' he said. I said, 'I can't find my book.' One of the bigger girls had stuck it in the stove and burned it up. Oh, I cried and cried. He said, 'I'll make her get you another one.' She bought me a little tiny, thin book. I never liked her after that ... It was my first composition book."*[342] Today, this would seem like an overreaction but during the 1920s and 1930s at Hosanna School new school supplies were a rarity and valued highly.

And, thanks to Charles Cooley's misadventure, one day the Hosanna students had unexpected and uninvited visitors, *"The man came up from the south, Henderson, that bought the Berkley Farm from Charlie Andrew's estate. He went down south and brought two hundred goats up from down south and turned them loose on the river hills out there to clean up his honeysuckle and fencerows and what-not. Somehow I appropriated two dollars and ended up with a pair of goats from him, baby goats. A nanny goat and a billy goat, but I spent some time training them with harness and pulling a wagon ... but by the time I got them trained pretty good was the time I went to school. While I was at school [Darlington Academy], they run off—go in Hosanna School while the class was on. My mother was very unhappy with me when I came home from school because the teacher was a lady teacher in Hosanna then, and she come up across the field and over the wood stile that my father had built for me to go to my grandmother's to tell my mother that she'd have to come get those goats. They were running in the school and jumping on the desks*

GLADYS IRENE WILLIAMS
is one of the outstanding teachers remembered by those who attended Hosanna School. Retired from education, Miss Williams' impact and influence in educating the children of Harford County has culminated in her induction into the Harford County Educators Hall of Fame. While teaching at Hosanna School, in the early 1940s, she resided next door with the Kenton Presberry family. Her family has been influential in the community for many generations with her brother, Dr. Percy Williams, appointed as the Deputy Superintendent of the Maryland Department of Education. Her interview preserves explicit details of the daily life of a teacher in the one-or-two-room schoolhouse, especially teaching in an African-American school with inadequate funding, second hand books, and pay unequal to other teachers in Harford County. She continues to educate by telling these stories to all of the visitors who come to the Hosanna School Museum.

Interviewed 17 March 2000

and her desk and making a mess of the school. So, my mother wasn't too pleased with me and the goats."[343]

Two Hosanna School teachers, Elva Cain and Gladys Williams, were interviewed for the book. Gladys, one of the last Hosanna School teachers, graduated from Bowie State College where, "*They were training you to be elementary teachers in a rural setting and so you were prepared to teach in a one-room school. And so, while we were at Bowie, we also had to learn to play the piano because we were the people to teach music ... and if you didn't have a piano, you had a pitch pipe.*" When she arrived at Hosanna, "*I was custodian, the music teacher, the gym teacher ... I was the nurse. I was at school about eight o'clock because I went over to get things prepared ... I would put the work on the board, because we had the slate boards ... and I would have it from the first grade on. On Mondays, Christine's grandfather, Henry J. Presberry, would make the fire [in the potbelly stove] and then it was my job to make sure it stayed for the rest of the time ... In the wintertime, I was over there in time to make sure that the place was warm when the kids came, because the children walked. And some of them walked as far away as five and six miles.*" And, as Gladys Williams pointed out, the disparity in resources extended to the teachers, "*In 1927, a white teacher got ninety-five dollars a month, but a colored teacher only got sixty-five.*"[344]

In 1937 there was a petition from "colored teachers" for salaries equal to white teachers. The petition was refused on the grounds that all of the funds had already been allocated. It took until 1941 when a Federal Court order required white and colored salaries to be equal.[345]

The teachers at Hosanna School were graduates of Bowie State College, Morgan State College, Brooklyn College, and New York University. Thus, even with limited supplies and facilities the teachers with their excellent education and talents provided as strong an academic program as possible, often supplementing the curriculum and supplies from their meager and unequal salaries. They became such excellent role models that the majority of students who enrolled in college after attending Hosanna School went into teaching.

The minutes of a 1907 meeting of the Harford County Board of Education recorded this about Hosanna School: "the building for the colored school at Hosanna is totally unfit for use as a school-house."³⁴⁶ Nonetheless, the school remained in service with minimal repairs until January of 1946. The teacher that year, Elva Presberry Cain, became ill and was unable to continue teaching after the Christmas holiday. The decision was made to close Hosanna School. The students were transferred to Kalmia School, a two-room school for blacks near Hickory, about 10 miles from Berkley. This marked the first time black children had the opportunity to ride to school.

Prior to the closing of Hosanna School there was no public school transportation available for Berkley's black children. Therefore, getting a high school education required great sacrifice and expense for the family. Havre de Grace Colored High School opened in 1930 as the county's first high school for black students, and was followed five years later by the Bel Air Colored High School. However, without transportation to and from school before 1947, the hope of attending school beyond the seventh grade was dim. The process for going to high school, therefore, was similar to going to college. Parents had to send their children to live with relatives who lived near a high school or pay room and board for accommodations near a high school. Before Havre de Grace Colored High School opened, some students went to Cecil County where a high school had already been established for blacks. Later, some went to Havre de Grace Colored High School or to Baltimore, others to Pennsylvania. Elva Cain went to Baltimore to further her education, *"... My sister had gone to Baltimore before I did, and I just wanted more education. I went to live with my aunt* [Minnie Presberry Roberts] *as my sister had done before me. While I was a resident there, I attended the Baltimore schools ... I attended Booker T. Washington Junior High and Douglass High School. I graduated from Douglass in 1933. At Douglass I remember taking Latin and mathematics ... I did very well in French, I liked French."*³⁴⁷

The 1946 survey for the Harford County educational system conducted by Boston University documented that white graduates of Harford County schools engaged in such occupations as nursing (girls only), protective service workers (boys only), agriculture, fishing and lumbering, clerical and sales, manufacturing, defense, ordnance operators, and laborers. The lower expectations in the academic curriculum for black students served to cripple their aspirations. As the study explained:

> With adequate education, Negro boys could find jobs at better wages in such occupations as chauffeuring, auto servicing, janitorial service, hotel work, plastering, gardening and the like. Negro girls could command better wages in domestic employment if they had more adequate preparation in maid service, cooking, housekeeping, home nursing and childcare.³⁴⁸

Christine Tolbert remembered her reaction to the 1946 survey, *"I was struck by the comparison of the curriculum for the black schools compared to the curriculum of the white schools. We were extremely deficient. And one of the statements was that we really didn't need to learn these things because the only thing we were going to do would be maids and laborers and farmers, so we didn't need to learn things like algebra and languages ... The Board of Education had one vision for us, but our teachers had a completely different vision for us. And that's what saved a lot of us. I know that's what sent me to college."*³⁴⁹

The closing of Hosanna School marked the first time the black children of Berkley had an opportunity to travel to school at public expense. How they got to school was an entirely different matter. The ride to the Havre de Grace colored school was quite a journey. As William Presberry described it, *"Mr. Kenton Presberry would drive us to school ... We met him at his house at six-thirty every morning. We'd leave his house, get almost to Havre de Grace, and then he would unload us at a grocery store. We would wait there until he went to Gravel Hill and picked up kids, transferred them to Havre de Grace, then come back and pick us up and take us to Havre de Grace. It would be about eight-thirty, quarter to nine ... [when we arrived at school]."*[350]

After 1946, all of Berkley's children whether black or white had to travel a great distance. The white children went to Bel Air High School, and the black children traveled first to the Havre de Grace Colored High School and then transferred to the new Central Consolidated High School in Hickory when it opened in 1950. Shirley Dunsen recalls the turmoil surrounding the building of the new school, *"The Harford County Board of Education purchased some property out on U.S. Route 1 in the Hickory area ... to build a consolidated school. This lady who they were purchasing it from, found out they were going to build a colored school there. She went into a tizzy. She fought and fought but the school was built there. When the school was built she moved."*[351]

The black community was jubilant about finally having a brand new school building with a combined auditorium and gymnasium, a home economics room, and a shop but were disappointed to find the science labs unequipped. Furthermore, no foreign languages were scheduled to be taught, and there was to be no typing. Through successful lobbying under the leadership of Berkley's Alverta Presberry, who was president of Central Consolidated's PTA and William Presberry's mother, the 1952–53 school year began with foreign languages and typing in the curriculum.

In 1954, the Supreme Court decision in Brown v. Board of Education ruled the 1896 "separate but equal" decision unconstitutional. A new era in education began for blacks and whites. In Harford County, change was slow, arduous, gradual, and painful. By the time the dust settled and all of the children in Berkley, regardless of race, could attend Darlington Elementary School without going through an application and evaluation process, it was 1965.

Laura Bradford was still teaching first grade at Darlington Elementary School when integration began. Carole Kolker interviewed her and captured her feelings about teaching in an integrated classroom. *"I have picture of my groups. And I remember the one that had the first two or three little black ones in. I was glad I taught that long to be included in the change ... because they're cute little kids."*[352] And further, when asked if integration changed her teaching she replied, *"Well, not too much because you just didn't belittle the other race. They got along. Children do anyhow. They don't need to be told. They want to play ball, and come and grab the little black one or whoever's around."* She didn't recall any problems and attributed this to the people in the community, *"In the first grade, you wouldn't notice. You included them in everything. If there was play, they were part of it ... we have a nice group of black people in this community."*[353] Shirley Dunsen summarized school integration this way, *"A lot of people did not like it when integration came, but it was a pulling together of the blacks ... I wanted it, and I didn't want it. You know, because I could see it was a lot of hurt, a lot of people who really weren't ready. I'm not saying that there is a time, that you should be ready, but there it was ...*[354]

Leisure and Pleasures of Our Youth

During the last half of the twentieth century vacations became commonplace among the people of Berkley. No longer tied to the rural countryside by employment or limited transportation, they frequented the beach, flew to famous resorts and tourist attractions in the United States and around the world, stayed at luxury hotels or in their tents and campers.

However, in Berkley during earlier times vacationing was not a favorite or, in most cases, a possible pastime. Sunday afternoon buggy rides or motoring were more the norm, riding along winding roads and, hopefully, stopping at an ice cream stand for homemade, hand-dipped ice cream. Spending the day at the church for the afternoon social provided these hardworking people the opportunity to visit with neighbors, enjoy a communal meal, and, probably, discuss the weather. Farming communities required the presence of the family to tend crops and milk the cows. As a family, they would harvest, butcher and preserve these foods for market or to sustain themselves through the winter. As in other farming communities, those who lived in Berkley during the early to mid-twentieth century amused themselves with leisure activities that revolved around the family. Charles Cooley thought that was just fine, *"You stayed home and listened to, with the kerosene lamp, the Lone Ranger and Amos and Andy on the radio. The big deal was to get an Eskimo Pie on Friday nights."*[355] The children of Berkley got pleasure from the very simple and routine activities in life. Elva Cain joyfully remarked, *"We played games—different types of ball. I recall on Sunday afternoons we had hymnbooks—we would just sing hymns. One thing we certainly enjoyed was going to see grandmother on Sunday afternoons. And at that time, we rode in the buggy drawn by our horse, Mike."*[356] Jean Ewing's favorite summer pastime, probably the same for other children in the community, was riding her beloved horse, Missy, *"I spent a lot of the time wandering around on horseback on these little dirt roads. All these roads were dirt roads, except for Route #1."*[357] For Genevieve Jones, a highlight of the week was the horse and buggy ride out the Berkley Road with her family to get ice cream. Nostalgically, she recalled those special days, *"When we were small, on Sunday they would get us ready and get us in the buggy. Mom and my father would be up in the seat ... with one child on her lap. The rest of us were down around their feet. They would take us and get us some ice cream. We thought we had been in heaven. Yeah, but that's about as far as we got."*[358]

The responsibility of assisting on the farm left children less time for organized activities, but Berkley's youngsters always found a way to have fun. There were community and family picnics in the fields or at the river. Laura Bradford remembered coming to Berkley for day-long picnics and neighborly visits. Butchering time, in addition to being a time for preparing the meat for winter, was also a festive occasion that brought families and friends together. Neighbors came and assisted each other on butchering day. Farmers delighted in comparing their stock with their neighbors', as if it were some sort of contest. They would check to see who had the fattest hogs and who made the best apple butter or the best sausage and scrapple. It was a noisy, hardworking, yet gleeful time.

Large hardworking families were the norm so most children had sufficient playmates to enjoy a variety of group activities such as hide and seek, baseball, tag, and card games. They played in the barns swinging on a rope in the hayloft or shooting marbles. Activities were often gender specific. Girls played school and jumped rope. Dolls were often constant companions whether they were paper dolls cut from Sears and Roebuck catalogs, or made of cloth or costly porcelain. The dolls were usually birthday or Christmas presents. Christine Tolbert especially remembered her special Christmas dolls, *"The excitement of it all ... you always had a doll, and that was one of the things that I find when I read some things about black history, that I find were strange and different from mine because they always talked about not finding black dolls. Where my mother found them, I do not know, but I always had a black doll. I don't know how she found them, but she would pinch and save ..."*[359] Evangeline Ford loved playing dolls after she changed her clothes after school and she also had outside activities she enjoyed, *"My grandmother had a dog and a cat and we'd go out in the yard and play with the dog sometimes. She had chickens, and we'd chase the chickens ... We picked berries. You made jellies ... you made mud pies. You picked wildflowers. In my grandmother's yard she had, in the springtime, the most beautiful poppies I've ever seen in my life ... The whole area was covered with those beautiful poppies and we would sit out there on the porch, or in the yard, and look at those poppies. We had games of some sort for inside, and my grandmother had a piano which we were not allowed to bang on, but we would sit and listen when she was playing the piano. And we read a lot. We had oil lamps you read by. And you did your homework. There was not much to be done by young people in those days. You pretty much stayed put. You were quiet so you didn't disturb your elders."*[360]

Playing horseshoes, baseball, fishing and hunting usually attracted the boys. Hunting for Charles Cooley was an important part of his childhood, *"Most of my time was spent visiting with Bill Bostic. We became good friends because we both ended up with 22 rifles and we hunted the whole area from Darlington clear north to Glen Cove Road, over the river hills to Broad Creek, back down to river hills this side of the river clear to Shure's Landing, back to the cemetery and back home again. Rabbits, squirrel ... we had fox hounds. We run foxes and caught them. He and I went night hunting for two years in a row. I had a cross between a Chesapeake Bay and police dog. And he was death on skunks. We'd go out and walk these fields at night and catch skunks. The dog would run around in circles and we'd run in and catch them by the tail and pick them up and put them in a bag, live. We'd take them to Havre de Grace and sell them live—we got more money for them—a full black, he was worth three dollars. If he had a white stripe, he was only worth a dollar ... Mr. Bostic, Bill's father, before Christmas he used to take us all on a walking tour of the woods to get crowsfoot and mistletoe for Christmas. We always ended up at a big oak tree at the corner of Paddrick and Castleton Road that was called Upper Castleton. Now, he always cut the mistletoe, shot it out of the tree with a rifle. In fact, his daughter, Rosemary, got pretty good shooting a rifle and she could do it too"*[361]

Living near the Susquehanna River provided opportunities for both swimming and fishing. Sometimes the river beckoned so strongly it caused some people, including Clifford Trott, to give in to impulse, *"I used to go swimming at Glen Cove. In fact, I swam across the lake and back one night at ten o'clock … because it was a nice moonlight night and I wanted to swim … Everybody said how stupid I was, to go in by myself, but I did and I swam over and I felt pretty good, so I swam back."*[362]

The river could also bring the otherwise separate races of people together. According to Shirley Thompson's story, *"I can remember my Dad, he was friends with everybody and all these people in the area … He had fishing buddies and he went ice fishing … and trout fishing and rock fishing … My dad, my uncle and there were black guys too. They would rent a boat and go up the river. I remember Daddy, he called one (black guy) 'Old Clinton' … He called him Old Clinton because he was older than he [Daddy] was … They went fishing, they had good times together."*[363] William Presberry grinned and said, *"We had a ball fishin' that was our biggest, biggest fun, fishin'."*[364]

People ice-skated and sledded in the winter on the local farm ponds and on the river. Charles Cooley recalled, *"I can remember ice skating on the river in '40. Ice was fourteen inches thick. Go down there and take tires out on the lake, out at Glen Cove, build a fire at 2 or 3 o'clock in the afternoon and skate up through midnight and [the fire] still burned, wouldn't burn a hole in the ice. Had a car out there, Hoyt Culler and the Moxley boys took Model T's and A's out there and run around on the ice. Bill Bostic and I skated the whole way with a pair of foxhounds.—Well, it was only fourteen miles up the river. But there's patches of snow on the ice, so coming down I had a horsehide jacket. I said, 'Well, open that up.' So, I opened that up and it was just like a sail. I was going flying down the river. All of a sudden, I couldn't steer round this big pile of snow … flipped me right headfirst out in the snow bank, facedown … Skinned nose and chin, startled."*[365]

Lois Steele Jones reminisced about sledding, *"I remember we had the best sledding around. We could jump on our sleds at the top of the hill at Route #1, go through the four corners Berkley and ride all the way down to the barrier, just before you reach Glen Cove. It was a great ride, but a very long walk back. So, as a result, we only made one or two runs a night, and there wasn't any traffic that time of night and the adults were out sledding with us. And when the roads got bare spots on them and we couldn't whiz down the hill anymore, we often went to what I remember as Henderson's Hill on their farm and then we would sled in their field. And then often snow was drifted, and I can remember it was as high as the fencepost, which seemed very high to me as a small child, and it would often remain that way for a number days before we could get in or get out. And there was a friend and a neighbor [Gregory] who lived at the Red Gate Turkey Farm. I used to pal around with the daughter there, and they had an old sleigh there and they had work horses, and they would hitch these old workhorses to the sleigh, and then across the yard and the fields we would go with the bells ringing."*[366]

Much of the family focus was on church activities. David Gordon and Charles Cooley spoke glowingly about the annual camp meetings held by their churches. David who attended Hosanna A.M.E. Church, recalled, *"I got a kick out of … going to the churches … when they used to have camp meetings, and that was what we did"*[367] in the

131

The smiles of the Steele sisters, living in one of the crossroads houses in the early 50s, reflect what they said in their interview, "It was a great place to grow up."

summer and Charles remembered the Episcopal Church in Darlington, *"had what they called camp meetings where they had pavilions around ... Everybody sang hymns together."*[368] Sunday school, along with learning about the faith and how to practice it, provided the opportunity for socializing with neighbors and friends. Sunday schools sponsored trips for the youngsters to visit an amusement park or perhaps to travel to Washington, D.C. In the 1940s, black residents went to Rocky Springs Amusement Park near Lancaster, Pennsylvania for the annual family picnic trip. The Park set aside one Saturday a year for black patrons. Having worked all day, the women would stay up late into the night preparing a picnic lunch to take with them. There was great excitement on that day, with people laughing, chatting and hustling about as they boarded the buses. After about an hour's drive the children bounded off the buses eager to have this opportunity to get on the rides but just as anxious to be alone with their friends. Although they had to check in periodically with their parents, this was one of the few times children went their way and the adults went theirs. The annual Sunday school trip tradition continues at Hosanna A.M.E. Church, except its destination is more likely to Hershey Park or King's Dominion.

In the early part of the century, adults in Darlington and Berkley participated in and enjoyed the locally produced minstrel shows. Laura Bradford participated in some of them, *"We had a minstrel—Mr. Shread was one of the end men and Norman Gorrell was one of the men because they danced—and they were black-faced ... it was the Darlington Minstrel. We always had a minstrel, which I think that's wrong. We wouldn't do that [now]. I was showing somebody a picture of a Darlington Minstrel when I was in it too. And one of the men of the dam was a middleman. He sits in the middle, has a title and tells jokes with the end men. And we blacked up and that would be wrong to do because you're really belittling the other race."*[369]

David Gordon boxed. Like many blacks in Berkley, he did not have the opportunity to attend high school, but wanted to use the time to participate in wholesome activities and found a way to do it. *"I got myself engaged in a lot of little sports you know, cause I couldn't go to high school ... you know when you at fourteen, fifteen, what are you going to do with all that free time? They had an athletic club in Havre de Grace in that they had a boxing league. I would walk from Darlington to Havre de Grace ... Cause we got all beat up ... one of the instructors Johnny Dennison ... had a car and he would bring us back sometimes. Both blacks and whites belonged to the club.*" Gordon continued his athletic pursuits by playing baseball for the Kalmia All-Stars, "*... Then, we was mixed up with whites and blacks,*" Gordon said.[370] They played in Maryland, Pennsylvania, and Delaware.

Evangeline James Dorsey started a 4-H club for the intermediate grade black girls in the 1940s. According to Bernice Glover, *"Ms. Eva Dorsey was our 4-H leader. She would make ice cream and stuff and she would show us how to do things, like cooking and sew a little bit. ... Just girly things. We would meet at her house ... twice a month ... She took us on outings. One year we went up to the Luray Caverns. We had to wear pins and buttons. White and green was the colors, but I don't remember having any special uniform.*"[371]

Separate facilities for whites and blacks were the norm throughout most of the twentieth century. Although most of the facilities for entertainment were closed to black citizens, they were not deprived of wonderful opportunities for leisure activities. Segregation helped blacks to develop their own sources of entertainment. Blacks could make "take out" purchases at Gahagan's restaurant in downtown Darlington, but could not eat there. As a result, several dining facilities owned by blacks emerged during the twentieth century. One of the earliest was a restaurant established by John and Lillie Lee. It was near Street, Maryland and was known by blacks as "Out on the Branch." Herbert and Marie Gittings, parents of Shirley Dunsen, opened the Glen View Restaurant, which they first leased from John Lee in the 1940s. Located on U.S. Route 1, patrons could indulge in the good home cooking of "Miss Marie." After the Gittings died, Charles and Shirley Dunsen took possession of the restaurant and re-named it The Clock Bar and Grill and served a new generation of the community. In the 1950s the Cevis family opened still another eatery named Cool Spring. Wes and Lottie Thompson opened West's Restaurant also on U.S. Route 1. The sign is fading but the building still stands like a sentry guarding the memories of another era.

While many blacks were moving to the cities, especially to Philadelphia, to find employment and better living conditions, a young black man from Philadelphia named John Jaynes saw opportunity to the south and settled in Darlington. Jaynes proceeded

Glen View Restaurant, owned by Herbert and Marie Gittings and located on U.S. Route 1, had a strong local clientele as well as serving travelers. The Gittings were the parents of Shirley Dunsen.

Private collection of Shirtey Dunsen

to become the entertainment mogul for the black community. He opened restaurants, bars, and a sports arena. At John Jaynes' Blossom Inn from 1940 to 1948 blacks could enjoy food, spirits and music. In 1950, he opened Johnnie's Sports Arena. He brought professional boxing matches and roller-skating to Darlington. Johnnie's Sports Arena provided roller-skating during the week and movies on Monday nights. Shirley Dunsen loved those movies, and said, *"That was my first time ever going to a movie. ... I remember that's when I first started watching westerns. That's all I think he showed. And the people loved it."*[372] There was a time when a night for roller-skating was set aside for whites. Although they were permitted to come at any time, most whites preferred a night of their own.

There were dances and musical entertainment on weekends. If professional acts were not scheduled the roller-skating continued. Jaynes was especially remembered for bringing some of the twentieth century's most outstanding performers. Long before they had arrived in the national spotlight, Ray Charles, Little Richard, Fats Domino and James Brown came to his sports arena for all to enjoy. William Presberry chuckled and said, *"We got so tired of seeing James Brown, we wouldn't come half the time when he was there. The fee to see James Brown was a dollar and a half. But if Duke Ellington ... or Ray Charles came there it was three dollars. The funny thing about it was during the dances—the whites in the community would come to the dances. ... Johnny Jaynes was a person like this, he didn't care who you were—you could come in. When the whites would come in, they'd start dancing with the blacks ... [this was] back in the fifties. And if we would go to white places, we'd be turned away."*[373] Unfortunately, Johnnie's Sports Arena burned down in 1968. Jaynes rebuilt only enough of the original building to provide a home for his wife and himself, signaling the end of "Big-time Showtime" for Berkley's youth.

Today, neighbors are apt to talk about going "down the ocean" [Ocean City, Maryland], cruising the Bahamas, wintering in Florida, or visiting their out-of-state children and grandchildren. Yet the river still beckons. Canoes, John-boats, cabin cruisers, pontoon boats and day sailers are moored at the Glen Cove Marina or sit in the backyards of Berkley waiting for spring and summer pleasures on the Conowingo Lake. Fishing the lake and the rocky Susquehanna below the dam is still the favored relaxation for many anglers even though the miraculous catches of the past are but stories passed from another generation. The workhorses of yesterday have given way to horses ridden for pleasure along the many woodland horse trails that surround Berkley. One can still be entertained by Ray Charles, Little Richard, and James Brown but not for three dollars and not near Berkley. Gone are most of the black businesses, the racetrack, the minstrel shows; and the church camp meetings are but a memory. Ray Charles, Little Richard, and James Brown may not come anymore but today Berkley claims its own internationally known musical genius, Kim Watters, whose mother, Brenda Jackson Watters, his maternal grandparents, and his great-grandparents lived in Berkley. Kim returns frequently to visit his family and to perform benefit concerts in his home county.

Lafayette Remembered

Many people remember a very special national and international event in Berkley on May 2, 1931. Through the determination and leadership of J. Alexis Shriver, Secretary-Treasurer of the Historical Society of Harford County, and the generosity of Mr. and Mrs. Harold Jones, who owned Rigbie house at that time, Berkley celebrated the 150th anniversary of General Lafayette and his troops' encampment during the Revolutionary War. Preparation for the event engaged the Berkley community—period costumes were created and sewn, and carpenters, masons, farmhands, and other workmen in Berkley and Darlington were called upon to work on the many details necessary for such an event. According to John Clark, *"Shriver convinced the power company* [Philadelphia Electric] *that what they ought to do is to celebrate the one-hundred fiftieth anniversary of Lafayette's crossing the river in 1781. Apparently, they got a little money in hand. They convinced the Joneses to allow them to have the celebration here. They would come in and make some improvements to the house and just get it back to a state where it could be shown how it was then. And so they did."*[374]

Alexis Shriver, member of the Harford County Historical Society and coordinator of the Lafayette celebration in 1931, sits in a French carry-all similar to one that carried General Lafayette to Rigbie House in 1781.

Historical Society of Harford County (Alexis Shriver Collection)
ref.: 1706

Charles Cooley remembers the event and the work expended to get ready for this extraordinary affair in Berkley, *"Well, it never got to be called Rigbie House 'til 1931 or '32. And, at that time, a guy by the name of Shriver was into historical Maryland and he come in and talked to Harold Jones* [Charles Cooley's Uncle] *who lived there because Harold was living on the farm and farming it ... But he talked him into redoing the house because it has ten foot ceiling and the wall is paneled. The old colonial paneling. But it'd been plastered over. He talked him into tearing all that off. They tore it all off and had a big open shindig in '31 or 32. I have a picture of them all out in the yard up there."*[375]

The *Bel Air Times* gave additional details about this extraordinary event in Berkley:

Mr. J. Alexis Shriver, Secretary-Treasurer of the Historical Society of Harford County, has arranged with Mr. And Mrs. Harold Jones, who now own the Rigbie house, to allow the celebration there on May 2nd of this spring, when an encampment of troops will arrange themselves in the fields surrounding the old house, and where it is planned to have Monsieur and Madam Claudel, the French Ambassador and his wife from Washington, unveil the historic markers which are being erected by the Historical Society to commemorate this event and also Lafayette's descendants, who have been invited as the guests of the nation to celebrate the 150th anniversary of the Battle of Yorktown.

Colonial dress bedecked these local women in celebration of 18ᵗʰ Century life at Rigbie House. Front Row (l–r) Mrs. Sam Mason, Mrs. Walter Self, Mrs. Prigg, Mrs. B. J. Williams, Mrs. Bernard Knight, Mrs. Evelyn Mason Gregory; Second row (l–r) Miss Laura Bradford, Miss Mary Hopkins, Helen Whaling, Mrs. Johns Hopkins, Margaret Kenley, Ruth Ashton, Lucy Thomas, Goldie Smith, Mrs. Nina Ashton.

Private collection of Mr. and Mrs. Robert Riley

> The inventory of the estate of Col. James Rigbie has been studied in the Orphans'
> Court and the house will be refurnished as nearly as possible as it was at that time …
> The room in which Lafayette and his officers held their council, and condemned
> Walter Pigot as a spy, is beautifully paneled throughout and is one of the most
> interesting rooms in Harford County.[376]

Several residents have photos of the event. These cherished mementos picture women in colonial dress, Shriver sitting in a French Carry-all similar to Lafayette's, and the hundreds of people gathered at Rigbie House for the celebration.

In addition to this international celebration, the Jones family agreed to open their home to the public during the week following the event for the spring house and garden pilgrimage sponsored by the Federated Garden Clubs of Maryland. Proceeds from these garden tours were donated to help beautify the roads into Washington, D.C. in anticipation of the nation's commemoration of the 200ᵗʰ anniversary of George Washington's birth.

In the 1960s, John Clark opened Rigbie House at Christmas time for neighbors and friends. According to Clark, the colonial spirit rose again in dress and remembrance. *"I would have somebody—two, three people with dresses. All the women got older costumes of the times. And that sort of thing. And we would have a lot of pleasure with that and I thought it was educational."*[377]

Hosanna!—for Hosanna

The Hosanna School continued to be cherished by the Berkley black community who revered the school and recognized its importance in the community. In 1948, Edward C. Dorsey, Roland Dorsey's father, Alexander Webster, Kenton Presberry, Daniel Webster and Marvin Webster formed a corporation, The Hosanna Community House, Incorporated. The certificate of incorporation states the following:

> To organize, operate and maintain an association of resident and non-resident citizens at or near Darlington, Maryland, exclusively,—

> (a) To furnish a location for recreation, social meetings, and entertainment for the community; to cultivate fraternity, goodwill and good fellowship within the community; to provide a repository for the preservation of the history of the AFRO-American Community in Harford County and for other non-profit purposes, no part of any net earnings of which is to inure to the benefit of any member or members, and for the purposes, aforesaid, the Corporation shall have the following powers: (1) To purchase, rent, lease, hire or otherwise acquire, hold, mortgage, pledge, sell, transfer or in any manner encumber or dispose of goods, wares, merchandise, implements and other personal property or equipment of every kind, lawfully; (2) To receive gifts, purchase, rent, lease or otherwise acquire, hold, develop, improve, mortgage, sell, exchange, let or in any manner encumber or dispose of real property wherever situated; and (3) To provide an opportunity to educate youth regarding the history and culture of AFRO-Americans.

As a result of this incorporation and dedication, the recently closed Hosanna School became a community center for the black community. It was used for meetings and served as a headquarters for the Boy Scouts and other clubs until the mid-1960s. It was, by this time, however, a one-room schoolhouse. In 1954, hurricane Hazel tore off the roof and the second floor of the schoolhouse. With labor and materials from the community the remaining first floor was roofed and the building stabilized for the uses as originally established in the incorporation. By the mid-1960s, many of those who held an attachment to the school had either died or moved away and community interest waned. What followed was twenty years of benign neglect. The already unstable building had deteriorated to the point where it was dangerous to use. Even though the community no longer used the building, Edward Presberry who was president of the Corporation continued to pay the property taxes from his own funds to make certain the property remained in the hands of the community.

In 1980 Harford County State Delegate Barbara Kreamer contacted Christine Tolbert about the availability of state funds for the stabilization, restoration, and preservation of historic properties. Christine approached the all-male Hosanna Board of Directors about the state's interest in preserving Hosanna School, at which point she was elected the first woman board member and appointed as project manager for the effort. Joining with the McComas Institute, another Freedman's Bureau school for blacks in Harford County, the entourage from Hosanna and McComas went to Annapolis to support the bond bill introduced by Delegate Kreamer and successfully achieved modest funds to stabilize the properties until funds for restoration could be obtained. With this funding, Hosanna's foundation was repaired, a new door was installed, the old chimneys were removed to reduce the chance of fire, and some of the cedar shake shingles were replaced. The McComas Institute received one-half of a new roof. After Hosanna was stabilized, Marge Traband, a teacher at Forest Hill Elementary School, brought fourth graders and their teachers to visit the school every year as part of their study of local history.

In 1988, State Senators William Amoss and Catherine Riley sponsored a $100,000 bond bill to begin the restoration of the two historic schools. Unanimously supported by the Harford County Delegation, the funding was approved and Hosanna had $50,000 to begin the restoration. County Executive Eileen Rehrmann supported the project by placing the supervision and management of the restoration under the auspices of Harford County Government. Although the leadership of the two schools worked diligently to raise funds from individuals and other organizations, there was still not enough money to complete work. Because of Senator Amoss' devotion to the project, further state funding became available to complete the restorations, albeit, without the second floor of Hosanna School being reconstructed. Amoss later served on the Hosanna Board of Directors until his death. The most visible sign of the restoration was the removal of the cedar shakes that had been placed on the school at some point in its history, and, surprisingly, these shakes had preserved the original German siding of the school. When the shakes were removed, the school regained its early look.

In 1991, the Hosanna School was placed on the National Register of Historic Places, listed in the Register as the Berkley School. There was finally something preserved in the county that would be significant to the history of Harford County blacks. The grand opening to dedicate the nearly restored Hosanna School was held on September 10, 1994. It was a momentous and joyous occasion with people laughing, mingling, and talking to each other. It was also the first time in its one hundred and twenty-seven year history that the white and black community had come together to celebrate at Hosanna School.

The remaining first floor of Hosanna School after hurricane Hazel destroyed the roof and second floor of the school in 1954.

Soon after the grand opening an important relationship developed with the Harford County School System—a relationship that had begun with Marge Traband's fourth grade classes. The Harford County school administrators saw the relevance of using this historic site as an opportunity to enrich Harford County students' understanding of local history, of black history, and of what education was like in early America when one-room schools were the norm. As a result, thousands of Harford County students have made field trips to Hosanna School.

Only one more step remained in the restoration process—rebuilding the second floor. In the spring of 2000, Harford County Executive James Harkins visited Hosanna School and met with the executive director, Christine Tolbert, and members of the Board of Directors. He pledged his support to complete the restoration and encouraged Tolbert to meet with Harford County's State Senators and Delegates to begin the quest for funding for the final restoration of Hosanna School. The delegation embraced the project with enthusiasm and introduced funding legislation in the 2000 session of the Maryland General Assembly. A bond bill for $186,000 was approved by the state and County Executive Harkins, with the consent of the Harford County Council, included matching funds in the county budget of $186,000. Restoration was slated to begin in 2002. With the support of the State of Maryland, Harford County, and contributions from private citizens, Hosanna School will be completely restored, at last. As Hosanna Community House, Inc., it will continue to educate in a different, but a viable, way. No longer providing a place to educate only grade one through seven, it now reaches elementary, middle, and high school students, college students and adults of all races and ages.

Hosanna Community House has, indeed, become a center for community interaction, as well as a teaching environment for educators and historians. The first meeting of the community to begin its historic preservation project was held at Hosanna School, as have all subsequent ones. On November 11, 2000, the celebration that honored all of the people interviewed for the Berkley project brought over seventy-five people to Hosanna, including County Executive Harkins, State Senator Robert Hooper, and Councilman Lance Miller. The Darlington Branch of the Harford County Library has begun to use Hosanna School Museum for its educational programs and organizations such as the Daughters of the American Revolution and The Questers, an international women's history club, have come to hear the Hosanna Story. The Community House also continues to sponsor "Heritage Days" each summer for the children in area.

The Art of Peaceful Co-existence

By the early 1800s, with the Mason-Dixon line about ten miles north of Berkley, the hamlet was home to abolitionists and slave holders, the free, the enslaved, and the indentured, the rich and the poor, the entrepreneur and the farmer, the educated and the illiterate, the black and the white, the huge land holders, the small lot owner and the renter, the multi-generational and the newcomer. This place, where black and white properties rested side by side, did not create a community that was integrated socially. But for most of its two-hundred-year history it did produce an interdependence among its residents and a place where respect for each other was given and held and where there was, as Evangeline Ford said, *"no segregated feeling when it came to*   **139** *helping."*[378] This journey has been one of recording the events and daily lives of various Berkley residents without comment about how blacks and whites felt about one another. In the eighteenth and nineteenth centuries, one can only infer, from the facts and stories, how they got along. In the twentieth century, however, the voices of Berkley did speak to those relationships.

This interdependence was characterized as, *"Well, certainly they depended on our labor, and we depended on having a job ... It was like the boss and the worker, you know. You're the workers; we're in charge. And you know, this is your place; this is our place ... Now, people are beginning to talk to each other more as equals."*[379]

The kind of hostility and animosity between the races, as witnessed throughout the country in the twentieth century, was expressed infrequently in Berkley. Perhaps it was because there was really little to fight over. There was no segregated housing; black people as well as whites were landowners so they didn't fight over land. There was no movie theater to picket or boycott, no restaurants to integrate, and black people did not have to sit in the back of the local McMahon buses or the nationwide Trailways buses. It appears that all along the way there were fits and starts of coming together. An early picture of the Darlington Academy school children shows black and white students. A photograph of the arrival of the first "fire truck" to the Darlington Fire Company reflects white and black leaders in the community proudly standing in front of the truck. And a photograph of the Friday night taxi service at the Conowingo Dam showed local entrepreneurs of both colors ready to drive the workers to their weekend revelries.

More often than not it was neighbor helping neighbor, lending a hand when help was needed, *"My dad,"* said Shirley Thompson ... *"if one of the black men in the community or one of the neighbors needed something ... my dad would be there to help him, or they'd be there to help my dad."* Thompson spoke of Helen Terrell, her next-door neighbor, *"When you got to high school, she went to Central Consolidated. It was the school for black children. And I went to North Harford and that was the school for white children. Even though we went to different schools, we would come over and we would play dolls together ..."*[380]

Land was available to newly arrived or young adult blacks in Berkley because of the amount of land owned by black families. This land ownership, however, did not ensure that one could get a mortgage to build a house. Carlton and Christine Tolbert were unable to obtain a mortgage to build their first home in Berkley. They were rejected for other than financial reasons. So, Carlton, who had built nothing but a lamp and a cutting board in his high school shop class, started to build a house for his family on a pay-as-you-go basis. Gilpin Jourdan, who owned a construction and plumbing business in Darlington and Mace's Hardware in Rising Sun loaned him tools, gave him advice as he continued his on-the-job training, and, as Carlton recalled, *"Gilpin instructed his assistant, 'If Carlton comes in and needs something, give it to him.'"*

Bernice Glover, a resident of Holloway Road between Berkley and Darlington, remembered when the first white family moved to Holloway Road. *"She was my friend*

... I knew her. We worked at the sewing factory [Glen Eagle factory in Bel Air] *together. We didn't have any problems with her because she was a very nice lady. She just fit right in, friendly with everybody back here ... and then another family bought my sister's house. That was a white family and we didn't have any problems with them either. So ... everything was all right ... It's about half and half back here now. Everybody's friendly and everybody minds their own business ... it's just everyday living and everything is just all integrated, you know. Once you get used to it ... we all just one bunch of people in Darlington.*[381]

This oneness of today was brought home to Christine Tolbert when she was approached by a black truck driver recently who was passing through Darlington and asked, "Could you tell me where the black section is?" "There is no black section," she replied, "The community is mixed."

There were incidents of name calling between young people that were obviously hurtful. Shirley Dunsen recalled an incident when, as a youngster, she was walking to Hosanna school, *"I can't remember exactly what was in my heart, but I know there was hurt. There was a lot of hurt. When we would see those buses, used to ride right past us, we'd be walking to school and they would be going to school in a bus ... the key thing used to be if somebody called you the 'N' word. And that, that's what really got you fired up ... But, anyway, my brother and the rest of them, if we come home and tell my brother, he'd say, 'I'll go there and get them,'"* she laughed, *"but anyway, we used to fight, I don't remember us really getting in any fist fights."*[382]

There was also the time that mild-mannered Roland "Bus" Dorsey was called a "nigger." He broke the man's jaw, and the white person who witnessed the incident told the name-calling man that he deserved what Roland had done to him.

Megan Evans, whose grandparents, Bernard and Grace Waring, owned Swallowfield, recalled an incident that happened with her childhood friend, Christine Tolbert, *"... I remember when we came back to Swallowfield, that was the safe place and we could do everything we wanted to here. At one point we were going to the store, or you [Christine] were sent on an errand to go to the store at Berkley, the crossroads, and so I came along. I had been told not to go—it was that same tone of voice that they used to use, sort of, 'I don't think it's a good idea' tone. But I wasn't going to listen to that, so we went down there, we bought whatever it was, bread or orange juice ... And we were walking back and this car, I remember the guys, coming, and I remember they were sort of yelling as they came, and we were walking just on the side of the road, and they took the car and they swerved it very, very close to us. I mean, just missing us and they threw something at us. I don't know if it was a bottle."*[383]

Megan also remembered the time she wanted the family to take Christine with them on an outing, *"Christine was my good friend, and we were going down to Deer Creek with a big picnic, and Genevieve had made this huge picnic basket. And Gracie was trying to get everybody in Grampy's car. We had been playing all morning and I wanted her to come along. And Gracie and whatever other mothers and aunts were around said, 'No, she can't come' ... When I kept protesting and kept being really angry, they said, 'Megan, get in the car. We'll tell you.' They literally pushed me in. And I was very upset*

141

when they explained to me that other people did not like to see blacks and whites playing together or doing things together. And they said these people were stupid, but the whole thing was very upsetting to me."[384]

There were unsettling and scary events for the children of Berkley, also, especially if you were black. Harford and Cecil Counties experienced the presence of the Ku Klux Klan through most of the twentieth century. During the 1960s and 1970s the Maryland head of this organization lived in Rising Sun just across the Susquehanna River so from time to time, there would be flurries of Klan activity in the area. Shirley Dunsen, whose family lived on Castleton Road clearly remembered those days, *"Where we lived in the big farmhouse, we used to stand on the front porch and we could see what they called the Ku Klux Klan. They used to burn crosses on that road* [Castleton] *all the time. I think it was because we had a black school on that road and a lot of black people lived on that road … it was a frightening thing, you know."*[385]

Charles Cooley's childhood and his boyhood relationships were similar to others, *"We got along with everybody. There wasn't any problem with the colored. Bubbles* [Edward Presberry] *and Roland Dorsey grew up here. I grew up with them. There was a Junior Gray I used to pick tomatoes with in the field. Him black, me white, right along side of one another … I used to visit him in the cemetery [to play]."*[386] Shirley Thompson reminisced about her neighbors, *"We visited our neighbors … my mom, she would make a pie or something and we would take it to our neighbors. On one side of us was a black family and we were as close to them as we were our relatives. I mean, my mother and her, and my dad and him. They had one daughter, but there was all of us, but that black lady … she loved us."*[387]

John Clark, who moved to Berkley as an adult reminisced about his childhood, *"What I am saying is that I had grown up with black people, and I really kind of like them because one, they're always kind of funny, they've always got stories to tell, that sort of thing … When I came [to Berkley] I introduced myself, and I immediately starting getting along well with the blacks, don't you know … See it was difficult during the Civil War days, up until the Civil War freed the slaves. It was a great many things that blacks weren't permitted to do."*[388]

The Berkley children played together until they began high school and the social interaction was curbed. Stories and rumors suggest that some of the teenagers found ways to get together clandestinely. Although rumors abounded about certain white women who liked black men or black men who liked white women, these relationships never resulted in marriage. Out of fear of rejection or worse, members of the community adhered to the strict lines of the social mores of the time. The older residents also remembered the accepted and expected protocols in addressing one another in Berkley. Laura Bradford and Jean Ewing captured the essence of that practice. Laura said, *"We have a nice group of black people in the community. Black people had an unhappy life I think. I don't know if they will ever be accepted as equal. And I think the men were the underdogs. The black people who were working for the white people had a good relationship with them. I don't think the blacks ever called white people, like today, by their first names. In those days, it'd be Mr. Bernie or Mr. Harry. But you always called black people what their name was. You didn't call a black person Mr. ... I'd call them by their first name. But they didn't call me by my first name.*"[389] And Jean Ewing poignantly recalled the practice, *"I remember when Connie said something about Mrs. Jones having come over to Swallowfield to talk about working here for the Warings ... I said, 'I haven't any idea who Mrs. Jones is.' And Connie said, 'I think her first name is Genevieve.' I said, 'Ooh, of course, Genevieve is part of my life.' I didn't know her last name at all.*"[390]

When people were asked, "How did you get along?" it was clear from blacks and whites that, while respectful, they led their own lives, interacting mainly through employment or when help was needed. It is difficult in the interviews to determine which speakers are black or white since the sentiments were similar.

"[Our] parents didn't talk about segregation and racism. We stayed to ourselves and they stayed to theirselves and so we weren't having any problems."[391]

"I think we were friendly with them, even though we didn't go to their yard to play or anything. But, you know, with going up and down the road we'd always speak to one another and things like that."[392]

"Well, we were nice with them. I mean we would see them. We would speak to them and talk to them."[393]

"I don't remember any disturbances between the races ... had no interaction with whites."[394]

"Except for the Quaker families my mother and I worked for and the proprietors of the Berkley store I had little interaction with white people in Berkley. Most of them I only knew their names and I would venture a guess that none of them knew mine."[395]

"A lot of blacks said let's leave well enough alone. I think they were more or less afraid. They didn't want to hurt the people they worked for."[396]

The Darlington and Berkley communities were and are great responders to those in need. Cliff Trott exemplified that usually quiet but effective assistance, *"Well, it [Berkley] was predominantly white, but there was still Hosanna Church and all of the black people who were there. They were always very nice and polite with us and we always got along very well with them. And Marguerite Cain, of course, worked for us ... but I remember when Hosanna was vandalized, broken into, and I guess some other churches were doing something but I would not give anything through the church. I went down to Marguerite and gave her twenty bucks towards the church, and she was tickled to death. She calls us every Christmas anyway to wish us well, and we got the nicest letter from her at the church."*[397]

In the 1960s, Deer Creek Harmony Presbyterian Church experienced some controversy when a member of its congregation invited William M. Presberry and his family to attend the church. Presberry accepted and in 1966 he and his family began to attend. He shared his experience, *"They changed ministers in 1968. So, when they changed ministers, the new minister wanted to know how come they had a black family come here and you never asked them to join. So here come two elders to my house ... they felt bad about not asking us to join. So, finally, they said, 'Well, do you want to join?' So we said yes. During that time, a few people left, but we still stayed."*[398] Later, Presberry was elected to the trustee board of the church and served for six years. After serving another six years as an elder he returned to the trustee board for another term. His family is still the only black family that belongs to Deer Creek Harmony Church.

Overall, the Berkley voices remembered their relationships between the races as good but not close—an unwritten agreement, two-hundred years old, to peacefully co-exist.

The Civil Rights movement of the twentieth century and the influx of new residents with new ideas and different experiences brought some changes to Berkley. While the changes have been slow and are still emerging, they are positive. Something as simple as blacks and whites knowing each other's first and last names is significant growth. Mr. and Mrs. titles preceding names are now used mainly to denote seniority or "I don't know you well enough to call you by your first name." The traditional neighborliness continues in most instances. The end of separate schools has permitted black and white friendships to develop and endure beyond elementary school. In fact, in the mid-1970s, there was a melee at the Havre de Grace Middle School where Berkley and Darlington children attended. The first reports suggested that there was a race riot at the school, but as the children came home, parents learned the conflagration had not been a racial one. It was the Berkley and Darlington black and white children against the Havre de Grace children—a matter of country versus city. The black and white children of the Berkley/Darlington area did not like being called hicks and hayseeds.

Today, there are several inter-racial marriages. A couple of black families belong to previously all white churches in Darlington and a couple of white residents attend Hosanna A.M.E. church. Even so the civil rights adage still applies: eleven o-clock on Sunday morning remains the most segregated hour of the week. The churches do have several ecumenical gatherings and projects and the various community boards and councils are integrated. These include the Darlington Community Association and the Hosanna Community House Board that maintains the Hosanna School Museum. Most notable among these endeavors is the Darlington Apple Festival, an ecumenical effort of all of the churches in Darlington and the Hosanna Church in Berkley. Previously, all of the congregations in the area were having endless fundraisers to support their churches, and those efforts were labor intensive and not very productive, financially. In 1986, the churches came together to develop the Darlington Apple Festival—a fall event that now draws over 50,000 visitors and vendors to Darlington on the first Saturday in October each year. This collaboration has benefited all of the religious and community services in the area. Laura Bradford noted, *"Right now, we have an apple fest in the fall and the Berkley colored church has a part in it. They have tables where they sell their home-baked pies. They* [the Apple Festival Committee] *choose the Apple of Our Eye, whoever's outstanding in the community. And a black man has been selected on that."*[399] The black man was Edward Presberry, a resident of Berkley who participated in the interviews for this book. Wendell Baxter, another black man of Darlington, was also selected for the festival's annual Apple of our Eye award.

An event that most ardently proclaims the sense of community occurred in the late 1990s. When the Ku Klux Klan decided to march in Darlington, the community swiftly and vigorously rolled out the YOU ARE NOT WELCOME mat. Clearly, co-existence has become cooperative existence, a demonstration of equal and mutual respect, where neighbor helps neighbor to work and act together for the community's betterment.

Berkley Today

Peddler's Run

Private collection of Ann Gregory

Berkley's Ghost Story

No journey would be complete without the local ghost story. "The Headless Ghost" was published in the *Bel Air Times* in 1932. Written by James W. Harry, it also provides the genesis for the name of the local stream—Peddler's Run.

In colonial days a familiar figure often seen in the rural districts was the peddler. These "Merchants of the Road" carried huge packs on their backs consisting of an assortment of dry-goods, notions, jewelry, and all manner of small articles for sale. They traveled on foot from hamlet to hamlet in by-ways and paths offering their goods for sale to the country folk. Besides the great pack they carried, they always had with them a stout cane or stock. This served a dual purpose of keeping vicious dogs away from them and affording a convenient means of resting their weary backs.

The following story is about the murder of one of these peddlers whose ghost haunted the scene of his untimely death for many years afterward. I relate the story as told to me by my father whose grandfather told him, as related by his grandfather, an eye witness to the strange apparition.

In the upper part of Harford County, then Baltimore County, near the Susquehanna River, there is a small stream of water known today as "Peddler's Run." In the land grants of the Lord Proprietor it was called "Rock Run." It was on the banks of this stream of water that the ghost of the murdered peddler appeared and kept vigilance for years, until his wants became known and his desired satisfied.

In the year 1763 John Bryarly, a small land owner and a grist mill operator was on his way one morning in the early Spring of that year ... He suddenly came upon the prostrate form of a man laying in the pathway. He was horrified to find the man had been murdered. The body was headless ... His head was nowhere to be found ... The identity of the murdered man remained a mystery. He was buried where they found his headless trunk, by a rock, between the stream of water and the mill race.

Some months after the finding and the burial, a peddler's pack was found ... Only the canvas cover remained. The finding of the peddler's pack and cane, associated the murder of a few months before with a peddler ... It was recalled that at about the time of the murder two peddlers were seen together in the village of Castleton ... One was carrying a large pack on his back and the other a small handbag ... The one with the small handbag also carried at his waist. in a scabbard, a sword. It was supposed that the murdered man had been one of the peddlers and the murderer his companion. Both were foreigners, said to have been Syrians.

Later, the same John Bryarly was returning home from his work in the mill by the same path on which he had found the murdered man. It was between sunset and dark when he saw a figure of a man standing at the rock where the peddler had been buried. His back was toward Bryarly and he seemed to bend forward, while he kept thrusting a cane or stick deep into the grave. Brryarly was horrified to discover when the figure turned toward him, that it was without a head. The headless apparition then continued along the path some three hundred yards to a swamp, where it again stopped and again thrust its cane deep into the marshy land, and after a few moments vanished from sight ... Others from time to time saw the same figure. Great fear and consternation came upon the country folks ...

In the Spring of 1848, Joseph Warner, the owner of the farm on which the grave of the headless ghost was dug ... was digging near where the ghost was always seen poking his cane ... came across a skull of a man. It had been severed from the body, the cut was clean, with no ragged edges ... It had been buried with the top of the skull downward ... Warner had the grave of the peddler opened, placed the skull on the skeleton, and in a new oak box reburied the bones in the original grave ... Since then the "Headless Ghost of Peddler's Run" has not been seen. It was quite evident that the soul of the murdered one could not rest while his body was in on place and his head another, and in the very uncomfortable position of standing on his head. He was but trying to point to the place where his head had been cast by his murderer, and made his appeal to the living.

Berkley Today

At the beginning of the twenty-first century Berkley maintains its feel of an earlier time. The wildlife is diverse. Deer are still abundant, but the bears of the past are gone and so are the wolves that roamed the hills overlooking the river. Foxes, opossums, rabbits, groundhogs, and gray squirrels still catch the eye on a morning walk and, at times, grace the dinner table. Reptiles include at least four species of turtles, one species of lizard and several species of snakes including the venomous Northern Copperhead. The hellbender, one of the largest salamanders in North America, has been spotted in Peddler's Run by resident Warren Baity who confirmed this sighting with the Maryland Department of Natural Resources. A descendant of the first animals with backbones, this prehistoric amphibian is seldom seen and is endangered but one of its known habitats in Maryland has been along the Susquehanna and in fast moving streams that feed the river, like Peddler's Run.

The woodlands reflect an upper Piedmont forest with oaks and beeches and a lower Piedmont forest of ash and poplar. The woodlands above Glen Cove are a significant feature of Berkley's landscape and vista. The Day family, owners of an unsubmerged portion of the historic San Domingo farm already visited in this journey, has a conservation easement with the Maryland Forest Service. This wooded area buffers the cove, provides a scenic vista for the tourists and boaters, and helps clean the air, water, and soil. The goal of this easement is to support as many native life forms as the land can support, and Master Gardener Charles Day has managed to meet this challenge. Efforts were undertaken to limit the expansion of invasive species and to protect threatened species that have been identified on the property. The woodlands support the Zebra Swallowtail butterfly due to the presence of the caterpillar's only food, the pawpaw tree. Baltimore orioles, scarlet tanagers, warblers, and other interior forest dwelling birds find sanctuary in these woodlands every year and are one good indicator that the woodlands are working as they should. At least one threatened species of plant, Goldenseal, is found in this preserve. Four of the three hundred bi-centennial trees in Maryland are located in Berkley—all are white oaks that ranged in age from 204 to 248 years old in 1976, the year of America's two-hundredth birthday celebration. Three are located at the crossroads at the Howard residence, (204 and 215 years old), and the Hutchins residence, (248 years old). The fourth white oak, 245 years old, spreads its boughs at Rigbie House. All had been in existence at the time of the American Revolution.[400]

The Webster, Dorsey, Cooley, Cain, and Presberry names still appear on the mailboxes. Stephen Sauers, the great-grandson of Berkley's blacksmith, Samuel Sauers, has brought the family name back to Berkley by purchasing and restoring a house close to the crossroads. Susan Fisher Hutchins, who spent her childhood in Berkley, returned with her family to that same home, Oak Winds, the historic home of Senator Charles Andrews. There are children again at the crossroads with tire swings, badminton courts, and bicycles—their voices ringing through the hamlet from the Waugh, Hutchins, Green, and

Eacho yards. Today's workers include teachers, college professors, nurses, civil servants, specialty farmers, and a librarian. There are home-based businesses and many service sector workers, such as plumbers, and repair and maintenance specialists. The crossroads is rather "gray" since yesterdays' workers at the railroads, the telephone and electric companies, and the Federal Government, both civilian and military, are enjoying their retirements in Berkley.

Much of the surrounding farmland has been placed in state and local agricultural preservation programs, particularly John Clark's property, thus preserving Berkley's rural and pastoral heritage. Gardens are still important with plots plowed and planted in the spring for eating ripe "off-the-vine" tomatoes in the summer. The farmers plant the corn or soybeans each year so the residents can still experience "the growing season" of Berkley's farming heritage. Orchards bloom in the spring and the roadside daylilies, cornflowers, and Queen Anne's lace extolled by Samuel Mason in 1955 still bloom along the roadways into Berkley. While business isn't booming, Berkley has several enterprises that are compatible with the hamlet.

Rigbie Farm has the unique distinction of having seen the start of three new centuries and the significant changes that have occurred during those more than 270 years. Today, though physically smaller in size than the original land grant of Phillip's Purchase, Rigbie is thriving as a multi-faceted horse farm owned by John and Sharon Clark. With a resident population of approximately 150 horses, the business consists of boarding clients' horses, rehabilitating performance horses, and operating a U.S. government-approved quarantine station. Rigbie Farm receives about 200 horses from Europe each year to be screened for disease prior to being released to their owners who live throughout the United States. Rigbie House, still in use as a private residence, is a wonderful and graceful structure and a constant reminder of our country's history. In providing this information, Sharon Clark revealed her love of Rigbie, "As we go forth into the new millennium," she wrote, "It is our hope that Rigbie will continue to stand as a monument to our heritage and our birth as a nation. As stewards of the land and this small bit of history, we view it as our mission to ensure that Rigbie is protected and preserved for future generations to enjoy."

Glen Cove Marina, located at the water's edge at the foot of Berkley Road, has been in operation since 1958. On land owned by Exelon (formerly Philadelphia Electric), the marina was first operated by the Silver family of Darlington. In 1983, Byron "Butch" Young took over the management of the marina and continues that gratifying position today. As a young boy, Butch worked at the marina, where he carved his name on a beech tree overhanging the cove's waters and that carving is a daily reminder of his life-long love of the Glen

Cove. The marina serves over 1000 people each year—providing boat slips for some and boat services to the several hundred cabins that are nestled in the forested areas along the Conowingo Lake. In addition to the many locals and Marylanders who use the marina, boat lovers drive from Virginia, Delaware, New Jersey and New York to enjoy the peaceful surroundings of the lake. Moored at the marina are boats ranging from small runabouts to 40' pleasure crafts. Many of them are pontoon boats favored by the lake aficionados because they are good for exploring the many coves and cruising the lake, and they are great for partying. Many visitors to the marina recall their days on the lake in the '40s and '50s. These older visitors are in for a treat for Butch is apt to drop everything to take these seniors on a water cruise down memory lane. He loves catering to these "old-timers" to give them a few moments of pleasure and, in return, he becomes the repository of the lake's stories. He waxes enthusiastically as he explains his love of the lake. "No industry, no homes—just summer houses, cleanliness, access, atmosphere." He is proud of the most important qualities he looks for in the young people he hires for the summer—a willingness to serve with joy, good manners and an ability to extend one's friendship to the customers. Those criteria are important, because the customers are all Butch's friends.

SweetAire Farm, owned by Arthur and Cathleen Johnson, on Castleton Road supplies fresh fruits of all kinds and varieties that can grow in this region. They grow conventional fruits such as apples, peaches, and blueberries, and unconventional fruits such as currants, gooseberries, and kiwis. They have varieties that extend the season both earlier and later than is normal for the Berkley area. SweetAire Farm features about 50 varieties of peaches and 75 varieties of apples, including the best of old-time varieties and the  newest of the new. These fruits have been offered to customers at the Bel Air Farmers' Market on Saturday mornings since 1979, and their small self-serve, honor-system produce wagon at the farm entrance provides neighbors and travelers on Castleton Road the freshest and finest of fruits. SweetAire Farm is an ecologically friendly farm. A mixture of fruits and livestock provide mutual support without unnecessary imported supplies. Animal manures are used to fertilize the plants where possible, and plants provide nourishment for the animals. Rodents are controlled by natural predators in sheep-grazed orchards, and spray use is kept to the minimum necessary to raise acceptable crops. Many fruits receive no sprays at all. The owners were part of the founding committee of the Darlington Apple Festival and have been active participants in the festival since that time, both in organizing the festival and as a vendor of apples and other fall produce. In 2001, Art Johnson received Darlington's "Apple of our Eye" award for his service to the community. In their spare time, Art is a professor of engineering at University of Maryland, College Park, and Cathy is the head librarian at the Darlington library.

Environmental Evergreens Tree Farm is a unique business begun by Robert and Mary Chance in 1978. Located on Berkley Road, the property was previously owned by the McNutt family who ran the Berkley Store in the early 1920s and later by Clifford and

Marian Trott from whom the Chance family purchased the house and property. When they moved to Berkley from Bel Air, Bob, an environmental educator and local conservationist, immediately began planting various species of conifers. As the evergreens grew, the couple developed a plan for a "choose and cut" Christmas tree farm. They chose the name "Environmental Evergreens" to suggest that the trees to be chosen and dug up would enhance a landowner's habitat for shelter belts, wildlife homes, wind breaks, or property diversity. They have planted over a dozen species of trees on the 6.54 rectangular acreage including Norway, blue, Englemann and black spruce, Douglas, Canaan, Frazer, Turkish, Korean and concolor fir, and white, Scotch, Japanese black, Himalayan, and Austrian pine. Throughout the acreage, a series of ponds and connecting surface trenches trap rainwater into skyponds where rare, indigenous reptiles are bred and released into the Susquehanna watershed. Environmental Evergreens usually sells just under a thousand trees each Christmas season including some pre-cut North Carolina frazer firs that are trucked in. Approximately 30% of the trees are custom hand dug, placed in biodegradable burlap for planting soon after Christmas. Bob serves on the Board of Directors of the Maryland Christmas Tree Growers Association and strives to provide a special holiday experience for families by dressing as Santa Claus and putting antlers on his purebred collection of yellow Labrador retrievers.

Presberry Racing has been running the straight tracks since 1985. As members of the National Hot Rod Association (NHRA), William Presberry and his two children, Tanya and Kevin, have raced on tracks up and down the East coast from New Jersey to Florida and as far west as Indianapolis. Kevin, who owns his own business, is the race driver and Tanya, a graphic designer, has her own affiliated business in racing. While not yet winning a race, Kevin has just acquired a first class car for the year 2002 racing season and expects to find his name in the winning column in the near future. Their NHRA competition number, since 1985, has been 1617, which is displayed on their multi-colored racecar. Tanya's company, TP Graphics, creates designs that consist of painting schemes for racing logos and tee shirts for racing, and develops layouts for race uniforms, vehicles, and transporters for soliciting racecar sponsors. She travels with her brother and father to the races to cheer her brother in the competitions and to acquire more clients for her specialty in motor sports illustration. Classically trained at Western Maryland (now McDaniel) College, she is also a portrait painter. Her commissions include the former school superintendent of New Jersey, Earl Byrd.

Berkley Beauty, owned by June Bonham, is located just up from the crossroads on Castleton Road. She began her new career after her children were grown and hung her business sign out in

1986. Like Ethel Taylor's beauty shop in Berkley in the 1950s, June's shop is located in her home. Cutting hair for residents of Berkley, Castleton, and Darlington for almost twenty years, she has loyal customers and one is apt to leave her shop with not only a good "do" but fresh vegetables from the Bonham garden. She has also taken her salon talents to assisted-living facilities and nursing homes where she continues to care for her aging customers who can no longer live on their own. Of her business she says, "This is a wonderful time in my life."

The Berkley Open, a special annual event that has occurred in Berkley since 1978, revived tennis in the area. One of the first clay tennis courts in Harford County was constructed by the Clifford Trott family in Berkley during the 1930s and continues to be maintained and used by the Chance family. The Open is staged on this unique court plus a diamond dust court on the other side of Berkley road on the historic Andrew's property. The all-day tournament is a mixed, open doubles competition for amateur tennis players participating from across the county. Held each fall, usually simultaneously with the U.S. Open, participants and observers arrive early bringing favorite recipes in covered dishes. Shirts and hats are distributed and the tournament continues until sunset. At that time, trophies are awarded, and everyone continues to eat and celebrate under the tents well into the night.

Berkley still has a Caribbean influence. In the past, Berkley almost became known as Santo Domingo and Evelyn Gregory, owner of the Towpath Tea House, met her husband, Basil Gregory, in Jamaica. Today, Caribbean-born Velta and Edwin Mahan and their children came to reside in Berkley from Granada as part of the Deer Creek Harmony Presbyterian Church missionary work. Velta echoes what many others have said, "I love Berkley; it is a great place to raise children."

Berkley may no longer have a Justice of the Peace or High Sheriff but the unofficial Mayor and High Sheriff of Berkley, Stewart "Farmer" Rice, Jr., whose family has resided in Berkley for years, watches the crossroads, surveys every visitor, checks out strange cars and other vehicles, and visits most houses at the crossroads to determine if all is well in Berkley.

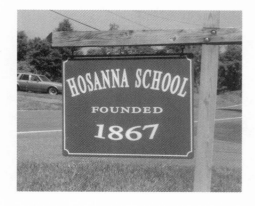

The Hosanna A.M.E. Church still lifts every voice in praise and song. The church has recently acquired additional property across the road thus signaling a healthy future. Berkley cemetery, with its well-maintained grounds, summons one to reflect as each holiday brings honor to those who rest there—flags for the patriots and flowers

153

for the loved ones. The Hosanna School Museum, with its manicured lawn, awaits its final "facelift," restoring it to its original size and appearance so those who attended the school may have a true look back at their childhoods and future generations will learn about the past as it really was. It continues to welcome visitors, young and old, to a living history of the one-room school experience and enrich their knowledge of black history.

The heyday of Berkley is long gone. Finding the bustling part of the hamlet's past is elusive and, by most accounts, there is no desire for it to bustle again. The architectural styles of its houses and other structures are the silent reminders of that earlier time which, to many, is ample documentation of the hamlet's past. Nearly everyone finds the quiet beauty of the landscape a haven for a peaceful, slow paced, nurturing environment in which to live, to raise children, and, hopefully, to continue on to a ripe old age.

By virtue of its past, Berkley has been deemed worthy by Harford County and the State of Maryland to be nominated as a Historic District to the National Register of Historic Places. As a Historic District and part of the Lower Susquehanna Heritage Greenway, the Berkley community now has some assurance that this small, rural hamlet at the crossroads, steeped in its nation's history, will remain a living testament to the past.

The Lower Susquehanna Heritage Greenway Hiking Trail Crossing Peddler's Run at Glen Cove.
Private collection of Byron Young

Epilog

This journey has ended. It has ended with the knowledge that the Berkley Cross-roads has been placed on the National Register of Historic Places designated as a Historic District. This designation will ensure the preservation of the vista, the historic structures and sites, and the physical presence of the past for future generations.

As the journey through Berkley traversed the years, more and more stories and information were moved to the side for future researchers and writers. Many paths that were tempting and interesting were not taken. Many times a paragraph could have become a major diversion, a full research project in and of itself. Some of these enticing quests involved the genealogy of families and the intricate transfers of land that occurred throughout the centuries. Others were mysteries:

* In starting the research, the existing literature cited Cupid Paca as the first free black to own land with his purchase in 1822 from the Rigbie family. Further research found him owning land six years earlier and that land was purchased from Moses Harrison, another free black. When did Cupid Paca really come to Berkley? Where did he come from? Who really was the first free black landowner?

* Late nineteenth century maps document a Friends Meeting House on Smith Road. Elva Cain remembered her ancestors saying it was a Quaker school. The structure still stands on Smith Road and recently was sold by the Cain family. No other documentation was found about the history of the small, well-proportioned structure. Who built it? Was it a Quaker school? A Quaker Meeting House? Was this a result of the split between the Hicksites and Orthodox Quakers in the nineteenth century? Was this another undertaking of the Smith Family, devout Quakers who owned Swallowfield and may have owned the land on which the structure sits?

Home of the Cain family believed to have been a Quaker School or Meeting House.

* Just how much industry was there along Peddler's Run? Judging from the remains along the Run, it was significant. What industries, needing energy from flowing water, were located there in addition to the ones identified in the book?

* According to Robert Riley of Darlington, his great-grandparents, Ashton and Clara Roussey, owned a house and general store across from the Hosanna School on Castleton Road. While Robert and his wife, Millie, have ephemera from this store, no one we have talked to has a clear memory of the store. It is uncertain if it were even open in the early 1880s when Charles Andrew

opened what was thought to be the first Berkley Country Store at the corner of Castleton and Berkley Roads. Ashton Roussey was born in 1848 and his wife in 1852, which gives some timeline to the possible existence of the store. The original Roussey house on a 28-acre tract no longer stands but a second Roussey house with it center peak remains. This house was owned later by the Thomas/Jones family, and now is occupied by its current owners, Warren and Barbara Baity. Charles Cooley's only memory of the merchant lives of the Rousseys is that there may have been a store on the property but he did remember that clothing was sold directly from the Roussey house. No other recollections have produced remembrances of this store. When did it exist? For how long? What did they sell? Did the wagons and carriages stop here also for sustenance and supplies while traveling or was it primarily for local trade?

* And a mystery that cannot be solved—what would Lillian Sauers, Leonard Burkins, and Mrs. George Scrivens have said in their interviews? They died before their lives and stories were shared.

This last mystery, the one of silence, is the saddest mystery and the one that carries with it a profound message for anyone interested in family or community history, particularly the stories of every day life and, in some cases, heroism. It was by word of mouth, half way through this book, that we encountered 95-year-old Gentry Phipps, a worker building the Conowingo Dam in his youth and, later in life, a hero, saving many from death in an explosion at Edgewood Arsenal during World War II. How sad it would be if his story had never been told. Or, Edward Presberry, who, out of love and devotion to his childhood school, paid the taxes on the Hosanna School property and building for over twenty years with faith and determination that one day it would be restored. His efforts would have been lost in the past without the recording of his life.

As the journey finishes, we note the passing of Laura Bradford, beloved school teacher; John Clark, a steward of the land and preserver of history; Jean Ewing, historic preservationist, advocate, and teacher; and David Gordon, a lover of education, baseball, and a civil rights fighter for justice and equality.

The stories and lives at the crossroads are continuing. There are more stories to be told, more historical facts and events to uncover, and more lives to be explored and celebrated. This new journey is bequeathed to the next generation—to capture the new stories, more old ones, and the memories of today's younger residents. Please do so, for it is an incredible journey.

Endnotes

1. John Smith, *The Generall Historie of Virginia, New-England, and the Summer Isles.*, (Ann Harbor, Michigan: Ann Arbor University Microfilms, Inc., 1966), 60 Originally printed in London, England, 1624.
2. George Alsop, *A Character of the Province Of Maryland.* Freeport, (New York: Books for Libraries Press, 1972), 76 Reprinted from the original edition of 1666.
3. Smith, 22
4. Doug Harper, "The Prehistoric Inhabitants of Lancaster County—Woodlands Indians" *The Intelligence Journal,* Lancaster, Pennsylvania. Thursday, 9 February 1995 A-8
5. Samuel Mason, Jr., *Historical Sketches of Harford County Maryland.* (Darlington, Maryland: Little Pines Farm, Private printing, 1955) 31
6. Albert P. Silver, *Lapidum: a Chapter of Harford County History.* Reprinted from original pamphlet prepared by Albert P. Silver, Esq., and read before the Harford County Historical Society on 8 April 1888. 3
7. Ibid. 3
8. C. Milton Wright, *Our Harford Heritage.*(Bel Air, Maryland: Privately printed. 1967) 14
9. Ibid. 15
10. Ibid. 9
11. Jean Ewing. Interviewed by Carole Kolker. 9 February 2000. 14
12. Mary Bristow, *Are There Ghosts at Rigbie House?* Monograph for Historical Society of Harford County, Inc. 1980
13. Wright, 15
14. George K. Fitch, "SUSQUEHANNA WATER, First of an Occasional Series of Tales of the Susquehanna River," *The Baltimore Engineer,* January 1967. 5
15. Ibid. 6
16. Ibid. 6
17. *Colonel Nathan Rigbie.* Monograph. Bel Air, Maryland: Historical Society of Harford County. July 1980.
18. Mason, Jr., 48
19. Ibid. 48
20. Ibid. 50
21. John Clark. Interviewed by Carole Kolker. 6 April 2000 8
22. Wright, 363
23. Edmund J. Bull, *Revolutionary Harford, Part I:*

A Bicentennial Project of The Steppingstone Museum. Privately printed, 1973 2
24. George B. Scriven. Transcripts of taped lectures at Darlington School of January 7, 14, 21, and 28, 1971. Harford County Library, 1971 25
25. Bull, 2
26. Scriven, 24
27. Silver, 15
28. Ibid. 16
29. Scriven, 24
30. Maryland Historical Trust Worksheet for nomination to the National Register of Historic Places, National Parks Service. Surveyor Jean Ewing. HA-1044, 1972 3
31. Elva Cain. Interviewed by Marya McQuirter. 15 January 2000 4–5
32. Shirley Thompson. Interviewed by Carole Kolker. 9 February 2000 7
33. Bull, 2
34. Ibid. 2
35. Ibid. 15
36. Ibid. 15
37. Ibid 16
38. This Post Road is today's Route 7. Located in southern Harford County, George Washington traveled this route many times since it was the main corridor between Virginia and Philadelphia.
39. Mason, Jr., 50
40. *The World Book Encyclopedia* (Chicago, Illinois: Field Enterprises Educational Corporation, Volume 12, 1965), 29–30
41. Mason, Jr., 50
42. Wright, 363
43. Christopher Weeks, *An Architectural History of Harford County, Maryland.* (Baltimore, Maryland: Johns Hopkins Press, 1996), 42
44. J. Alexis Shriver, *LaFayette in Harford County —Memorial Monograph 1781–1931(An accounty of the events of the Marquis de LaFayette and his troops through Harford County in 1781 and subsequent events, to the Surrender of Cornwallis at Yorktown.* (Privately printed, 1931), 28–29
45. Weeks, 42
46. Charles Cooley, Interviewed by Carole Kolker. 21 February 2000 42.
47. Bristow, 2
48. Weeks, 43
49. Wright, 84–85
50. Scriven, 104

51. Ibid. 104–105
52. George Johnson, *History of Cecil County* (Baltimore, Maryland: Regional Publishing Company. 1967), 345 (Originally published Elkton, 1881)
53. Ibid. 379
54. George Scriven. *Transcript of Presentation at Darlington Elementary School.* (Bel Air, Maryland: Historical Society of Harford County, February 7, 14, 21, and 28, 1971), 33
55. Mason, Jr., 43
56. "Deer Creek Friends Meeting House Opening June 2, 2001," *The Aegis.* May 2001
57. *Harford Historical Bulletin, Number 81* (Bel Air, Maryland: Historical Society of Harford County, Summer 1999), 46
58. Thomas F. Cline and Dale H. Neeper, *Harford County Historical and Geographical Atlas* (Bel Air, Maryland: Harford County Public Schools, 1988) (Originally researched and written by Dale H. Neeper and Charles L. Robbins, 1977).
59. Mason, Jr., 71–72
60. Darlington Lions Club, *Know your Darlington.* (Darlington, Maryland: Privately printed, n.d.) 12
61. Liber HDX Folio 55, Harford County Land Records, Bel Air, Maryland, 10 August 1812
62. Liber HD HDZ Folio 420, Land Records, Bel Air, Maryland, 9 October 1816
63. Christine Tolbert. Interviewed by Carole Kolker, 21 February 2002 2
64. Several iterations of Paca's name appear in documents. Originally found was Paca, which evokes the most interesting possibility of a connection to William Paca, Harford County Signer of the Declaration of Independence, then Peca, Peco, and finally, over time it became Peaker. The descendents of Cupid Paca, today, spell the name Peaco.
65. Weeks, 102
66. Ibid. 102
67. Ibid. 102
68. Ibid. 102
69. Land records of Harford County, HD 14/290. 24 September 1831.
70. Jeffrey R. Brackett, *.The Negro in Maryland.* (Baltimore, Maryland: Johns Hopkins Press, 1889), 187
71. Independence Hall Association, "Mother Bethel A.M.E. Church" 1996–2001, 25 Nov 2001 <http://www.ushistory.org. 3
72. Ibid. 3
73. Ibid. 7
74. Roland Dorsey, Interviewed by Christine Tolbert, 28 March 2000 32
75. *Celebrating 150 Years, St. James African Methodist Episcopal* Church, n.p. n.d. 8
76. A Jew's Harp is a small musical instrument having a flexible steel tongue and held between the teeth to play. It has also been called a "Juice" Harp.
77. Harry Webb Farrington, *Kilt to Togs—Orphan Adventure* (New York, New York: The MacMillan Company, 1930), 257
78. Ibid. 258
79. George W. Hensel, "REMINISCENCES of Harford County," (Read by Him on 28 January 1888 before the Harford County Historical Society at Bel Air.) *Harford Historical Bulletin No. 37.* (Bel Air, Maryland: Historical Society of Harford County, Inc., Summer 1988), 79.
80. Hensel, 79
81. John Lamb. Annotated notes on Historical Society of Harford County Bulletin No. 37, Summer 1988
82. Weeks, 85
83. Mason, Jr., 148–149
84. Wright, 106
85. Henry C. Rauch, "All Wood and a Mile Wide," *The Baltimore Sun*, n.d.
86. John W. McGrain. "Letter to the Editor." *Baltimore American.* 18 September 1820
87. John Lamb, Interviewed by Christine Tolbert. 26 November 2001.
88. A mile marker for this route is still standing along this old route as identified by John Lamb.
89. Andrew Guilford, *Our Country Schools.* Third edition (Niwot:University of Colorado Press) 45
90. James E. Pickard, *A Brief History of Deer Creek Friends Meeting.* 2001
91. Hensel, 74
92. W. Stump Forwood, M.D., *Darlington Academy, 1841–1890:An Historical Address, Delivered on the Occasion of Laying the Cornerstone of the New Academy* (Bel Air, Maryland: Historical Society of Harford County, 16 September 1890)
93. Spellings of the name appear elsewhere as Pervell or Purviel.
94. Forwood, Op.cit.
95. Hensel , 75
96. Wright, 254–255
97. Forwood, Op. cit.
98. Wright, 342. Also see Charles Cooley Interview,21 February 2000
99. Wright, 258
100. http://home.earthlink.net/earthalive/family.stories/hughjones.html 3 December 2001, 1–2
101. Forwood, Op.cit.
102. Hensel. 77–78
103. Tolbert, 1
104. Tolbert, 2

105. Wright, 121–125
106. George B. Scrivens , *"The Susquehanna and Tidewater Canal."* (Bel Air, Maryland: Historical Society of Harford County, Maryland. n.p., n.d.,) 2
107. Mason, Jr., 94
108. Ibid. 94
109. Ibid. 94
110. David Graham, "Years Ago, Covered Bridges Spanned the Susquehanna" *The Record*, Havre de Grace, Maryland. 28 January 1976
111. Ibid.
112. Mason, Jr., 71
113. Ibid. 71
114. Ibid. 53
115. Land records of John Lamb. Privately owned.
116. Elizabeth Newlin Smith Ewing. *Swallowfield: Stories by Elizabeth Newlin Smith.* Darlington, Maryland, n.p.,1936. 9
117. Jean Ewing, *Register of Historic Places Inventory—Nomination Form HA 361.* 1972
118. Ibid.
119. Ibid.
120. Benjamin Stump Silver and Frances Aylette (Bowen) Silver, *Our Silver Heritage* (Gatesville, Texas: Gatesville Printing Company, 1976), 3408–9
121. Ibid. 3409
122. Bernard Waring. Taped interview by family member. 1954
123. Dorothy Sharpless Strang. Interviewed by Constance Beims and Christine Tolbert. 23 January 2002. 22
124. Henrietta Buckmaster, *Let My People Go: The Story of the Underground Railroad and The Abolitionist Movement (Boston: Beacon Press, 1941), 58–59*
125. Ewing, 8–9
126. Weeks, 347
127. Mason, Jr., 38
128. Waring, 1–2
129. Tolbert, 39–40
130. Buckmaster, 30
131. Mason, Jr., 118
132. William Still, *The Underground Railroad* (Chicago: Johnson Publishing Company, 1970) v
133. Ibid. 433
134. Ibid. 433
135. Ibid. 434
136. Ibid. 434–435
137. Ibid. xiii
138. Ibid. vii
139. Silver, Chapter IV
140. Agnes Kane Cullum, "Corporal Philip Webster: A Civil War Soldier," *Harford Historical Bulletin No. 35* (Bel Air, Maryland: Historical Society of Harford County, Inc. Winter 1988), 4–5
141. Ibid 6
142. Ibid. 6
143. Mason, Jr., 114
144. Ibid,114
145. Elizabeth Newlin Ewing. Brief notes. Historical Society of Harford County. Bel Air, Maryland. n.d, n.p.
146. Waring, 11–12
147. Silver, 8595
148. Ibid. 8595
149. Ibid. 3603
150. Wright, 233
151. Booker T. Washington, *Up From Slavery* (New York: Oxford University Press, 1995), 18
152. In addition to his many architectural achievements in Philadelphia, Walter Cope, a relative of the Smiths at Swallowfield, designed many of the significant stone dwellings in Darlington, including two "modern" houses in Berkley.
153. Weeks, 347–48
154. Mason, Jr., 69
155. Ibid. 69
156. Weeks, 336
157. Mason, Jr., 73
158. R. G. Rincliffe, *Conowingo The History of a Great Development on the Susquehanna* (New York, San Francisco, Montreal: The Newcomen Society in North America, 1953), 13
159. Mason, Jr., 73
160. Darlington Lion's Club. *Know Your Darlington-Dublin Area* n.p., n.d. 9
161. Mason, Jr., 73
162. Scrivens, 6
163. Ibid. 6
164. Ibid. 342, 348
165. Fred C. Jones, *The Old Paper Mill* Monograph. n.p., 1940, 1–8
166. Farrington, 268–269
167. Ibid. 271
168. Mason, Jr., 73
169. Fred C. Jones, Op.cit.
170. In addition to the Cooley House, John Lamb constructed many local buildings including the Berkley Chapel owned by Charles Andrew, the Darlington Academy, now the Masonic Lodge and doctor's office in Darlington and his great-great-grandson's home on Conowingo Road. Lamb was a veteran of the Civil War and worked as a carpenter until his retirement.
171. Charles Cooley, 2–3
172. *Portrait and Biographical Record of Harford and Cecil Counties Maryland (*New York and Chicago: Chapman Publishing Co. 1897 278

173. Ibid. 278
174. Farrington, 259
175. Mason, Jr., 72
176. Lois Steele Jones. Interview by Constance Beims, 29 February 2000 11
177. Ewing, 23
178. Cooley, 13
179. Farrington, 186–87
180. Harford County Land Records Index, County Court House, Bel Air, Maryland
181. Wright, 393
182. Personal papers of Mrs. Jerry Miller, Glenview Farm, Darlington, Maryland.
183. *Harford Historical Bulletin #85* (Bel Air, Maryland. Historical Society of Harford County, Summer 2000) 23
184. Wright, 131
185. George Hilton, *The Ma & Pa: A History of the Maryland and Pennsylvania Railroad.* (Berkeley, California: Howell-North, 1963), 38
186. Ibid. 39
187. Mason, Jr., 138
188. Wright, 109
189. "Historical Notes," *The Rising Sun Herald.* Rising Sun, Maryland. 25 October 1989 10
190. Richard J. Sherrill, *The Tidewater Canal: Harford County's Contribution to the "Canal Era"* Harford County Bulletin Number 58. (Bel Air, Maryland: The Historical Society of Harford County, Bel Air, Maryland, Fall 1993), 175
191. Ibid. 177
192. Ibid. 177
193. Mason, Jr., 129–130
194. David Graham, "Years Ago Covered Bridges Spanned the Susquehanna," *The Record*, Havre de Grace, Maryland, 28 January 1976
195. Ibid.
196. On July 26, 1775, members of the Second Continental Congress, meeting in Philadelphia agreed "… that a Postmaster General be appointed for the United States, who shall hold his office at Philadelphia …" That first Postmaster General under the Continental Congress was Benjamin Franklin. His efforts produced the United States Postal Service that today traces its origin to that time.
197. http://www.usps.gov/history/his2.htm. *History of the U. S. Postal Service 1775–1993* 1–2
198. http://www.uwpw .gov/history/his2.htm. 2
199. Waring, 5–6
200. "The New Darlington Academy: Its Corner Stone Laid," *The Aegis & Intelligencer.*19 September 1890
201. Information provided by John Lamb, descendent of John T. Lamb. December, 2001
202. "The New Darlington Academy: Its Corner Stone Laid," *The Aegis & Intelligencer, September 19, 1890*
203. Waring, 6
204. Ewing, 18
205. James Pickard, *"A Brief History of Deer Creek Friends Meeting"* 2001
206. Ewing, 12
207. *History of the Deer Creek Harmony Church n.p.,* 1972 4
208. Ibid. 5
209. Ibid. 5
210. Elva Cain, *One Hundredth Anniversary Souvenir Journal of Hosanna Church—1880–1980.* Darlington, Maryland. 21 September 1980 1
211. Ibid. 1
212. James T. Wollon, Jr., A.I.A., *Grace Memorial Church, Deer Creek Parish, Darlington, Harford County, Maryland"* a Brief History. Unpublished monograph. Undated. 1
213. Ibid. 1
214. Ibid. 2
215. Ibid. 2
216. Wright, 193
217. Wollon, Jr., 2
218. Weeks, 340
219. Elizabeth Gorrell, *History of Darlington Methodist Church.* Monograph. n.p., n.d., 1
220. Cooley, 20
221. Laura Bradford. Interviewed by Carole Kolker. 13 June 2000 36
222. Genevieve Jones. Interviewed by Carole Kolker. 15 January 2000 35
223. Weeks, 141
224. Weeks, 343
225. Excellent early cemetery records are kept at the Historical Society of Harford County in the Family History Section.
226. Clark, 22
227. Tolbert, 41–42
228. David Gordon. Interviewed by Marya McQuirter. 27 February 2000, 11
229. Clark, 16–17
230. Cooley, 8
231. John L. Lamb, Jr. Unpublished Notes. July 1, 2001
232. Fred C. Jones. 9–10
233. mike@mdroads.com
234. www.us-highways.com
235. *The Automobile Blue Book: A Touring Handbook of Motor Routes in New Jersey, Pennsylvania and the Southern Atlantic States.* Chicago, Illinois: The Automobile Blue Book Publishing Company. 1913
236. Ibid.584–85
237. Ibid.585

238. Ibid.245–46
239. Ibid. 246
240. Ewing, 24
241. Gentry Phipps. Interview by Constance Beims. 26 January 2002 3
242. John Lamb. Unpublished notes 2002
243. Phipps, 13–14
244. Charles Cooley. Second Interview by Constance Beims. 16 November 2000
245. Wright, 290
246. Ewing, 23
247. The McNutt family has a long and interesting history in Berkley and Darlington. An extensive genealogy of the family is archived at the Historical Society of Harford County.
248. Bradford, 5
249. Cooley, 12
250. Cooley, 24
251. Evangeline Ford. Interviewed by Carole Kolker. 6 April 2000. 25–26
252. Lois Steele Jones 3–4
253. Ibid. 20
254. Gwyneth Howard. Unpublished monograph. 13 May 2002 1
255. Cooley, 10
256. Thompson, 40–41
257. Bradford, 6
258. Phipps, 9–10
259. John Sauers, *An Incident from Life in Berkley in the Twenties. n.p. June 2002*
260. Cooley, 24
261. Cooley, 24
262. Mason, Jr., 164
263. Ann Gregory, notes from Interview of Jean Ewing . n.p.1998
264. Phipps, 2–3
265. Jean Ewing, 16—and follow-up telephone interview October 2001.
266. Cooley, 12
267. Frank Steward, *History of Post Offices of Harford County* (Harford County, Maryland: Privately published. December 1991) 7
268. *The Chesapeake and Potomac Telephone Company Telephone Directory*. Historical Society of Harford County. Bel Air, Maryland 1910. 13
269. Ewing, 18
270. *1920 Census Tract, Election District of Dublin, Maryland*. 10 January 1920. Maryland Archives, Annapolis, Maryland
271. Photograph owned by Mr. Edwin Kirkwood, Street, Maryland
272. Land records of Harford County WSF 117/123
273. Walter Charlton Hartridge, "Refugees from the Island of St. Domingo in Maryland," *Maryland Historical Magazine*. Vol. 96, No. 4, Winter 2001 475

274. Ibid.475
275. Ibid. 478
276. Ibid. 486
277. Harford County Land Records WSF 117–123&124. Bel Air, Maryland
278. Edward Presberry, Interviewed by Marya McQuirter. 4 March 2000 34
279. Ewing, 21
280. Ewing, 21
281. Dorsey, 14
282. Genevieve Jones, 12
283. Tolbert, 55
284. Cooley, 21
285. Ford, 26–27
286. Lois Jones, 7–8
287. Ewing, 11
288. William M. Presberry. Interviewed by Marya McQuirter. 3 March 2000 2
289. Genevieve Jones, 12
290. Dorsey, 15
291. Bernice Glover. Interviewed by Marya McQuirter and Christine Tolbert. 10 June 2000 23
292. David Gordon, Interviewed by Marya McQuirter. 27 February 2000 19–21
293. Edward Presberry, 30
294. Nicolas B. Wainwright. *History of the Philadelphia Electric Company 1881–1961*. Philadelphia, Pennsylvania. 1961 167
295. _____ *The Aegis*. Bel Air, Maryland, 27 January 1923
296. Philadelphia Electric Company Archives, Philadelphia, Pennsylvania.
297. R. G. Rincliffe. 19
298. _____ *Journal of Commerce*. Philadelphia, Pennsylvania: Philadelphia Electric Company Archives. February 1925
299. Phipps, 35
300. Clifford Trott. Interviewed by Gwyneth Howard. 30 June 2000 2
301. Cooley, 13
302. Genevieve Jones, 21
303. Shirley Gittings Dunsen. Interviewed by Marya McQuirter. 17 March 2000 9
304. _____, *Baltimore News*, July 20, 1923
305. Mason, Jr., 114
306. _____, "Conowingo Project," *The Baltimore Sun, 29* November 1927
307. Rincliffe,19
308. Phipps, 4–5
309. Joyce Gahagan Crothers. Interviewed by Gwyneth Howard. Spring 2002
310. Alexander Wilson, "The Conowingo Hydro-Electric Development of the Susquehanna River," *American Society of Civil Engineers,* Paper No. 1710 1929

311. Stone & Webster, Inc. *Conowingo* Privately printed. n.d., 11

312. _____, "Old Conowingo Span Wrecked by Explosives," *The Baltimore Sun*, 29 November 1927

313. David Healy, "Dam's Rising Waters Claimed Conowingo Village in 1928," *The Cecil Whig*, 13 May 1989 3a

314. Bradford, 24

315. Ewing, 29

316. Mason, Jr., 43

317. Edward Presberry, 42

318. Annabelle Burkins, Interviewed by Gwyneth Howard, December 1999 19

319. Phipps, 20

320. Cooley, 42–43

321. Phyllis Price. Interviewed by Constance Beims. 29 February 2000 6

322. Annabelle Burkins, 10

323. Dunsen, 4

324. Price, 6

325. David Healey, 3a

326. Thompson, 49

327. Cooley 16–17

328. Shirley Thompson, 18–20

329. Bradford, 26

330. Dorsey, 10

331. Shirley Dunsen, 18

332. William Presberry, 15

333. Dunsen, 21

334. Gordon, 10

335. Tolbert, 28

336. Dunsen, 38

337. Bernice Glover, Interviewed by Marya McQuirter. 10 June 2000. 9

338. Genevieve Jones, 26

339. Cain, 11

340. Edward Presberry, 11

341. Gordon, 8

342. Ibid. 25–26

343. Cooley 2–9

344. Gladys Williams. Interviewed by Marya McQuirter, 17 March 2000, 32, 35–37

345. Roy O. Billett, et.al. *A Survey of the Public Schools of Harford County, Maryland*, Bel Air, Maryland: Harford County Board of Education, 1946 204

346. Ibid. 202

347. Cain, 12–13

348. Billett, 168

349. Tolbert, 23–4

350. William Presberry, 16–17

351. Dunsen, 34

352. Bradford, 25–26

353. Ibid. 26

354. Dunsen, 35

355. Cooley, 2–3

356. Cain, 2–3

357. Ewing, 7

358. Genevieve Jones, 20

359. Tolbert, 56

360. Ford, 14–15

361. Cooley, Interview 2. 6 & 11

362. Trott, 31

363. Thompson, 15

364. William Presberry, 8

365. Cooley Interview 2, 15

366. Lois Jones, 19

367. Gordon, 14

368. Cooley, 20

369. Bradford, 7

370. Gordon, 34–37

371. Glover, 15

372. Dunsen, 17

373. William Presberry, 51–52

374. Clark, 7

375. Cooley, 4

376. _____, "Historical Society of Harford County Will Celebrate the Sesqui-Centennial of Lafayette Passing Through Harford Co." *The Bel Air Times*. February 22, 1930

377. Clark, 11

378. Ford, 24

379. Tolbert, 60

380. Thompson, 28–29

381. Glover, 29–30

382. Dunsen, 46

383. Megan Evans. Interviewed by Christine Tolbert and Constance Beims, January 2002 30

384. Evans, 29

385. Dunsen, 42–43

386. Cooley, 27

387. Thompson, 18

388. Clark, 19

389. Bradford, 40

390. Ewing, 11

391. Glover, 27

392. Lois Jones, 8

393. Trott, 19

394. Cain, 20

395. Tolbert, 43

396. William Presberry, 40–41

397. Trott, 19

398. William Presberry, 41

399. Bradford, 26

400. Maryland Forestry Service, Maryland Department of Natural Resources, *Maryland's Bicentennial Trees and a listing of Species of Trees Believed to be Living in Maryland in 1776* .n.p., n.d.

Bibliography

Published References

Alsop, George, *A Character of the Province of Maryland*. Freeport, New York: Books for Libraries Press, 1972. (Original edition: 1666.)

... American Automobile Association, *The Automobile Blue Book: A Touring Hand-book of Motor Routes in New Jersey, Pennsylvania and the Southern Atlantic States*. Chicago, Illinois: The Automobile Blue Book Publishing Company, 1913.

Billett, Roy O., et al. *A Survey of the Public Schools of Harfrod County, Maryland*. Bel Air, Maryland: Harford County Board of Education, 1946.

Brackett, Jeffrey R., *The Negro in Baltimore*. Baltimore, Maryland: The Johns Hopkins Press. 1989

Buckmaster, Henrietta, *Let My People Go: The Story of the Underground Railroad and the Abolition Movement*. 1941

Bull, Edmund J., *Revolutionary Harford, Parts I and II: A Biennial Project of the Steppingstone Museum*. Privately printed, 1973.

————, *Revolutionary Harford, Part III: A Gentleman's Journal*. Final editing by Mary C. Wright and Mary R. Bristow. Privately Printed, 1977.

Bunting, Elaine and Patricia D'Amario. *Our Maryland Counties Series: Counties of Northern Maryland*. Centerville, Maryland: Tidewater Publishers, 2000.

Chesapeake and Potomac Telephone Company, *Telephone Directory 1910*.

Cline, Thomas F. and Dale H. Neeper, *Harford County Historical and Geographical Atlas*. Monograph prepared for Harford County, Maryland, School System, 1988. (Originally researched and written by Dale H. Neeper and Charles L. Robbins, 1977)

... "Conowingo—Light and Power for Harford—3800 Workman Began Construction in 1926," *The Aegis,* Bel Air, Maryland, 16 August 1973.

Cook, Ebenezer, *The Maryland Muse*, (1667–1732). Facsimile, with introduction by Lawrence C. Wroth, 1935.

Cullum, Agnes Kane. "Corporal Philip Webster: A Civil War Soldier," *Harford Historical Bulletin number 35*. Bel Air, Maryland: Historical Society of Harford County, Inc., winter 1888.

Darby, A. K. Untitled column on Conowingo Dam. *Baltimore News,* 18 July 1923.

... Darlington Lions' Club. *Know Your Darlington-Dublin Area*. Privately printed, n.d.

... "Deer Creek Friends Meeting House Opening, June 2,2001." *The Aegis*. Bel Air, Maryland, May 2001.

Farrington, Harry Webb. *Kilts to Togs: Orphan Adventures*. New York: The MacMillan Company, 1930.

Fitch, George K. "Susquehanna Water, First of an Occasional Series of Tales of the Susquehanna River," *The Baltimore Engineer,* Baltimore, Maryland, January 1967.

Garnett, William G. *Tidewater Tales*. Dunnsville, Virginia: Tidewater Publishing Company, 1927.

Goldberg, Edna, "Traffic Flows Again over the Conowingo." *The Baltimore Sun*. n.d.

Graham, David. "Years ago, Covered Bridges Spanned The Susquehanna," *The Record*. Havre de Grace, Maryland, 28 January 28, 1976.

Guilford, Andrew. *Our Country Schools*. 3rd Ed. Niwot: University of Colorado Press.

Harper, Doug. "The Prehistoric Inhabitants of Lancaster County: Woodlands Indians," *The Intelligencer Journal*, Lancaster, Pennsylvania, 9 February 1995.

Hartridge, Walter Charlton. "The Refugees from the Island of St. Domingo in Maryland." *Maryland Historical Magazine*, Vol. 96, No. 4, winter 2001.

Healey, David. "Dam's Rising Waters Claimed Conowingo Village in 1928," *The Cecil Whig,* Cecil County, Maryland, 13 May 1989.

Hensel, George W. "Reminiscences of Harford County, read by him on January 28, 1888 before the Harford County Historical Society." *Harford Historical Bulletin number 37*. Bel Air, Maryland: Historical Society of Harford County, Inc., summer 1988.

Hilton, George W. *The Ma & P: A History of the Maryland and Pennsylvania Railroad*. Berkley, California: Howell-North, 1963.

... "Historical Notes," *The Rising Sun Herald*. Rising Sun, Maryland, 25 October, 1989

... "Historical Society of Harford County Will Celebrate the Sesqui-Centennial of Lafayette Passing Through Harford County." *The Bel Air Times*. Bel Air, Maryland, 22 February 1930.

... Independence Hall Association. *Mother Bethel A.M.E. Church 1996–2001*. n.p., November 2001

Johnson, George. *History of Cecil County*. Published by County Directors of Maryland, Inc. 1956. (Reprint 1981)

Jones, Edward C. "Hugh Jones of Harford County: Excerpts from *Recollections.* http://home.earthlink.net/~earthalive/familystories hugh jones.htm c. 1998–2001

Jones, Fred C. *The Village of Darlington in Harford County, Maryland*. Privately published, 1947.

——. "Susquehanna Memories," *Pennsylvania Farmer*. Lancaster, Pennsylvania, 23 January 1947.

… *Journal Of Commerce*. Philadelphia, Pennsylvania: Philadelphia Electric Company Archives, February 1925.

… Lane, R. A. "Operators' Village at Conowingo is Real Utopia," *Current News*. Philadelphia, Pennsylvania, 1928.

… Maryland Forestry Service, Maryland Department of Natural Resources, *Maryland's Bicentennial Trees and a Listing of Species of Trees Believed to be Living in Maryland in 1776. n.d.*

Mason, Samuel, Jr. *Historical Sketches of Harford County Maryland*. Lancaster, Pennsylvania: Intelligencer Printing Company, 1940. (Reprinted 1955)

McGrain, John W., "Letter to the Editor, *Baltimore American*. 18 September 1820.

Morrison, Don. "They Helped Build the Conowingo Dam. *The Aegis*. Bel Air, Maryland, 31 March 1993.

Myers, Richmond E., *The Long Crooked River (The Susquehanna)*. Boston, Massachusetts: The Christopher Publishing House, 1949.

… "New Darlington Academy: Its Corner Stone Laid," *The Aegis and Intelligencer*. Bel Air, Maryland, 19 September 1890.

… "Old Conowingo Span Wrecked by Explosives," *The Baltimore Sun*, 24 November 1927.

Peden, Henry C., Jr., "Harford County Place Names, Past and Present—Their Location, Origin and Meaning—Part I: A-J. *Harford Historical Bulletin number 78*. Bel Air, Maryland: The Historical Society of Harford County, Inc., fall 1998.

… *Portrait and Biographical Record of Harford and Cecil Counties, Maryland*. New York and Chicago: Chapman Publishing Co., 1897.

Preston, Walter W. *History of Harford County*. Privately Printed, 1901.

Rauch, Henry C. "All Wood and a Mile Wide." *The Baltimore Sun*. n.d.

Rincliffe, R. G. *"Conowingo!" The History of a Great Development on the Susquehanna*. New York, San Francisco, Montreal: The Newcomen Society in North America, 1953.

Rouse, Paul E., Jr. *The Great Wagon Road From Philadelphia to the South*. Richmond, Virginia: The Deitz Press, 1995.

Sarudy, Barbara Wells, Editor. *History Matters! Interpretive Plan for the Lower Susquehanna Heritage Greenway*. Baltimore, Maryland: Maryland Humanities Council, 2001.

Sawyer, Jeffrey K. and Charles Lee Robbins. "The Pursuit of Justice in Early Harford County," *Historical Bulletin number 81*. Bel Air, Maryland: Historical Society of Harford County, Inc., Summer 1999.

Searight, Thomas B. *The Old Pike: A History of the National Road with Incidents, Accidents, and Anecdotes Thereon*. Uniontown, Pennsylvania: privately published, 1894. (Reprinted—Bowie, Maryland: Heritage Books, Inc., 1990.)

Sherrill, Richard J. "The Tidewater Canal: Harford County's Contribution to The Canal Era," *Harford Historical Bulletin number 58*. Bel Air, Maryland: The Historical Society of Harford County, Inc., fall 1993.

Shriver, J. Alexis. *Lafayette in Harford County— Memorial Monograph 1781–1931*. Baltimore, Maryland: Privately printed, 1931.

Silver, Albert P., *Lapidum: Another Chapter in Harford County History*. Text read before Harford County Historical Society on April 8, 1888. Bel Air, Maryland: Historical Society of Harford County Archives.

Silver, Benjamin Stump and Frances Aylette Silver. *Our Silver Heritage*. Gatesville, Texas: Gatesville Printing Company, 1976.

Smart, Jeffrey K. "Suppressing Rebellion in Harford County In 1861, Part 2," *Harford Historical Bulletin, number 84*. Bel Air, Maryland: Historical Society of Harford County, Inc., spring 2000.

Smith-Brown, Fern. *The Beckoning Hills*. Darlington, Maryland: Ltd. Edition Press, 1984.

Steward, Frank. *History of Post Offices in Harford County*. Harford County, Maryland: Privately published, December 1991.

Still, William. *The Underground Railroad*. Chicago: Johnson Publishing Company. 1970

… Stone and Webster, Inc. *Conowingo*. Philadelphia, Pennsylvania: n.p., 1928.

Wainwright, Nicholas B. *History of the Philadelphia Electric Company 1881–1061*. Philadelphia Electric Company, 1961.

Washington, Booker T. *Up From Slavery*. New York: Oxford University Press, 1995.

Weeks, Christopher. *An Architectural History of Harford County, Maryland*. Baltimore, Maryland: Johns Hopkins University Press, 1996.

——"Harford's black history: Two modest buildings hosted some significant happenings," *The Record*. Havre de Grace, Maryland, 11 February 1987.

Wilson, Alexander. "The Conowingo Hydro-electric Development on the Susquehanna River,"

Transactions, Volume 93. American Society of Civil Engineers, paper #1710. Philadelphia, Pennsylvania, 1929.

Wilstach, Paul. *Tidewater Maryland*. New York: Blue Ribbon Books, 1931.

Wright, C. Milton. *Our Harford Heritage: A History of Harford County, Maryland*. Privately published, 1967.

Unpublished References

Documents

Bristow, Mary. *"Are There Ghosts at Rigbie House?"* Monograph. Bel Air, Maryland: Historical Society of Harford County, Inc., 1980.

Cain, Elva. *One-Hundredth Anniversary Souvenir Journal 1880–1980—Hosanna Church*. September 21, 1980

Cox, Geraldine et al. *Celebrating 150 Years, St. James African Methodist Episcopal Church*. 1999

Ewing, Elizabeth Newlin Smith. *Swallowfield Stories by Elizabeth Newlin Smith*. Berkley, Maryland. Privately owned, 1936

——, *Brief Notes*. Bel Air, Maryland: Historical Society of Harford County, n.d.

Ewing, Jean S. *Red Gate*. National Register of Historic Places Inventory—Nomination Form, survey number—HA-208, 1972.

——*Swallowfield Ice House*. National Register of Historic Places Inventory—Nomination Form, survey number—HA-359. Repository: Maryland Historical Trust, 1972.

——. *Swallowfield Barn*. National Register of Historic Places Inventory—Nomination Form, survey number—HA-360. Repository: Maryland Historical Trust, 1972.

——. *Swallowfield Springhouse*. National Register of Historic Places Inventory—Nomination Form, survey number—HA-361. Repository: Maryland Historical Trust, 1972.

——. *Swallowfield Smokehouse*. National Register of Historic Places Inventory—Nomination Form, survey number—HA-362. Repository: Maryland Historical Trust, 1972.

——. *Berkley Store*. National Register of Historic Places Inventory—Nomination Form, survey number—HA 1027. Repository: Maryland Historical Trust, 1973.

——. *Howard-McNutt Log House*. National Register of Historic Places Inventory—Nomination Form, survey number—HA-1028. Repository: Maryland Historical Trust, 1973.

——. *Thomas House*. National Register of Historic Places Inventory—Nomination Form, survey number—HA-1030. 1973

——. *The Mackleveny House*. National Register of Historic Places Inventory—Nomination Form, survey number—HA-1031. Repository: Maryland Historical Trust, 1973.

——. *Curtis Byrd House, Site of Berkley Chapel*. National Register of Historic Places Inventory—Nomination Form, survey number—HA-1034. Repository: Maryland Historical Trust, 1973.

——. *John Clark's Tenant House*. National Register of Historic Places Inventory—Nomination Form, survey number—HA-1044. Repository: Maryland Historical Trust, 1973.

——. *Cooley House*. National Register of Historic Places Inventory—Nomination Form, survey number—HA-1045. Repository: Maryland Historical Trust, 1973.

Forwood, W. Stump. *Darlington Academy, 1841–1890: An Historical Address on the Occasion of Laying the Cornerstone of the New Academy*. Bel Air, Maryland: Historical Society of Harford County, Inc. 16 September 1890.

Gorrell, Elizabeth. *History of Darlington Methodist Church*. n.p., n.d.

Gregory, Ann. *Notes from Interview with Jean Ewing on the Towpath Tea House*. 1998

Howard, Gwyneth B. *A Berkley Experience*. 13 May 2002.

Howard, Stephen P. M. *Anatomy of a Sow's Ear*, 12 December 1985.

… *"Colonel Nathan Rigbie."* Monograph. Bel Air,Maryland: Historical Society of Harford County, Inc., July 1980.

Jones, Fred C., *The Old Paper Mill*. Bel Air, Maryland: Historical Society of Harford County Inc. Reference Number: HC 664.72 J, n.d.

Pickard, James. *A Brief History of Deer Creek Friends Meeting*. 2001

Sauers, John. *An Incident from Life in Berkley in the Twenties*, n.p. June 2002.

Scrivens, George B. *The Susquehanna and Tidewater canal*. n.p, n.d.

Wollon, James T., Jr. *Grace Memorial Church, Deer Creek Parish, Darlington, Harford County, Maryland: a Brief History*. n.p., n.d.

Interviews

The audiotapes and transcripts of the interviews conducted for this project are archived with the Maryland Historical Trust, The Historical Society of Harford County, Inc., and available for borrowing through the Harford County Library system. The interviews were numbered for the project as BX-OH (Berkley Crossroads Oral Histories).

Laura Bradford. Interviewed by Carolyn Kolker. BX-OH-017, 13 June 2000.

Annabelle Dow Burkins. Interviewed by Gwyneth Howard. BX-OH-018, 7 December 1999.

Elva Cain. Interviewed by Marya McQuirter. BX-OH-002, 15 January 2000.

John Clark. Interviewed by Carolyn Kolker. BX-OH-015, 16 June 2000.

Charles Cooley. Interviewed by Carolyn Kolker. BX-OH-005, 21 February 2000.

Roland Dorsey. Interviewed by Christine Tolbert. BX-OH-013, 28 March 2000.

Shirley Dunsen. Interviewed by Marya McQuirter. BX-OH-011, 17 March 2002.

Megan Evans and Dorothy Sharpless Strang. Interviewed by Christine Tolbert and Connie Beims. BX-OH-020, 30 January 2000

Jean Ewing. Interviewed by Carolyn Kolker. BX-OH-03, 9 February 2000.

Evangeline Ford. Interviewed by Marya McQuirter. BX-OH-014, 6 April 2000.

Bernice Glover. Interviewed by Marya Mcquirter and Christine Tolbert. BX-OH-016, 10 June 2000 and 25 June 2000.

David Gordon. Interviewed by Mary McQuirter. BX-OH-007, 27 February 2000.

Genevieve Jones. Interviewed by Marya McQuirter. BX-OH-001, 15 January 2000.

Lois Steele Jones and Phyllis Steele Price. Interviewed by Connie Beims. BX-OH-008, 29 February 2000.

Gantry Phipps. Interviewed by Connie Beims. BX-OH-021, 26 February 2002.

Edward Presberry. Interviewed by Marya McQuirter. BX-OH-010, 4 March 2000.

William Presberry. Interviewed by Marya McQuirter. BX-OH-009, 4 March 2000.

Shirley Thompson. Interviewed by Marya McQuirter. BX-OH-004, 9 February 2000.

Christine Tolbert. Interviewed by Carolyn Kolker. BX-OH-006, 21 February 2000.

Clifford Trott. Interviewed by Gwyneth Howard. BX-OH-019, 30 June 2000.

Gladys Williams. Interviewed by Marya McQuirter. BX-OH-012, 17 March 2000.

Index

The Authors

Constance Ross Beims

Connie Beims, a resident of Berkley, is retired from public service having served in several positions including Executive Director of the Maryland Commission for Women, Appointments Officer and Deputy Chief of Staff for Maryland Governor Harry R. Hughes and Vice-President and Executive Assistant to the President at the University of Maryland Baltimore County (UMBC). Connie was editor of *Harry R. Hughes: The Legacy* and author of *The Chesapeake Bay: Conflict or Challenge,* a publication of the National Oceanic and Atmospheric Administration. A graduate of Harford Community College and Goucher College, she was inducted into the Maryland Women's Hall of Fame in 1998. She and her husband, Bill, have four grown children and two granddaughters. For the past thirty years they have been the stewards of Swallowfield, a documented stop on the Underground Railroad. She is a member of Phi Beta Kappa and currently serves on the Harford County Historic Preservation Commission.

Christine Presberry Tolbert

Christine is a seventh-generation descendant of the early blacks who settled in Berkley. As a child she attended Hosanna School, as did her mother and grandmother. Christine earned her BS degree from Bowie State Teachers College and MEd from Loyola College. She began teaching in Harford County when the schools were still segregated. Moving from the elementary school classroom Christine became a high school guidance counselor and later Supervisor of Elementary and Secondary Education for Harford County Schools until she retired. She has served on the Harford County Human Relations commission, the Historic Preservation Commission and for the past 20 years as the volunteer Executive Director of the Hosanna Community House, Inc. encouraging and overseeing the restoration and preservation of Hosanna School. She continues her role as educator by educating all of the children and adults who visit the restored historically black school. In 2001 she was inducted into the Harford County Educators Hall of Fame. Christine and her husband, Carlton, are parents and grandparents.